PUBLIC SPEAKING:

A RHETORICAL PERSPECTIVE

In speech-making, as in life,
not failure, but low aim, is crime.

WAYLAND MAXFIELD PARRISH

PUBLIC SPEAKING:

Prentice-Hall, Inc., Englewood Cliffs, New Jersey

A
RHETORICAL
PERSPECTIVE

JANE BLANKENSHIP

University of Massachusetts

Jane Blankenship

PUBLIC SPEAKING: A RHETORICAL PERSPECTIVE

© 1966 by PRENTICE-HALL, INC.
Englewood Cliffs, N. J.

Current printing (last digit):

10   9   8   7   6   5   4   3   2

Library of Congress Catalog Card Number: 66-13532
Printed in the United States of America   73889-C

PRENTICE-HALL INTERNATIONAL, INC., *London*
PRENTICE-HALL OF AUSTRALIA, PTY., LTD., *Sydney*
PRENTICE-HALL OF CANADA, LTD., *Toronto*
PRENTICE-HALL OF INDIA (PRIVATE) LTD., *New Delhi*
PRENTICE-HALL OF JAPAN, INC., *Tokyo*

The central function of rhetorical theory is to provide an understanding of the factors contributing to free and enlightened choices by those responding to persuasion—to answer the questions: "*Why* is one speaker more effective than another? *Why* may a suggested procedure win a desired response?" This book will, in a limited way, answer the question "Why?" Whenever possible, theory is integrated with illustrations from great speeches of the past and from speeches given in the classroom. The assumption is that the relationships between theory and skills are many and varied and that principles are useful only as they find practical application in speeches.

The purpose of this book is to provide the student with both principles and applications which he can use in his own speaking. Part One offers a brief discussion of communication in general and persuasive speech in particular. Part Two discusses each of the five canons of rhetoric and considers some central ideas of both classical and modern theory which provide the student with an approach to public speaking and which will help him develop a "rhetorical perspective." And, since a beginning student will probably hear more speeches than he will give, Part Three

PREFACE

discusses speech criticism and offers a commentary on brief samples of student speeches. Appendix A provides a text on which the student can try his own critical abilities.

The book includes collateral reading lists for additional reading by interested students. Since it is useful, even for the beginning student, to be exposed to as wide a range of materials as possible, I have included references to journals as well as books. My own students have enjoyed hearing about recent experimental studies which related to what they are studying. From time to time we have duplicated an experiment, or part of it, in the classroom. This kind of activity provides not only additional information with a real sense of immediacy but also variety in kinds of activity. The more the student reflects carefully about *why* his speeches or the speeches he hears are effective or not, the more his speaking becomes a truly conscious art.

The rationale and subject matter of the book reflect the heavy debt to rhetoricians of the past who have conceived and taught a rhetoric in the tradition of humane studies. The speakers of the past who have so often eloquently pleaded "the cause of human dignity and the rights of free men" have contributed to no less an extent. Whatever part of this book is worthwhile is due to their good counsel.

Many of my own students have also participated very directly in the preparation of this book. A number of them have read it in whole or in part and have discussed it, sometimes vigorously, with me. I would especially like to thank those whose outlines and speeches are included in the text, particularly Anne and Janet Roede whose materials form a large part of the last chapter.

I also owe a debt of thanks to the Mount Holyoke College Library staff, to Martha Cobb of Prentice-Hall, to Christian Kay, and particularly to Judith Hopkins of the Yale University Law Library for editorial help with the manuscript. And finally, I would like to thank all those who read the text and whose rigorous dialogue often stimulated me to clarify my thinking and writing.

JANE BLANKENSHIP

PART ONE

Definitions and Implications   1

I.   THE NATURE OF COMMUNICATION   3

The Process of Communication, 3
The Communicative Event, 8

II.   THE NATURE OF RHETORIC   23

A Definition of Rhetoric, 24
The Nature and Scope of Rhetoric, 25
Rhetoric as Participation, 28
The Relationship of Rhetoric
to Other Subjects, 29

PART TWO

Principles and Applications   35

III.   RHETORICAL INVENTION:
PRELIMINARY PLANNING   37

First Steps, 37
Developing Lines of Argument, 43
Modes of Presenting Material, 46

CONTENTS

IV.   RHETORICAL INVENTION: SELECTION OF PROOFS   51

Ethical Proof, 52
Logical Proof, 56
Emotional Proof, 68

V.   ARRANGEMENT OF MATERIALS   75

Speech Organization, 76
Sequencing Materials, 91
Proportion, 92
Direct Suggestion, 92

VI.   STYLE: SOME THEORETICAL CONSIDERATIONS   98

Language in Use, 99
The Users of Language, 101
The Meaning of Meaning, 104
Semantic Meaning, 105
Structural Meaning, 109
Sound Meaning, 111

VII.   STYLE: SOME PRACTICAL APPLICATIONS   121

Clarity, 122
Appropriateness, 129
Impressiveness, 132
Style and Purpose, 139
Style and the Three Modes of Proof, 146
Oral and Written Style, 149

VIII.   REMEMBERING YOUR SPEECH   153

Relation to Invention, 154
Relation to Arrangement, 155
Relation to Detail, 157
Relation to Style, 158
Relation to Delivery, 159

IX.   DELIVERY   161

The Basic Elements of Good Delivery, 164
Special Problems of Beginning Speakers, 166

PART THREE
Analyses and Criticism 179

X.   EVALUATING SPEECHES   181

Guide Questions, 182
Sample Criticisms, 184

APPENDIX   203

"OUR BROKEN MAINSPRING,"
BY ADLAI E. STEVENSON

INDEX   215

PUBLIC SPEAKING:

A RHETORICAL PERSPECTIVE

PART ONE

DEFINITIONS AND IMPLICATIONS

Speech is civilization itself ... it is
silence which isolates.

THOMAS MANN

I   As students interested in public speaking, you are
       about to explore one of the oldest studies in the
history of Western education. Since about 450 B.C. in Sicily,
when Corax wrote the first known treatise on rhetoric, every
generation has devoted much time and effort to exploring
the theory and the practice of public speaking. Writers on
rhetoric include Plato, Isocrates, Aristotle, Cicero, Quintilian, St. Augustine, and Francis Bacon, as well as many
distinguished contemporary public figures.

In this chapter, however, rather than review the tradition
of rhetoric and public speaking, we shall consider two
questions: (1) What does it mean to say we are "communicating" with one another? and (2) What are the elements
of the communicative situation?

The Process of Communication

The word "communication" comes from the Latin *com-
munis*—common. When we communicate with someone we
are attempting to share information, ideas, or attitudes.
Communication is the process through which this sharing
is possible, the process of sending and receiving ideas by
means of verbal symbols.

THE NATURE
OF COMMUNICATION

The basic pattern of communication is stimulus-response:

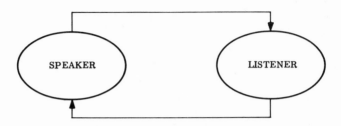

The simplicity of this diagram is deceptive. Whenever there is more than one listener, members of the audience tend to control their reactions according to those of the other listeners in the situation. Thus the diagram must include not only interstimulation between the speaker and the listener but also the additional interstimulation among other listeners.

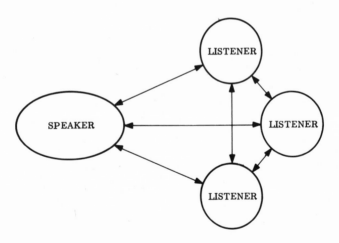

This return process can be termed "feedback." Feedback tells us how our message is being interpreted. The hearer may say, "That's right, I agree." He may frown, look puzzled, smile. He may look as if he were losing interest or nod in agreement. As the speaker is speaking, he also listens to the sound of his own voice and to what he is saying. He himself may say, "What I meant to say was . . . ." Here, he is responding to his own message. James A.

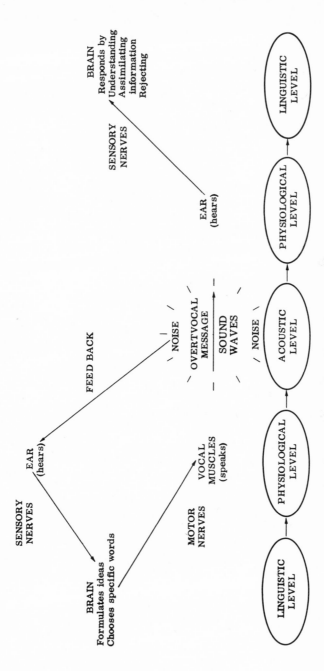

An Overview of the Communicative Event

Winans tells the story of the nineteenth-century lawyer, Rufus Choate, who reiterated the arguments and pleas in one of his jury addresses for hours after eleven men were won, until he saw the frowning face of the twelfth juror relax in sympathy. He comments: "Many a passage of good oratorical prose can be turned into a dialogue by writing out the questions and objections that lie plainly between the lines. The . . . speaker can do no better for himself than to fix firmly in mind that *a speech is a dialogue* and emphasize constantly the part of the audience, anticipating and watching for its response." [1]

Viewing the communicative event in more detail, we see that it consists of three different levels: (1) the linguistic level; (2) the physiological level; and (3) the acoustic level. (See page 5.) At the linguistic level the speaker chooses to express one of the ideas in his mind. He makes specific language choices and "says" them aloud. Let us suppose Mr. Z is walking down the street and sees a friend. He could mention the weather, talk about a committee meeting they had both attended the evening before, or mention some news item he just heard or the baseball scores he read in the morning paper. From all available subjects, he chooses the weather. He could say, "Isn't it a beautiful day?" or "Nice weather we're having" or could select one of a dozen other ways of saying essentially the same thing.

The saying aloud, the physiological level of speech, is a special problem in itself. When we speak, sound waves are actually the "primary message." This "primary message" conveys information on a variety of levels. It gives the listener words to decode. It emphasizes some words and not others. It presents words in a pattern of timing and of intonation which helps to communicate the final meaning. Even the quality of voice—loud, soft, rasping, light, deep, shrill, high—carries information about the speaker and what he is saying. The listener hears the sounds, arrives at a meaning, and responds in some way to what has been said. If there is no response at all, there has been no communication.

All the steps in the communicative process must be taken with a

[1] James A. Winans, *Speech-Making* (New York: Appleton-Century-Crofts, 1938), pp. 13–14.

relatively high degree of efficiency if communication is to be successful; it can be no stronger than the weakest link. Communication can fail at any one of many points:

(1) The idea may be "fuzzy"; that is, the speaker may not have adequate, clear information.

(2) The message may not be expressed in accurate, effective, transmittable words.

(3) Noise (any interference with transmission) may obscure all, most, or some of the message, so that the speaker's message may not be the one received by the decoder. The speaker may speak too softly to be heard. Someone in the audience may cough. A plane may pass overhead. Noise may also be thought of in a nonmechanical sense. It can be any type of distortion by the speaker, such as poor word choice or excessive "slanting" of materials.

(4) The message may be heard accurately, but may not mean the same thing to the listener as to the speaker. At the receiver's end, noise can be misinterpretation resulting from the listener's biases and emotions or his lack of information.

The circles represent the accumulated experiences, emotions, and motivations of two people trying to communicate. The source (speaker) can encode and the destination (listener) can decode *only* in terms of his experience. If we have never learned any German we can neither encode nor decode in that language. If a South African tribesman has neither seen nor heard of television, he can only decode the sight of a television set in terms of whatever ex-

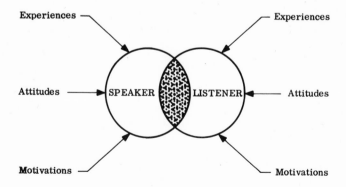

perience he has had. If the circles do not meet, if there is no common experience, then communication is impossible. If the circles have only a small area in common, then it will be very difficult for the speaker to convey his intended meaning to the audience.

The Communicative Event

Now let us view the communication act by considering the elements of the communicative situation and discussing eight of them: speaker, audience, place, time, purpose, content, style, and delivery.[2]

THE SPEAKER

In every oral communication, from the simple "Let's go get a cup of coffee" to a complex speech before the General Assembly of the United Nations, someone, some "I" is doing the speaking. We have already mentioned that the speaker is the sum total of his environment; that is, he has a certain character, a certain personality. The audience may or may not "know" the speaker. If the speaker is known, he may be known in a variety of ways. When former Soviet Premier Khrushchev spoke to the United Nations, the ways in which he was known, the ways he was listened to because of his identity were diverse. Each one of you may be known in a different way, hence listened to in a different way by each person in your audience.

When Daniel Webster spoke, he was called, not altogether admiringly, the "Great Expounder." One group of people knew him as the "great champion of the Constitution," whose views were of "the most enlarged and liberal description" and which derived from feelings "of the purest patriotism." To another he was a "cordial and undeviating hater of democracy," the "champion of localities," whose views were "the opposite extreme of a liberal" and which were lacking in "ardor and sympathy." [3] Some knew him as a mixture of the two descriptions, and some probably moved from one view to the other as issues and times changed.

[2] This treatment follows one suggested by Marie Hochmuth, "The Criticism of Rhetoric" in *A History and Criticism of American Public Address*, ed. Marie K. Hochmuth (New York: Longmans, Green and Co., Inc., 1955), III, 1–23.

[3] Wilbur Samuel Howell and Hoyt Hopewell Hudson, "Daniel Webster" in *A History and Criticism of American Public Address*, ed. William Norwood Brigance (New York: McGraw-Hill Book Company, 1943), II, 665–733.

A speaker may make himself known in two ways: by what he brings to the speech, his character, his personality, his reputation; and by what he says in the speech, the topics he chooses to talk about, the way he views the great concerns of the day, and the materials he uses to support his argument. Primarily he is a selector. He selects:

(1) a reason for speaking, that is, his purpose
(2) the parts of his resources: materials, ideas, and meanings which serve his purpose in a speech of any given length
(3) the best way to compose and arrange the patterns of his ideas
(4) the details, the means of supporting his ideas, and the ways of polishing them for final presentation.

THE AUDIENCE

On every occasion a particular audience is present. The listener has been described as the sum total of his environment. Each audience has an already established system of values which conditions the way in which listening occurs, or whether or not it does occur. Value systems tend to differ with educational level, age, sex, economic and social group, political heritage, special interests, and ambitions.

An audience comes to a speech for a reason, with certain expectations and moods. Theodore Roosevelt, speaking to an outdoor audience in 1910, used the occasion to give some advice on improving farms. The audience, which expected a "rousing political speech," grew restless and started to leave. Realizing what was happening, Roosevelt ad-libbed colorfully and rearoused its interest. As soon as the audience had settled back on the grass, its expectations fulfilled, he continued with his manuscript speech.[4]

The student who has had two classes in a row may not be ready for a third one. A PTA audience, the members of which have come from discussing a variety of subjects, may not be "keyed up" to listen to a speech concerning funds for planting shrubbery around the local high school. Or, when a speaker says to someone in passing, "Beautiful day, isn't it?" his "audience" may not be receptive to that question if he has had a particularly bad day at the office.

[4] Richard Murphy, "Theodore Roosevelt" in *A History and Criticism of American Public Address*, III, 313–64.

Recent studies in the social sciences reveal some general characteristics of audiences. Six dominant societal influences on the American audience today are:

(1) conformity, concern for the appropriate, respect for accepted ideas
(2) materialistic self-interest: "How may I benefit?"
(3) respect for timesaving efficiency
(4) respect for progress
(5) search for personal adjustment
(6) straining for superiority or status.

Certain "needs" are also shared by all people. These may be arranged in a hierarchy of importance. As each basic need is fulfilled others emerge. They are:

(1) physiological needs (food, water, sex, and so forth)
(2) safety needs (tangible measures of well-being; these may range from the mother's support of a child to insurance of various kinds —medical, unemployment)
(3) love and belongingness needs
(4) esteem needs
(5) self-actualization, self-fulfillment needs.[5]

A speaker, using this mode for analyzing human behavior, can gain insights into the nature of his particular audience. For example, the Goodyear Tire and Rubber Co. published for national circulation an article called "Selling Appeals." Their advice was to make people want to buy by appealing to the instinct for self-preservation; by appealing to self-interest—for example, "Use your pencil to show the truck owner how your retreads give him lower cost per mile"; by appealing to interest in family—for example, "Your children will thank you for the rest of their lives for having safe tires on your car." This kind of appeal is not very different from the days of the elixir sellers, the medicine men, the hucksters: "Buy Dr. Hower's Magic Tonic and cure your aches and pains, live ten years longer, grow two inches more of hair, fill yourself with pep and vitality," all for the price of one dollar. In both, the speaker appeals very directly to the needs of his audience.

[5] This treatment is based on an analysis by Abraham H. Maslow, *Motivation and Personality* (New York: Harper and Row, Publishers, 1954).

THE PURPOSE

The speaker has a reason for speaking. A speech results from a need; it is a response to a specific situation. Most people do not speak merely to hear themselves talk. Classroom speeches should serve purposes other than filling the allotted time, getting a grade, or satisfying a requirement. Consider the purposes of the following speeches:

(1) Patrick Henry's speech in 1775 before the Virginia Convention:

> [*To encourage the Convention to pass a resolution to put Virginia "in a state of defense" by raising and equipping an army*] Sir, we have done everything that could be done, to avert the storm which is now coming on. We have petitioned; we have remonstrated; we have supplicated; we have prostrated ourselves before the throne, and have implored its interposition to arrest the tyrannical hands of the ministry and Parliament. Our petitions have been slighted; our remonstrances have produced additional violence and insult; our supplications have been disregarded; and we have been spurned, with contempt, from the foot of the throne. In vain, after these things, may we indulge the fond hope of peace and reconciliation. There is no longer any room for hope. If we wish to be free—if we mean to preserve inviolate those inestimable privileges for which we have been so long contending—if we mean not basely to abandon the noble struggle in which we have been so long engaged, and which we have pledged ourselves never to abandon until the glorious object of our contest shall be obtained, we must fight! I repeat it, sir, we must fight! [6]

(2) Daniel Webster's speech in 1830 before the United States Senate:

> [*To refute the argument that states have a right to nullify acts of Congress which they consider unconstitutional*] . . . the people have wisely provided, in the Constitution itself, a proper suitable mode and tribunal for settling questions of constitutional law. There are in the Constitution grants of power to Congress, and restrictions on these powers. There are, also, prohibitions on the States. Some authority must, therefore, necessarily exist, having the ultimate jurisdiction to fix and ascertain the interpretation of these grants, restrictions, and prohibitions. The Constitution has itself pointed out, ordained,

[6] From *The World's Great Speeches*, Lewis Copeland and Lawrence Lamm, eds., and rev. ed. (New York: Dover Publications, Inc., 1958), p. 233.

and established that authority. How has it accomplished this great and essential end? By declaring, Sir, that *"the Constitution, and the laws of the United States, made in pursuance thereof, shall be the supreme law of the land, anything in the constitution or laws of any State to the contrary notwithstanding."*

This, Sir, was the first great step. By this the supremacy of the Constitution and laws of the United States is declared. The people so will it. No State law is to be valid which comes in conflict with the Constitution, or any law of the United States passed in pursuance of it. But who shall decide this question of interference? To whom lies the last appeal? This, Sir, the Constitution itself decides also, by declaring, *"that the judicial power shall extend to all cases arising under the Constitution and laws of the United States."* These two provisions cover the whole ground. They are, in truth, the keystone of the arch! With these, it is a government; without them it is a confederation.[7]

(3) U Thant's speech, when, as Secretary General of the United Nations, he spoke to a 1963 college commencement audience:

[*To persuade his audience that education must go beyond the development of the potentiality to do good*] What we need is a synthesis of . . . values—spiritual and moral as well as intellectual—with the aim of producing a fully integrated human being who is inward looking as well as outward looking, who searches his own mind in order that his nobler self may prevail at all times, and at the same time recognizes his obligations to his fellow men and the world around him; because while the world is shrinking, humanity is multiplying, and each of us has to recognize his essential kinship to every other member of the human race.[8]

Whatever end the speaker has in mind, his specific purpose is to speak with persuasive effect toward that end. He has a *reason* for speaking, and everything the speaker says must be directed to fulfilling that purpose.

A consideration of purpose can suggest a potential problem. Is a speech which does not prompt immediate response successful? Perhaps fulfillment of specific purpose is not the only test of "success." For example, although the members of an audience may not act in precisely the way a speaker intends, they may be considering new problems and different solutions to old problems, their predispositions may be changed, and their minds alerted.

[7] Wayland Maxfield Parrish and Marie Hochmuth, eds., *American Speeches* (New York: Longmans, Green and Co., 1954), p. 221.

[8] Mimeographed press release courtesy of the Mount Holyoke College News Bureau.

THE TIME

A speech is given at a time. Time represents more than 4 o'clock in the afternoon; it represents a stage in the life of problems. Time is reflected in the choice of topic and in the way it is handled. Note the change in what speakers have been saying about the Cuban problem from 1959 to the present.

Observe how changes in time are reflected by the events about which the speaker speaks. The speeches of Adlai E. Stevenson from July 21, 1952 to November 5, 1952 are an example: [9] On July 21, in his welcoming address to the Democratic Convention, he said:

> As Governor of the host state to the 1952 Democratic Convention, I have the honor of welcoming you to Illinois.

On July 26, in his speech accepting the presidential nomination, he said:

> I accept your nomination—and your program. . . . I have not sought the honor you have done me. I *could* not seek it because I aspired to another office, which was the full measure of my ambition. One does not treat the highest office within the gift of the people of Illinois as an alternative or as a consolation prize.

On August 14, at the Illinois State Fair, shortly before beginning his campaign for the presidency, he said:

> I am about to leave you on a long journey, and the route, by the way, won't be a military or a political secret. I intend to cover as much ground as time and strength and our resources permit.

On October 23, in Cleveland, Ohio, as the campaign drew to a close, he said:

> The hour is growing late in this autumn of our political decision. But I find it necessary to talk here tonight of things which are more fundamental than the immediate political questions before us.

On November 1, in Chicago, a few days before the election, he said:

> Tonight, we have come to the end of the campaign, and a long, long journey—and I have come home to old friends and to familiar surroundings. . . . There have been times when I have wondered whether

---

[9] From *Major Campaign Speeches of Adlai E. Stevenson, 1952.* Copyright 1953 by Random House, Inc. Reprinted by permission.

you, my friends here in Illinois, couldn't have found some easier way of getting rid of me.

On November 5, at his campaign headquarters in Springfield, Illinois, on radio and TV, he conceded defeat:

> I have sent the following telegram to General Eisenhower. . . . "The people have made their choice and I congratulate you. That you may be the servant and guardian of peace and make the vale of trouble a door of hope is my earnest prayer. . . ." Someone asked me, as I came in, down on the street, how I felt, and I was reminded of a story that a fellow-townsman of ours used to tell—Abraham Lincoln. They asked him how he felt once after an unsuccessful election. He said he felt like a little boy who had stubbed his toe in the dark. He said that he was too old to cry, but it hurt too much to laugh.

Observe the way in which one speaker responds to changes in a specific policy. Recall William Pitt (Lord Chatham), twice Prime Minister of Great Britain, on British policy concerning the American Colonies between 1766 and 1778.[10] On January 14, 1766, after news of the colonies' resistance to the Stamp Act, he spoke on the subject of taxing the American colonies:

> There is an idea in some that the colonies are *virtually* represented in the House. I would fain to know by whom an American is represented here.
>
>   ❊   ❊   ❊
>
> Upon the whole, I will beg leave to tell the House what is my opinion. It is, that the Stamp Act be repealed absolutely, totally, and immediately. That the reason for the repeal be assigned . . . because it was founded on an erroneous principle. At the same time, let the sovereign authority of this country over the colonies be asserted in as strong terms as can be devised, and be made to extend to every point of legislation whatsoever; that we may bind their trade, confine their manufactures, and exercise every power whatsoever, except that of taking their money out of their pockets without their consent.

On May 27, 1774, in ill health, but deeply troubled by British desire to quarter troops in the homes of the colonists, he said:

> The Americans had almost forgot, in their excess of gratitude for the repeal of the Stamp Act, any interest but that of the mother country. . . .
>
>   ❊   ❊   ❊

[10] Chauncey A. Goodrich, *Select British Eloquence*, photo offset edition (Indianapolis: The Bobbs-Merrill Company, Inc., 1963), pp. 103–42. Reprinted by permission of The Bobbs-Merrill Company, Inc.

But, my Lords, from the complexion of the whole of the proceedings, I think that administration has purposely irritated them into those late violent acts, for which they now so severely smart, purposely to be revenged on them for the victory they gained by the repeal of the Stamp Act. . . .

❋   ❋   ❋

This, my Lords, though no new doctrine, has always been my received and unalterable opinion, and I will carry it to my grave, *that this country had no right under heaven to tax America.* It is contrary to all the principles of justice and civil polity, which neither the exigencies of the state, nor even an acquiescence in the taxes, could justify upon any occasion whatever.

On January 20, 1775, he spoke again, this time to urge the immediate removal of troops from Boston homes:

When I urge this measure of recalling the troops from Boston, I urge it on this pressing principle, that it is necessarily preparatory to the restoration of your peace and the establishment of your prosperity.

❋   ❋   ❋

[I]f the ministers thus persevere in misadvising and misleading the King, I will not say that they can alienate the affections of his subjects from his crown, but I will affirm *that they will make the crown not worth his wearing.* I will not say that the King is betrayed, but I will pronounce *that the kingdom is undone.*

On May 30, 1777, in one last effort to end the contest with America, Pitt said:

My Lords, this is a flying moment; perhaps but six weeks left to arrest the dangers that surround us. The gathering storm may break; it has already opened, and in part burst. It is difficult for government, after all that has passed, to shake hands with defiers of the King, defiers of the Parliament, defiers of the people. . . . They are rebels; but for what? Surely not for defending their unquestionable rights!

❋   ❋   ❋

You have been the aggressors from the beginning. . . . You have made descents upon their coasts; you have burned their towns, plundered their country, made war upon the inhabitants, confiscated their property, proscribed and imprisoned their persons. . . . A repeal of those laws, of which they complain, will be the first step to that redress.

On November 18, 1777, he protested allowing mercenaries to attack the colonists:

> My Lords, no man wishes for the due dependence of America on this country more than I do. To preserve it, and not confirm that state of independence into which *your measures* hitherto have *driven them*, is the object which we ought to unite in attaining. The Americans, contending for their rights against arbitrary exactions, I love and admire. It is the struggle of free and virtuous patriots. But, contending for independency and total disconnection from England, as an Englishman, I cannot wish them success. . . .
>
>   ✿   ✿   ✿
>
> Spain armed herself with blood-hounds to extirpate the wretched natives of America, and we improve on the inhuman example even of Spanish cruelty; we turn loose these savage hell-hounds against our brethren and countrymen in America, of the same language, laws, liberties, and religion, endeared to us by every tie that should sanctify humanity.

On December 11, 1777, he spoke of his fears about the outcome of the war:

> I tremble for this country. I am almost led to despair that we shall ever be able to extricate ourselves. At any rate, the day of retribution is at hand, when the vengeance of a much-injured and afflicted people will, I trust, fall heavily on the authors of their ruin. . . .

On April 7, 1778, little more than a month before his death, Chatham urged the Parliament:

> In God's name, if it is absolutely necessary to declare either for peace or war, and the former can not be preserved with honor, why is not the latter commenced without delay? . . . Let us at least make one effort, and, if we must fall, let us fall like men!

THE PLACE

The speaker and the audience assemble in a place. And place helps determine both what the speaker says and how an audience will react. People do not react in a crowded, smoky convention hall the way they do in the more dignified atmosphere of the Senate gallery, although the day in 1856 when, on the Senate floor, Preston Brooks struck Charles Sumner on the head with a cane may be one exception.

Washington's farewell to his troops on a battlefield contrasted with his inaugural address in the Senate chambers; and it was only because he was delivering a speech in Faneuil Hall, Boston, that Wendell Phillips in 1837, protesting against the death of Elijah Lovejoy, an abolitionist editor, said: [11]

> Sir, when I heard the gentleman lay down principles which place the murderers of Alton side by side with Otis and Hancock, with Quincy and Adams, I thought those pictured lips [pointing to the portraits in the hall] would have broken into voice to rebuke the recreant American—the slanderer of the dead.

and:

> James Otis thundered in this hall when the King did but touch his pocket. Imagine, if you can, his indignant eloquence had England offered to put a gag upon his lips.

It is place, the cemetery at Gettysburg, which allowed Lincoln to say: [12]

> We are met on a great battlefield of that war. We have come to dedicate a portion of that field as a final resting place for those who here gave their lives that that nation might live. It is altogether fitting and proper that we should do this.

> But, in a larger sense, we cannot dedicate—we cannot consecrate— we cannot hallow—this ground. The brave men, living and dead, who struggled here, have consecrated it, far above our poor power to add or to detract.

THE CONTENT

The substance of the speech calls for particular attention. Speeches may be made on any subject, but some subjects are more likely to prompt speeches than others. For example, a man may write a lyric poem because of the beauty of moonlight shining on a lake, but he is rarely moved to give a speech about it. People generally give speeches in three situations: (1) when they are deciding whether or not to act; (2) when they are trying to determine the way in which they ought to act; and (3) when they are trying to evaluate their methods of action. To recognize something as a problem, to determine that some courses of action are better solutions than others, and to decide if a solution has actually alleviated the problem call for value judgments by the speaker. He perceives what things constitute a threat to his welfare, his institutions, his progress toward achieving his goals. Because he values some goals more than

---

[11] *The World's Great Speeches,* p. 281.
[12] *Ibid.,* p. 315.

others he decides which problems should be dealt with first. Because
he views some courses of action as more satisfactory than others,
he determines what alternative solutions are possible. Thus, the
speaker is concerned with: (1) those forces, events, and ideas which
prompt men to act; (2) alternative ways of acting; and (3) evaluating actions which have taken place.

Whatever his topic, the speaker is responsible for each statement
he makes, for the facts he selects, and for the inferences he draws
from those facts. Each public statement is a commitment. Observe
how the statements below imply certain humane values as their
basis:

(1) The future towards which we are marching, across bloody fields
and frightful manifestations of destruction, must surely be based
upon the broad and simple virtues and upon the nobility of mankind. It must be based upon a reign of law which upholds the
principles of justice and fair play, and protects the weak against
the strong if the weak have justice on their side. (Winston
Churchill, speaking to the House of Commons in 1944) [13]

(2) I believe that man will not merely endure: he will prevail. He is
immortal, not because he alone among creatures has an inexhaustible voice, but because he has a soul, a spirit capable of
compassion and sacrifice and endurance. The poet's, the writer's,
duty is to write about these things. It is his privilege to help man
endure by lifting his heart, by reminding him of the courage
and honor and hope and pride and compassion and pity and sacrifice which have been the glory of his past. (William Faulkner,
accepting the 1949 Nobel Prize in Stockholm, Sweden) [14]

THE SPEAKER'S STYLE

The style of a speech must also be considered. Style in the narrow
meaning, the effective use of language, is in no sense "magic." In
a broad sense it is an overt manifestation of the speaker's general
outlook on life. Whether you define style as "the man himself" [15] or
"proper words in proper places," [16] style is a means of persuasion,
a way of identifying the speaker's attitudes, ideas, and so forth, with

[13] F. B. Czarnomski, ed., *The Eloquence of Winston Churchill* (New York:
The New American Library, 1957), p. 178.

[14] *The World's Great Speeches*, p. 638.

[15] "Discourse on Style" reprinted in *Theories of Style*, ed. Lane Cooper (New
York, 1907). Republished as *The Art of the Writer* (Ithaca, N.Y.: Cornell
University Press, 1952).

[16] "A Letter to a Young Clergyman" also reprinted in Cooper, *The Art of
the Writer*.

those of his audience. Consequently, the speaker first determines what effect he wants to achieve and selects the words and structures which will best achieve it. Lincoln, for example, in his "First Inaugural Address" was seeking unity. When one of his assistants suggested the phrase "passion has strained," Lincoln changed it to "passion may have strained" because he wanted to temper his words. Because he wanted to appear direct and friendly, he said "we are not enemies, but friends" rather than "we are not, we must not be aliens or enemies but fellow countrymen and brethren." The first is simple and kind; the second is less positive and less personal.[17]

Listen to the speeches, the conversations around you and consider these questions: (1) What did the speaker hope to achieve? (2) By what linguistic "strategies" did he try to achieve his purpose? (3) How else could it have been done? (4) Which of the alternative suggestions are better? (5) Why are they better? Frances Perkins tells of the time [18] she suggested this sentence to Franklin Roosevelt during a speechwriting effort: "We are trying to construct a more inclusive society." President Roosevelt simplified and clarified that statement when he changed it to: "We are going to make a country in which no one is left out." Why? Because he was working to attain directness and clarity.

Almost every participant in a recent high school oratory contest quoted President John F. Kennedy's statement, "Ask not what your country can do for you—ask what you can do for your country." [19] The same thought has been expressed thousands of times, by many writers and speakers, but a distinctive use of language added vitality to the thought.

THE SPEAKER'S DELIVERY

Obviously, communication cannot occur if the speaker talks too softly to be heard, or mumbles so much that the audience can only guess at what he is saying. The most brilliant idea, the most effective style are lost if the speech is not heard. If the audience is conscious of delivery itself—whether good or bad—it is not paying complete

[17] See Marie Hochmuth, "Lincoln's First Inaugural" in *American Speeches*, pp. 21–71.

[18] Frances Perkins, *The Roosevelt I Knew* (New York: The Viking Press, Inc., 1946), p. 113.

[19] Ernest J. Wrage and Barnet Baskerville, eds., *Contemporary Forum: American Speeches on Twentieth-Century Issues* (New York: Harper and Row, Publishers, 1962), p. 320.

attention to the "message" of the speaker. For example, Cicero criti-cizes the delivery of one of his contemporaries because of "ridiculous gestures." He ridicules another because in shifting his weight from side to side he looked as if he were "speaking from a boat." On the other hand, he praises still another because his actions corresponded to the meaning of every sentence.[20]

The more natural the delivery, the more likely it is to be effective as a means of persuasion, in the sense that it does not call attention to itself. It was commonly said of Wendell Phillips, the great nine-teenth-century abolitionist orator, that his voice "had the effect of 'finding' its auditor . . . . as if it were speaking to each one as an un-known friend," [21] that it was as if he simply repeated in a little louder tone what he had just been saying to a friend at his elbow.

Delivery reveals very directly the "workings" of the speaker's mind. For example, Theodore Roosevelt's voice and manner have been described as "consistent with the rough-and-ready vigor of his personality." He had a "strong, direct voice, slightly strained and rasping, but not unpleasant in quality." His "whole manner was vigorous, suggestive of his moods." [22] Critics recall that William Pitt had "[s]uch . . . power of his eye, that he very often cowed down an antagonist in the midst of his speech, and threw him into utter confusion, by a single glance of scorn or contempt." [23]

In addition to telling the audience something about the speaker, delivery also gives the listener cues as to what is important in the message. The comments about Lincoln's "First Inaugural Address" include: [24] He had "firm tones of voice" and spoke with "great de-liberation and precision of emphasis." A writer in the *Chicago Daily Tribune* noted that "With great solemnity of emphasis, using his gestures to add significance to his words," Lincoln remarked: "*You* have no oath registered in Heaven to destroy this Government, while I shall have the most solemn one to preserve, protect, and defend it." Emphatic delivery made prominent Lincoln's main point, that his duty was to keep the Union whole.

[20] Cicero, *Brutus*, trans. G. L. Hendrickson, The Loeb Classical Library (London: William Heinemann Limited, 1939), LXIII, LX, XXXVIII.

[21] Cited in: Willard Hayes Yeager, "Wendell Phillips" in *A History and Criticism of American Public Address*, I, 359.

[22] Murphy, "Theodore Roosevelt," *A History and Criticism of American Public Address*, pp. 355, 358.

[23] Goodrich, *Select British Eloquence*, p. 71.

[24] Hochmuth, "Lincoln's First Inaugural," *op. cit.*, pp. 44–45.

Summary

The communicative situation is not a simple one. In each speech is reflected, both directly and indirectly, a particular speaker, speaking to a particular audience, at a particular time, in a particular place, for a particular purpose. How well or how poorly a speaker succeeds is often a result of how well or how poorly he analyzes his unique communicative situation and the ways in which he responds to the challenge of his analysis.

Rhetorical Exercises

(1) Give a three to five minute speech in which you: introduce yourself; or, give your political or social attitude toward something; or, describe your main area of interest.

(2) Attend a speech on or off campus and write a description of it in terms of the eight elements in the communicative situation. Read your descriptions aloud in class and compare notes on the kinds of things observed. Consider these questions:

   (a) *About the speaker:* Was the speaker known or unknown? How did this affect the way in which people listened to him?

   Was there an introduction to explain the speaker's qualifications for speaking on his topic? Do you think this introduction influenced the audience's way of listening to him?

   What did he say in the speech to reveal his character, his personality and general outlook?

   (b) *About the audience:* Did the audience share certain characteristics: Age? Sex? Educational development? Economic class? Social strata? Political heritage? Special interests?

   Do you think the audience had certain expectations about the speaker and his topic? Do you think they were fulfilled?

   (c) *About the purpose:* What was the speaker's specific purpose? Was it explicitly stated or implied?

   Do you think he fulfilled his purpose?

   (d) *About the time:* At what time was the speech given? How was time likely to affect the audience?

   Was time reflected in how the speaker handled his subject? In what he said?

   (e) *About the place:* Where was the speech given? Did it condition the audience's reactions?

   Did the speaker make special reference to it?

   (f) *About the content:* What were the speaker's main points? How did he support them?

Was the content adequate? Varied? Appropriate to the audience? Interesting?

(g) *About the style:* Was the speaker's style clear? Was it appropriate to the occasion and to the audience? Was it impressive?

(h) *About the delivery:* Was the speaker direct? Fluent? Was he animated and communicative?

(3) Compare two speeches given in class. Which one was better? Why? How could the other one have been improved?

Collateral Readings

Berlo, David K., *The Process of Communication.* New York: Holt, Rinehart and Winston, Inc., 1960. Especially "A Model of the Communication Process" and "The Fidelity of Communication: Determinants of Effect," pp. 23–70.

Hochmuth, Marie K., ed., *A History and Criticism of American Public Address,* III. New York: Longmans, Green and Co., Inc., 1955. See "The Criticism of Rhetoric," pp. 1–23.

Schramm, Wilbur, ed., *The Process and Effects of Mass Communication.* Urbana: University of Illinois Press, 1954. See "How Communication Works," pp. 3–10.

*If rhetoric teaches nothing else, she requires that her
student make up his mind, that he take decision
only after search and full inquiry, that he speak from
his convictions with all the skill he can acquire.*

KARL R. WALLACE

II   Ours is a rhetorical world. We are virtually sur-
rounded by talk; we are talking or listening a large
part of our day. We may be discussing last weekend's football scores over coffee or debating the role of the federal
government in higher education or listening to a professor
discuss the "Tragic Vision in Contemporary Literature."
The Senate may be holding open committee hearings on
syndicated crime in the United States, and the spokesmen
for many nations may be meeting to discuss disarmament
agreements.

How well or how poorly we cope with our problems
through talk determines whether or not we can fulfill our
aspirations. How expeditiously we deal with our problems
determines how many of our needs we can satisfy. How well
or how poorly each man participates in this "great conversation" of trying to solve our common problems determines,
in the end, the overall quality of the human condition in
a free society. The beginning speaker would do well to
remember the words of Isocrates in the fourth century
B.C.:

> ... in the other powers which we possess, we are in no
> respect superior to other living creatures; nay we are in-

THE NATURE
OF RHETORIC

ferior to many in swiftness and in strength and in other resources; but, because there has been implanted in us the power to persuade each other and to make clear to each other whatever we desire, not only have we escaped the life of wild beasts, but we have come together and founded cities and made laws and invented arts; and, generally speaking, there is no institution devised by man which the power of speech has not helped us to establish. For this it is which has laid down laws concerning things just and unjust, and things honourable and base; and if it were not for these ordinances we should not be able to live with one another. It is by this that we confute the bad and extol the good. Through this we educate the ignorant and appraise the wise; for the power to speak well is taken as the surest index of a sound understanding. . . . With this faculty we both contend against others on matters which are open to dispute and seek light for ourselves on things which are unknown. . . . [W]e shall find that none of the things which are done with intelligence take place without the help of speech, but that in all our actions as well as in all our thoughts speech is our guide, and is most employed by those who have the most wisdom.[1]

This book is concerned with one kind of speech, public speaking: public speaking not in the sense of discussion or debate (or discontinuous discourse), but in the sense of giving *a speech* (with continuous discourse). The art of rhetoric, of public speaking, has existed since the fifth century B.C. The ancients, the eighteenth-century and nineteenth-century theorists, and our contemporaries have all attempted to interpret the term "rhetoric" in order to determine its proper use. Through the centuries it has been called a synonym for bombast; sophistry; elocution; style, especially as exemplified by the "purple passage"; the theory of spoken and written discourse; Freshman English; and recently "the study of misunderstanding and its remedies." Since there is so much confusion about the term, let us first determine what we are studying and then its relation to other disciplines.

A Definition of Rhetoric

Aristotle defined rhetoric as "the faculty of observing in any given case the available means of persuasion." [2] This definition has useful

---

[1] Isocrates, *Antidosis*, trans. George Norlin, The Loeb Classical Library (London: William Heinemann, Limited, 1929), 253–57.

[2] Aristotle, *Rhetoric*, trans. W. Rhys Roberts (New York: Random House, Inc., 1954), 1355b 26–27.

implications for today's beginning speaker. Rhetoric is, according to this definition, a *faculty*, an ability. All too often we hear about "the natural born speaker," but it is doubtful that such a creature exists. Skill in speechmaking usually results from a rigorous study program rather than some happy accident or native faculty. Most distinguished speakers have either systematically studied the principles of effective speechmaking or have deduced these principles through constant practice and careful analysis of their own failures and successes. Skill in speechmaking has always been sought by young men and women working to make their ideas known. Recall the almost legendary story of Demosthenes practicing by the seashore with pebbles in his mouth to correct his stutter. Or of the young Henry Clay, who so often practiced giving speeches to imaginary juries that he once began a speech before a Kentucky town assembly with "Gentlemen of the jury—." Or of the shy young Eleanor Roosevelt patiently listening to the suggestions of her husband's advisors.

Rhetoric is a particular kind of faculty: It is the faculty of observing in any given case the available means of persuasion. Aristotle suggests that the faculty of rhetoric is the faculty for observing, that is, the speaker should consider the widest possible variety of materials available on his topic for inclusion in his speech.

The speaker, however, does not only determine the materials for his speech according to his topic. He must also consider the specific audience and specific occasion. He surveys each speech situation, each "given case," to decide which materials will be most appropriate and most impressive.

Finally, the Aristotelian definition of rhetoric suggests that the speaker must have a thorough grasp of "all the available means of persuasion." A description of the "means of persuasion" forms the major substance of this book. The arguments, the organization, and the style of the speech and the manner of delivery are all included as means of persuasion. They help the speaker accomplish his specific purpose.

The Nature and Scope of Rhetoric

Rhetoric is used quite practically to direct men's thoughts and actions toward the realization of a particular course: to present a plan which will provide medical care for the aged, to encourage interest in student government organizations, to offer support to the

Organization of American States. Thus, rhetoric operates as an instrument of social control.

One writer on the subject of oral communication asserts that there is a twofold approach to it: one, rhetorical; the other, evaluative. He notes: "Through a study of rhetorical principles the student learns to organize and present his thoughts according to acceptable standards of composition. Through the evaluative approach he learns to weigh carefully the validity and accuracy of his statements. He learns to talk sense, not nonsense." [3] By suggesting the rhetorical and the evaluative as two separate approaches to the study of oral communication, this writer is almost suggesting that rhetoric may teach nonsense as long as it is well composed nonsense. What he forgets is that evaluation is part of the rhetorical act.

We have already emphasized the role of the speaker as *selector*. At each stage in the rhetorical process he selects from many alternatives: one subject out of many, one set of opinions instead of others, one structure of arguments and not another. When he selects, he makes a choice. Implied in the word choice is evaluation. Each of the speaker's statements is based on an assumption he makes about values. Consider the commitments made in these statements:

(1) by John Marshall in 1788 when he stood before the Virginia Convention to urge the ratification of the new national constitution and affirmed that the underlying principles of good government were "[a] strict observance of justice and public faith, and a steady adherence to virtue." [4]

(2) by Daniel Webster when, not quite half a century later, at the early signs of discord between North and South, he stood before the Senate to plead not for "liberty first, and union afterwards" but "liberty and union, now and forever, one and inseparable." [5]

(3) by Clarence Darrow, speaking in 1926 on housing segregation, when he said: ". . . the last analysis is, what has man done?—and not what has the law done?" [6]

These statements were prompted by the necessity of making decisions in order to act or making judgements in order to appraise the nature of the action. Rhetoric, as the study of purposive speech

[3] Glenn Capp, *How to Communicate Orally* (Englewood Cliffs, N.J.: Prentice-Hall, Inc., 1961), p. ix.

[4] Lewis Copeland and Lawrence Lamm, eds., *The World's Great Speeches*, 2nd rev. ed., (New York: Dover Publications, Inc., 1958), p. 240.

[5] *Ibid.*, p. 278.

[6] Arthur Weinberg, ed., *Attorney for the Damned* (New York: Simon and Schuster, Inc., 1957), p. 233.

about the human condition, requires intense feeling, powerful intellect, and direct, responsible judgment. The search for arguments,
evaluation and decisions about which are good and which bad, and
the framing of those arguments in the best possible language all
share equally in the domain of rhetoric.

With what kinds of topics does the speaker concern himself? With
what class of subjects is rhetoric properly concerned? Aristotle, in
his *Rhetoric* says:

> Every other art can instruct or persuade about its own particular
> subject-matter; for instance, medicine about what is healthy and
> unhealthy, geometry about the properties of magnitudes, arithmetic
> about numbers, and the same is true of the other arts and sciences.
> But rhetoric we look upon as the power of observing the means of
> persuasion on almost any subject presented to us; and that is why
> we say that, in its technical character, it is not concerned with any
> special or definite class of subjects.[7]

What are the proper topics for speeches? The examples of statements from the speeches of the past indicate that they were statements about courses of action or about evaluation of those actions
or about basic assumptions underlying those courses of action. Thus,
the speaker is concerned with judgments about the conduct of human affairs, judgments which enable man to adjust to his environment and, perhaps more importantly, which allow him to change
his environment.

One writer has commented that rhetoric is the "organizing and
animating principle of all subject matters which have a relevant
bearing on [public] decision." [8] To this extent, rhetoric is bound to
all other subject-matters. Whenever human affairs are directed toward a predetermined end in any area, ethics, politics, and others,
the situation is rhetorical. As rhetoric works toward a particular
intent, as it provides a basis for public decision, ultimately it determines the very structure of men's thoughts and actions as they
operate to mold the entire pattern of society. Thus rhetoric is concerned with the principles of persuasion, and the essence of persuasion lies in the content of the subject under discussion.

Although we have primarily stressed the persuasive intent, not
all speeches are governed primarily by it. Some speeches are de-

[7] *Rhetoric,* 1355b 28–36.
[8] Donald C. Bryant, "Rhetoric: Its Function and Its Scope," *Quarterly
Journal of Speech* (December, 1953), p. 408.

signed primarily to give information: to describe a process, a place, a person, or an event; to tell about personal experiences; to clarify concepts, materials, ideas. In these cases, the speaker's purpose is not mainly to arouse his listeners to action or to change their attitudes and opinions, but to give them new knowledge (which may well eventually arouse them to action). But even in speeches of exposition and narration the speaker is, at a very basic level, trying to get the audience to accept him as a good source of information. The speaker wants the audience to accept the method he is describing as an effective method, to accept the materials of his speech as accurate. Thus, to a certain extent the persuasive intent is present by the very nature of the speech act: stimulus seeking to elicit a predetermined response.

Rhetoric as Participation

To let only a few lead, to let only a few speak is to have too narrow a view of public speaking and of the function of men in our contemporary democratic society. Thomas Jefferson wrote in a letter to John Tyler: "No experiment can be more interesting than that we are now trying, and which we trust will end in establishing the fact, that man may be governed by reason and truth...." [9] This experiment is still going on in our day. The speaker, in a sense, is the catalyst, the activating agent in this experiment. The basic difference between the rationale of liberal democracy and the rationale of totalitarian forms of government is that democracy has always held to the belief that men of good will and intelligence can reach agreement and understanding through general communication. A liberal democracy permits men to function together as they work to secure the common good.

The speaker, as a participator in a liberal democracy, should not be misled by the contention that rhetoric is solely a technique and as such has no inherent morality. It is vitally concerned with the end to which it subscribes as well as with the means to that end. Rhetoric demands responsible commitment. Central to it is the power of ideas as manifested by the conceptions, the choices, the value judgments of the speaker. So, the speaker needs to raise very early and very seriously these questions: "What values should I apply when

[9] Adlai E. Stevenson, *Major Campaign Speeches of 1952* (New York: Random House, Inc., 1953), pp. xxx–xxxi.

choosing ends?" "What values should I choose for the means to that end?"

There is, as such, no generally accepted code of ethics. Wallace has, however, suggested four responsibilities of the speaker:

(1) duty of search and inquiry
(2) allegiance to accuracy and fairness
(3) revelation of individual motives
(4) tolerance of dissent [10]

In the final analysis, ethics and persuasion cannot be separated. At the most basic level, man's ageless enemies must be conquered if he is to fulfill his potential for growth and development. Disease must be overcome. Poverty must be alleviated. Illiteracy must be wiped out. Survival must be assured in an atmosphere conducive to free, creative enterprise, rather than in the shadow of nuclear war, conducive only to the disintegration of human values. These goals can only be met through the vigorous and free exchange of ideas, through verbal agreements and persuasions. Ethical rhetoric thus has the potential of creating the kind of communication which helps man to be the best he can become. The responsibility of the public speaker is a tremendous one, and the study of rhetoric is not an easy task; but it is essential to public and private decision-making.

The Relationship of Rhetoric to Other Subjects

Rhetoric is inextricably bound to other disciplines, as indeed they are to it. Let us explore these relationships a bit more thoroughly.[11]

HISTORY

The study of history attempts to recover the past and to make the present more intelligible through interpretation of the past. Since the speech grows out of a need, it occurs in time. Time here refers in its largest sense to time in the life of problems. The speaker must understand the background relevant to the speech. He may discuss either the chronological life of a problem, its history or one aspect of its history. The time at which a speech occurs may well be called

[10] Karl R. Wallace, "An Ethical Basis of Communication," *Speech Teacher* (January, 1955), p. 9.
[11] The author is heavily indebted to Prof. Karl Wallace for this treatment of the relationship between rhetoric and other disciplines.

the environment of that speech, the environment of a problem or of a solution.

Speakers have been catalysts in history. Surely the United States without Samuel Adams, James Otis, Patrick Henry, Henry Clay, John C. Calhoun, Daniel Webster, the abolitionist orators, and Abraham Lincoln would be different. Britain without Sir Winston Churchill, William Pitt, and Edmund Burke would not be the same as it is today. It is hard to envision Greece without Demosthenes and Rome without Cicero. All these men, speaking out in their times, have undoubtedly helped to shape the destinies of their nations. As Landor has Pericles say:

> Show me how great projects were executed, great advantages gained, and great calamities averted. Show me the generals and the statesmen who stood foremost, that I may bend to them in reverence; tell me their names, that I may repeat them to my children . . . place History on her rightful throne, and, at the sides of her, Eloquence and war.[12]

The impact of Churchill, speaking to the House of Commons, indeed to all of Great Britain, in the "gathering storm" of World War II, cannot be overemphasized. Recall his words:

> The whole fury and might of the enemy must very soon be turned upon us. Hitler knows he will have to break us in this island or lose the war.
>
> If we can stand up to him all Europe may be freed and the life of the world may move forward into broad sunlit uplands; but if we fail, the whole world, including the United States and all that we have known and cared for, will sink into the abyss of a new dark age made more sinister and perhaps more prolonged by the lights of a perverted science.
>
> Let us therefore brace ourselves to our duty and so bear ourselves that if the British Commonwealth and Empire last for a thousand years, men will still say "This was their finest hour." [13]

POLITICAL SCIENCE

The end of political science is to understand political ways of life and the processes which provide effective political power. The speaker may be speaking on a political subject. He needs at least

[12] Sidney Colvin, ed., *Selections from the Writings of Walter Savage Landor* (London: Macmillan and Co., 1882), p. 277.
[13] *The World's Great Speeches*, p. 446.

a basic knowledge of political behavior and the ways of influencing it. To influence, he must try to grasp the national character of audiences and their political allegiances.

The speaker may be a political speaker, a professional politician. Never before have so many politicians appealed directly to the people; for example, the much publicized Nixon-Kennedy debates. As one political commentator has noted: "Eloquence and greatness are by no means the same, but in politics the former is almost always the indispensable tool of the latter." [14]

The political scientist can often use the tools of audience analysis developed by rhetorical theorists. He can gain insight into specific strategies and the effects of those strategies on different kinds of audiences. Lasswell, for example, has pointed out that "one of the principal problems of political science is the study of the factors making for the restriction or diffusion of political doctrine and formulas. . . ." [15] Political scientists, Leiserson says, should not overlook "the value of communications studies for their own work in political-party and pressure-group publicity, communications between representatives and constituents in policy-making, administrative public relations and . . . revolutionary and war propaganda." [16] In a still larger sense, Godkin has pointed out that in the United States, England, and France "the work of bringing the popular will to bear in filling the offices of government, and in performing any act of government . . . needs almost constant attention." [17] In a democratic society political processes are carried out by rhetorical means.

PSYCHOLOGY

The end of psychology is to understand sensory and motor experience, emotional and symbolic experience in their physiological and neurological setting in the human organism. Thus, it shares with rhetoric a need for knowledge of basic mechanisms such as those involved in organically centered motivations and desires and those entailed in emotion; knowledge of such compensatory mechanisms as rationalization and identification; knowledge of the character of

[14] *The New York Times Magazine* (February 25, 1962), p. 71.

[15] Harold D. Lasswell, ed., *Language of Politics* (New York: G. W. Stewart, 1949), p. 14.

[16] Avery Leiserson, "Problems of Methodology in Political Research," *Political Science Quarterly* (December, 1953), p. 576.

[17] E. L. Godkin, *Problems of Modern Democracy* (New York: Charles Scribner's Sons, 1898), p. 287.

belief, conviction, opinion, attitude; knowledge of the conditions of learning, retention, recall, and so forth.

SOCIOLOGY AND
SOCIAL PSYCHOLOGY

The end of sociology is to understand the behavior patterns of large groups; the end of social psychology is to understand the behavior of small groups and the interaction of the group and the individual. They share with rhetoric the need for knowledge of the institutional character of audiences, institutional motivations, and values; knowledge of the ways in which the individual is affected by the presence of others; knowledge of what motivates a group to listen, what kinds of proof a given group is most likely to accept.

PHILOSOPHY

The relationship between rhetoric and philosophy is very old and very close. We need only to list a few of the philosophers who have written treatises on rhetoric: Plato devoted not one but several of his works to rhetoric; Aristotle wrote perhaps the soundest rhetoric ever conceived; the list continues through St. Augustine to the present day. In ancient Greece, for example, the whole of the educational system was built around the study of Politics-Ethics-Rhetoric. In the medieval trivium plan of education, it was Rhetoric-Logic-Grammar.

There is an especially close relationship between rhetoric and two branches of philosophy: ethics and logic. The end of ethics is to discover ways of evaluating conduct on a scale labeled good-bad, to provide individuals with methods of making acceptable choices among values. The speaker's selection of topics and arguments reveals his character. On the other hand, values are animated, disseminated by the speaker.

We have mentioned that the chief tool of rhetoric is logical proof. In turn, rhetoric offers a practical way for utilizing the forms of logic. Both studies share a common vocabulary: argument, probability, validity, induction, premise, and so on.

FINE ARTS

One may secure a deeper appreciation of the art of public speaking when he sees it as one of many arts. The artist brings an object into being which stimulates others to respond. The relation of rhetoric to literature especially needs to be mentioned. The speech may be literature if the language and form have lasting value: (1) the speeches within a piece of literature, for example, the famous "Friends, Romans, countrymen" speech in Julius Caesar; (2) the speeches within a history, for example, the Pericles oration for the dead Athenian soldiers as recorded by Thucydides; (3) the speech as a speech, for example, Cicero is included in studies of Latin literature, Edmund Burke, in many studies of English literature. Many of Emerson's "essays" were speeches, delivered orally before they were printed. Faulkner's "Nobel Prize Acceptance Speech" is included in numerous volumes of collected essays. And, not long ago, Winston Churchill was awarded a Nobel Prize for Literature, in part, for material that first appeared as speeches.

Summary

As students of rhetoric, we are studying what people say when they want to have an effect upon others. The key word is effect, for speech is purposive. It is a response to needs which have grown out of a time, a place, and a subject. Men give speeches when they are trying to decide whether to act, when to act, how to act, and when they are evaluating actions. The conversation Adlai Stevenson records with Albert Schweitzer points to the main task of our time for speakers:

> . . . he told me that he considered this the most dangerous period in history. I said, "In contemporary history?" "No," he said, "in all human history." "Why?" "Because," he said, "heretofore nature has controlled man in the last analysis, but now man has learned to control elemental forces of nature—before he has learned to control himself." [18]

As communication facilitates social control, it makes adjustment and readjustment possible.

Rhetorical Exercises

(1) Give a five-minute informative speech in which you: Describe a process, place, person or event; or, give a five-minute speech about one of the related fields of rhetoric.

(2) Nichols points to the essential confusion concerning the meaning of the term "rhetoric" when she contrasts two comments concerning

[18] Adlai E. Stevenson, *Putting First Things First* (New York: Random House, Inc., 1960), p. 29.

Lincoln. Parrington remarks: "Matter he judged to be of greater significance than manner. Few men who have risen to enduring eloquence have been so little indebted to rhetoric. Very likely his plainness of style was the result of deliberate restraint, in keeping with the simplicity of his nature." Basler, on the other hand, writes: "It would be difficult to find in all history a precise instance in which rhetoric played a more important role in human destiny than it did in Lincoln's speeches of 1858." [19] Parrington uses the word "rhetoric" to mean style. Basler uses it to mean much more. Note the various ways in which the word "rhetoric" is used by contemporary writers. How many different uses could you find?

(3) Discuss the place of rhetoric in our contemporary society. Can you find direct support for the statement that ours is a rhetorical world?

(4) Think of the various codes of ethics which many professions have. Suggest a code of ethics for a public speaker? Discuss your code with the other members of the class.

Collateral Readings

Arnold, Carroll C., Douglas Ehninger, and John C. Gerber, *The Speaker's Resource Book*. Chicago: Scott, Foresman and Co., 1961. See Arnold's "Speech as a Liberal Study," pp. 2–5 and William G. Carleton's "Effective Speech in a Democracy," pp. 5–11.

Baskerville, Barnet, "The Place of Oratory in American Literature," *Quarterly Journal of Speech* (December, 1953), pp. 459–64.

Bryant, Donald C., "Rhetoric: Its Function and Its Scope," *QJS* (December, 1953), pp. 401–24.

———, "Aspects of the Rhetorical Tradition: The Intellectual Foundation," *QJS* (April, 1950), pp. 169–76.

Hunt, Everett Lee, "Rhetoric as a Humane Study," *QJS* (April, 1955), pp. 114–17.

Lee, Irving J., "Four Ways of Looking at a Speech," *QJS* (April, 1942), pp. 148–55.

Nichols, Marie Hochmuth, *Rhetoric and Criticism*. Baton Rouge: Louisiana State University Press, 1963. See "Rhetoric and Public Address as Humane Study," pp. 3–18.

Nilsen, Thomas R., "Free Speech, Persuasion, and the Democratic Process," *QJS* (October, 1958), pp. 235–43.

Parrish, Wayland Maxfield, "The Tradition of Rhetoric," *QJS* (December, 1947), pp. 464–67.

Wallace, Karl R., "The Substance of Rhetoric: Good Reasons," *QJS* (October, 1963), pp. 239–49.

Wieman, Henry Nelson and Otis M. Walter, "Toward an Analysis of Ethics for Rhetoric," *QJS* (October, 1957), pp. 266–70.

[19] Marie Hochmuth Nichols, *Rhetoric and Criticism* (Baton Rouge: Louisiana State University Press, 1963), p. 69.

PART TWO

PRINCIPLES AND APPLICATIONS

. . . when anyone elects to speak or write discourses which are worthy of praise and honour, it is not conceivable that he will support causes which are unjust or petty or devoted to private quarrels, and not rather those which are great and honourable, devoted to the welfare of man and our common good. . . .

ISOCRATES

III   A person becomes a speaker not when he stands up to speak, but long before, when he begins to select a topic to talk about. In this chapter let us discuss some of the preliminary problems involved in planning a speech. The speaker must first carefully consider what he knows about audiences in general and what he knows about *his* audience in particular. On the basis of what he wants to accomplish in his speech and what he thinks he *can* accomplish because of the nature of his audience, he decides on his specific purpose and the lines of argument he wants to advance. Only then is he ready to select the specific materials and proofs he will present.

First Steps

The first steps in preliminary planning are crucial to the overall effectiveness of the speech. They form the foundation for all the decisions the speaker will have to make as he decides *what* to say and the most effective ways of saying it.

ANALYZING ATTITUDES

In selecting a topic (indeed throughout the whole rhetor-

RHETORICAL INVENTION: PRELIMINARY PLANNING

ical process), it is important to recall that audiences do not assemble in a vacuum nor have they come from one. Socrates admonishes a student in the *Phaedrus:* "Since it is ... the function of speech to influence souls, a man who is going to be a speaker must know how many types of souls there are." [1] So to determine what response a speaker thinks he *can* get from an audience, he must perform an audience analysis. For this analysis he determines the characteristics of his audience, by decribing it in terms of age, sex, economic status, educational development, and group affiliation (both informal and formal groups). Knowledge of group allegiances is especially important because many attitudes stem from group membership.

Four kinds of relationships should be explored:

(1) the relationship of the group to its individual members
(2) the relationship of the group to the speaker and of the speaker to the group
(3) the relationship of the speaker to individual members of the group
(4) the relationship of the audience to the subject.

These relationships give the speaker real insight into the attitudes an audience brings with them to the speech. Attitudes are *"the inferred bases for observed consistencies in the behavior of individuals."* [2] We don't "see" the attitudes, only the overt results of them. A somewhat expanded definition is offered by Young. According to him, an attitude is "a learned and more or less generalized and effective tendency or predisposition to respond in a rather persistent and characteristic manner usually positively or negatively (for or against) in reference to some situation, idea, value, material object or class of such objects, or person or group of persons." [3]

Attitudes generally possess four dimensions: direction, degree, intensity, and salience. (1) Direction: How do the members of the audience feel toward the speaker? Toward his subject? Do they respond favorably? Unfavorably? Or are they undecided? Neutral? (2) Degree: Are they very favorable? Or only slightly so? Are they

[1] Plato, *Phaedrus*, trans. W. E. Helmbold and W. G. Rabinowitz (New York: The Liberal Arts Press, Inc., 1956), 271.

[2] Eugene L. Hartely, Ruth E. Hartely, and Clyde Hart, "Attitudes and Opinions," in *The Process and Effects of Mass Communication*, ed. Wilbur Schramm (Urbana: University of Illinois Press, 1954), p. 221.

[3] Kimball Young, *Social Psychology* (New York: Appleton-Century-Crofts, 1944), p. 122.

opposed? Or only mildly so? (3) Intensity: With what degree of firmness do they hold these attitudes? If they are favorably disposed, will they only give "lip service"? Or actively demonstrate their predispositions? (4) Salience: How significant is this attitude? Is it really important? Does it vitally concern them? Do they feel a real sense of involvement?

Earlier we mentioned that it is important for the speaker to have knowledge of group allegiances. Just as some individuals are more resistant to external influence than others, some groups resist new ideas, suggestions, information. These questions will help give insight into the group:

(1) How highly does the group value its own opinions and attitudes?

(2) How dependent are the individuals in the group upon the opinion of the group?

The second question is important because the more strongly the individual is motivated to be a member of a group, the greater his identification with the opinions and attitudes of that group will be.

As the speaker prepares to approach his topic, he should keep these pointers in mind:

(1) Attitudes are learned.

(2) They can be changed, but not easily.

(3) Any given attitude may well have three bases, and the relative proportion of each basis may vary greatly:
   (a) a logical basis: observing, reasoning
   (b) a social, cultural basis: examples and pressure of other people in the community
   (c) an emotional basis: personal anxieties, conflicts, and so forth.

There must, in any event, be an area of common ground between the speaker and his audience if he is to have his information accepted or to change attitudes.

SELECTION OF SUBJECT

Ideas for a speech come from observing, from experience, from conversation, from listening, and from reading. The first prerequisite of good speaking is curiosity, questioning: What is going on? Why? How can it be changed or supported? Thomas Huxley once said,

"No one who has lived in the world as long as . . . I have can entertain the pious delusion that it is engineered upon principles of
benevolence. . . . But for all that, the cosmos remains always beautiful and profoundly interesting in every corner—and if I had as many
lives as a cat I would leave no corner unexplored." [4] Exploring—
through conversation, through experience, through reading—is the
speaker's starting place. When a speaker says, "I know something
about the subject," "I would like to learn something more about this
subject," "I think it should be talked about—" he is in a sense saying:
This subject is important to me.

It has been said of Lord Chatham, twice Prime Minister of England and defender of the rights of the American Colonists in Parliament, that his "mind [was] all aglow" [5] with a subject. We can not
always be "all aglow" with a subject, but we can be genuinely interested in those subjects that have a natural urgency. What is being
talked about? What needs to be talked about? If the speaker is not
interested in his topic, how can he expect an audience to be or to
become interested in it?

Since the speech occurs in a social situation, selection of subject
is influenced by the audience for which it is intended. The speaker
asks: "What does my audience know?" "What are they talking
about?" "What should they be concerned with?" A potential speech
subject can be found in the "common ground" which exists between
the speaker and his audience, the common ground of interest, of
feeling, and of belief. [6]

The audience gains insight into the speaker's mind and his attitude
toward his audience by the topic he selects. When a man speaks he
is occupying someone else's time. When one man is speaking, another cannot speak and probably cannot think his own thoughts.
Thus the speaker assumes responsibility for using his own and his
listeners' time in a useful and productive manner. A trivial topic
indicates that the speaker does not value the audience's time very
highly. The speaker, by selecting a topic of importance, brings to
his audience a real sense of dignity and of respect.

Our ability to communicate through speech helps us to do more

[4] Cited in "Is Liberal Education Still Needed?" a speech delivered by
Gordon N. Ray. Printed in pamphlet form by Houghton-Mifflin Company.

[5] Chauncey A. Goodrich, *Select British Éloquence*, photo offset edition (Indianapolis: The Bobbs-Merrill Company, Inc., 1963), p. 73.

[6] James A. Winans, *Speech-Making* (New York: Appleton-Century-Crofts,
1938), pp. 335f.

than adjust to our environment; it enables us to change our environment, to reconstruct it so that we can bring it closer to the way we would like it to be. In our human context, then, the important subjects are those that allow us to discover what man can be. The speaker's task is to challenge his audience in the tradition of civilized people everywhere on the assumption that man can and will respond to an appeal of reason and imagination. The speaker must give *good reasons* [7] why men should act, why they should act in certain ways, and why they should evaluate their actions according to certain criteria.

The speaker, when selecting his topic also asks: "What topic can gain and maintain attention?" More specifically, "What can gain my audience's favorable and undivided attention?" No one perceives everything that is in his immediate environment. Our mental apparatus simply does not organize materials in such an indifferent manner. It does not give equal importance to all stimuli. We are vaguely aware, for example, of colors, shapes, sounds, smells, textures, and so forth, all at one time. In fact, it has been suggested that man's brain can receive up to 1,000 impressions in one-tenth of a second. More stimuli come to the listener than he is able to attend to. He feels the room temperature, he hears a plane pass overhead, he is aware of the people around him, but from each complex of stimuli the listener *selects*.

We "scan" our environment much as we scan newspaper headlines. Headlines provide a quick survey of what is in the newspaper. The articles which are most likely to catch the attention of the reader are those which serve his immediate purpose. He selects what he will read on the basis of his needs, expectancies, attitudes. In different situations, he selects different articles (stimuli). Thus, as the speaker searches for ways to gain and maintain attention, he must consider whether or not his topic meets the audience's needs and interests at each particular time and for each particular occasion.

FOCUSING ON A PURPOSE

Since most of us speak to achieve certain responses from our hearers, the audience assumes that each speaker has a reason for giving his particular speech. The reason may be partly due to the occasion, but whatever the occasion, the speaker's primary purpose

[7] Karl R. Wallace, "The Substance of Rhetoric: Good Reasons," *Quarterly Journal of Speech* (October, 1963), pp. 239–49.

is to elicit a response. The most general purpose a speaker has is to establish the commonness of which we spoke earlier, to share an idea, an attitude, some information. The first question the speaker asks here is: "What do I want my audience to think? To understand? To say? To feel? To do? To value?

If the speaker's topic is the concept of economic community, the desired response may be an understanding of the term. The specific statement of purpose could be explained in this way: To describe the concept of economic community. If a speaker wants to persuade the audience to support U.S. membership in an economic community his specific purpose would be: To show the advantage of the United States's forming a close trade alliance with the European Economic Community.

In any event, the purpose must be limited by what can be done in the time allotted for the speech: what can be done at the time of the speech (the stage in the "life" of the problem under discussion); and what approaches can be taken with the audience hearing the speech.

As the speaker seeks to find specific ways of guiding responses, he moves still another step toward fulfilling his purpose. Generally, a speaker can guide responses in three ways: He can inform; he can persuade; he can entertain. Many times he does all three, but generally one of the three ways is dominant.

While every speaker wants to succeed, no premium can be placed on success. The speaker's success, his effectiveness, is judged not only by how many boxes of Zap Soap Powder he can sell in one year, but also by the *quality* and long term effects of his speech. Many times the odds are against immediate accomplishment of purpose; the difficulties may simply be insurmountable. For example, although Franklin Roosevelt's "Happy Warrior Speech" in 1924 nominating Al Smith for the presidency was much cheered and well received, Smith was not nominated. Burns, in *Roosevelt: The Lion and the Fox*, comments: ". . . no speech could affect that convention. Ballot after ballot dragged on in the smoky heat of Madison Square Garden until it became clear that neither the forces centered in the East supporting Smith nor the forces centered in the South and West behind McAdoo could muster the vital two thirds. . . . [T]he 103rd ballot gave John W. Davis the nomination." [8] Thus in a political

[8] James MacGregor Burns, *Roosevelt: The Lion and the Fox* (New York: Harcourt, Brace and World, Inc., 1956), p. 94.

campaign, although an audience does not vote the way a particular candidate wants, it may be considering new problems and different solutions to old problems. Its dispositions may be changed. Its minds may be opened.

Developing Lines of Argument

After the speaker has selected his topic, determined his specific purpose, and considered his audience, he is ready to select the particular lines of argument suitable for his unique speech situation. The lines of argument for a speech can best be approached by raising a series of questions about *the basic nature of the situation* in which the speech is going to be given. Relevant questions would include: "What is my speech a response to?" "Is there a problem which should be considered?" "Is one solution better than another for this problem?" "What kind of difficulties will be met in trying to solve the problem?" "Does the problem involve an immediate and serious threat?" "Does some worthwhile cause or group need support?" "Can some group profitably use information on a process, a place, a concept?"

We shall discuss six situations [9] which are likely to prompt speeches:

(1) the information-giving situation
(2) the difficulty situation
(3) the goal-oriented situation
(4) the barrier situation
(5) the threat situation
(6) the identification situation.

(1) In the information-giving situation the group wants to learn something new, for the sake of acquiring new knowledge, if not for the sake of changing its opinions and attitudes. A speaker may choose:
   (A) to describe a process, place, person, or event
   (B) to tell about his personal experiences
   (C) to clarify concepts, material, ideas
   (D) to discuss the specific works of someone such as a writer, painter, composer.

[9] This scheme represents, in part, a modification of a method presented by Otis M. Walter in "Toward an Analysis of Motivation," *Quarterly Journal of Speech* (October, 1955), pp. 271–78.

(2) In the difficulty situation the group perceives a problem. A speaker may:

   (A) acknowledge that the problem exists

      (1) by pointing out the importance of the problem

      (2) by locating and more precisely defining the problem

      (3) by pointing to the causes of the problem.

   or

   (B) not acknowledge that the problem exists

      (1) by denying that there is a problem

      (2) by belittling the importance of the problem.

(3) In the goal-oriented situation the group attempts to formulate a solution. A speaker may:

   (A) urge the acceptance of a certain solution by pointing out:

      (1) that the solution will meet the problem

      (2) that the solution will work; that it is practicable

      (3) that the solution holds certain other advantages.

   or

   (B) urge the rejection of a certain solution by pointing out:

      (1) that it will not meet the need

      (2) that it is impracticable

      (3) that there are more disadvantages than advantages

      (4) that another solution is better.

(4) In the barrier situation the solution may become complicated by a barrier between the group and the goal. Here, the speaker may urge:

   (A) that the barrier is not a deterrent to action, because

      (1) the goal is worth achieving regardless of the barrier

      (2) the barrier has been unnecessarily raised

      (3) the barrier is not really crucial.

   or

   (B) that the barrier is a deterrent to action, because

      (1) the barrier is insurmountable

      (2) even if the barrier can be surmounted, the goal is not worth the time and energy

      (3) even if the barrier can be surmounted, so many disadvantages would result that would make the situation worse, rather than better.

(5) In the threat situation action is needed because of some threat. The speaker may point out:

(A) that the threat is great, because
    (1) the threat is dangerous
    (2) the threat is immediate.
or
(B) that the threat is not really great, because
    (1) the threat is not dangerous
    (2) the threat is not immediate.

(6) In the identification situation one group acts for the sake of another group. The speaker may urge:
    (A) that Group A help Group B, because
        (1) there is a relationship between the two groups
        (2) there should be a relationship between the two groups
        (3) the group deserves to be helped—they perform useful tasks.
    or
    (B) that Group B not be helped by Group A, because
        (1) there is no relationship between the two groups
        (2) the problem faced by the other group is not really serious—they can solve it themselves
        (3) helping the other group would weaken this group.

In each motivational situation there are other alternatives, other lines of argument. The information situation is, in a way, present in all the others. The difference is one of dominant purpose. In the first case the speaker gives information to acquaint the audience with new materials and new facts that can be assimilated and become somehow useful. In the others he gives information to persuade people to accept a specific course of action or way of thinking.

A locus or line of argument may be found whenever there is potential disagreement. The point of disagreement may be called a *stasis*, a point beyond which discussion cannot proceed until one view or another is accepted as the one proved to be right. The reason for deciding upon a specific line of argument is that the speaker can at the beginning narrow the focus of what he intends to say to the point or points which specifically concern the matter he is discussing. Determining the *stasis* helps the speaker choose the line or lines of argument he will use in his speech. He should carefully select a few lines of argument since maximum impact comes from developing the best arguments and making as vigorous a defense as possible.

At what points in the discussion of any subject is a *stasis* likely to occur? There are at least four general ones:

(1) At a point of conjecture: Is something a fact or not?
(2) At a point of definition: Is this what it means or not?
(3) At a point of policy: Is this what we should do or not?
(4) At a point of value: Is this worthwhile or not?

These four general areas of disagreement, coupled with the nature of the specific motivational situation out of which the speech grows, determine the speaker's line of argument or approach to his subject.

Modes of Presenting Material

After the speaker selects his line or lines of argument, he must consider one other factor before evaluating his specific proofs and choosing those which best serve his purpose. He must decide whether or not to present the arguments on both sides of the issue. We shall discuss two of the many experiments designed to find an answer. The first study indicates that:

(1) Presenting the arguments on both sides of an issue was found to be more effective than giving only the arguments supporting the point being made, in the case of individuals who were *initially opposed* to the point of view being presented.
(2) If people are *already convinced* of the point of view being presented, the inclusion of arguments on both sides was found to be less effective for the group as a whole than presenting only the arguments favoring the general position being advocated.[10]

Another study also indicated that a one-sided presentation was more effective with subjects initially favoring the advocated view.[11]

Because of such findings and his own observations about what persuades him when other people speak, the speaker chooses the technique best suited to his topic and to his audience. If he decides to

[10] Carl I. Hovland, Arthur A. Lumsdaine, and Fred. D. Sheffield, "The Effect of Presenting 'One Side' versus 'Both Sides' in Changing Opinions on a Controversial Subject," in Schramm, *The Process and Effects of Mass Communication*, p. 274.

[11] Nathan Maccoby, "The New 'Scientific' Rhetoric," in Schramm, *The Science of Human Communication* (New York: Basic Books, Inc., Publishers, 1963), pp. 43–44.

use the "both-sides presentation" he should then take special care
to do two things:

(1) be abundantly clear about which side he is discussing at all
times; and
(2) be sure that he develops the argument in support of the
proposition he advocates. The listener should never leave a
speech feeling like a man who, after a tennis match, has a
neck so sore that he forgets the particularly good lob in the
third game or the marvelous baseline game Joe X played.

Following are two examples of the effective use of the both-sides
presentation. At one point in his single term in the United States
Congress, Abraham Lincoln took exception to the often repeated
Presidential position on the Mexican War. He refuted one of the
President's statements in this way:

> His next piece of evidence is that "The Republic of Texas always
> *claimed* this river (the Rio Grande) as her western boundary [.]"
> That is not true, in fact. Texas *has* claimed it, but she has not *always*
> claimed it. There is, at least, one distinguished exception. Her state
> constitution . . . makes no such claim. But suppose she had always
> claimed it. Has not Mexico always claimed the contrary? so that
> there is but *claim* against *claim*, leaving nothing proved, until we
> get back of the claims, and find which has the better *foundation*.[12]

One student in a classroom speech used the technique as follows:

> Yes, it is true that there are many loan funds for needy college stu-
> dents, but there are also many restrictions which, in reality, make it
> difficult and often impossible for the students who need the loans—
> the poorest students—to borrow from these funds.

> Yes, it is true that there are scholarships available and that some of
> them are going unused. Why? Because there are also sometimes very
> stringent restrictions and that's why they aren't used—not because,
> as the previous speaker inferred—those students were simply too
> lazy to apply for them. What he, in fact, failed to tell you is the
> single most relevant fact about scholarships and that is, that while
> enrollments are increasing, scholarships are not increasing at the
> same rate—but at a much slower pace.

Both of these examples represent the refutative technique. If the
speaker decides to use this technique, either for the entire speech or

[12] Roy P. Basler, ed., *The Collected Works of Abraham Lincoln* (New
Brunswick, N.J.: Rutgers University Press, 1953), I, 434.

for a small portion of it, he will need to select materials that will fit the technique he has chosen.

Narrowing the method of handling materials is one of the most important steps in preliminary planning whether the speaker aims at a one-sided or two-sided presentation of materials on a controversial subject or at giving information. Just as all the steps in the rhetorical act are made with reference to the audience for which the speech is aimed, so are the decisions: (1) on whether or not to use the two-sided presentation; and (2) on how to use it for maximum effect.

Summary

Rhetorical invention begins with very careful preliminary planning. From the moment the speaker decides on his topic he is faced with a series of questions. How well or how poorly he answers these questions may determine the success of his speech. A speech cannot succeed without careful consideration of the basis on which the speaker will build. The foundation for a speech is the selection of a topic. That first act reveals much about: (1) what interests the speaker; (2) what the speaker knows; and (3) what he thinks is appropriate for public discussion. As Weaver has suggested: "Nowhere does a man's rhetoric catch up with him more completely than in the topics he chooses to win other men's assent." [13]

After he has selected his topic, the speaker continues to build a firm foundation for his speech by analyzing his audience to determine what common ground he can find between himself and his listeners. Then he is ready to develop the specific lines of argument in his speech and to select his mode of presentation. His preliminary planning done, he can select the specific supporting materials of his speech.

Rhetorical Exercises

(1) Give an eight to ten minute persuasive speech in which you (a) make the audience aware of a problem area they may not have considered before; or, (b) suggest a solution to a much discussed problem.

(2) Recall the topics on which you have heard speeches lately. What were they? Could you gain insight into the speaker's mind by them? Did they reflect how he regarded his audience?

[13] Richard Weaver, *Ethics of Rhetoric* (Chicago: Henry Regnery Co., 1953), p. 114.

(3) Stop to think over some of the topics you would like to speak about in class. How did you pick them? What areas of common ground can you find between you, your topics, and your audience?

(4) Listen to the speeches in class with a view to answering this question: "Did the speaker take into consideration the audience's attitudes and opinions on his subject?" Then answer the question: "Did the speaker understand them very well?"

(5) Check your library for materials relating to attitude and opinion. Report on a particularly interesting article or book.

(6) Select a problem area. Then discuss the nature of the problem, the causes of the problem, and the solution to it. How many different lines of argument can you find? Try doing this exercise in class and writing the lines of argument on the board. How would you determine which are the best ones? Is there general agreement in the class on which lines of argument are the best? If there is disagreement, analyze why it has occurred. Finally, after each member of the class has delivered his speech, discuss the lines of argument used in each. Can you suggest others which might have been used?

Collateral Readings

Berlo, David K., and Halbert E. Gulley, "Some Determinants of the Effect of Oral Communication in Producing Attitude Change and Learning," *Speech Monographs* (March, 1957), pp. 10–20.

Bunch, Marion E., "The Concept of Motivation," *Journal of General Psychology* (1958), pp. 189–205.

Hovland, Carl I., Irving L. Janis, and Harold H. Kelley, *Communication and Persuasion*. New Haven: Yale University Press, 1953. See "Group Membership and Resistance to Change" and "Personality and Susceptibility to Persuasion."

Jarrett, R. F., and Alex C. Sherriffs, "Propaganda, Debate, and Impartial Presentation as Determiners of Attitude Change," *Journal of Abnormal and Social Psychology* (1953), pp. 33–41.

Katz, Daniel, ed., *Public Opinion Quarterly*, special issue on "Attitude Change" (Summer, 1960).

Maccoby, Eleanor E., Nathan Maccoby, A. K. Romney, and J. Stacy Adams, "Social Reinforcement in Attitude Change," *Journal of Abnormal and Social Psychology* (1961), pp. 109–15.

Maslow, Abraham H., *Motivation and Personality*. New York: Harper and Brothers, 1954.

Peak, Helen, and H. William Morrison, "The Acceptance of Information into Attitude Structure," *Journal of Abnormal and Social Psychology* (1958), pp. 127–35.

Rosenberg, Milton J., and others, *Attitude Organization and Change*. New Haven: Yale University Press, 1960.

Sherif, Muzafer, and Carl I. Hovland, *Social Judgment: Assimilation and Contrast Effects in Communication and Attitude Change.* New Haven: Yale University Press, 1961.

Walter, Otis M., "Toward an Analysis of Motivation," *Quarterly Journal of Speech* (Oct., 1955), pp. 271–78.

Facts cannot be selected without some personal conviction as to what is truth.

IV   Whatever end the speaker has in mind, his specific purpose is to speak with persuasive effect toward that end. Thus, he is concerned both with the end and the means of securing that end. He is faced with the necessity for responsible commitment as he seeks to determine the "available means of persuasion." What are the means of persuasion? Let us begin the answer by recalling a very simple fact about communication. When we speak, we assume the responsibility for usefully filling up the duration of our speech, either for one minute or for a full hour. Each time we say something, we are, in effect, asking people to listen to us and we generally "say" one of these:

(1) Listen to me because of who I am.
(2) Listen to me because of what I know.
(3) Listen to me because, as a human being, I share certain motives, certain emotions, certain ambitions with you.

All three of these we may call a speaker's credentials, his proof that he is using the time wisely, that what he is saying is of value.

RHETORICAL INVENTION: SELECTION OF PROOFS

The word "proof" is closely bound to the Greek word *pistis* which is associated with trust, faith. Proof is what we offer to secure belief. The term implies reciprocity: Something must be offered and *accepted* to be proof; somebody must show that he is reliable and somebody must trust. The three kinds of proof are not mutually exclusive and, in fact, are difficult to separate.

Ethical Proof

In a sense we began our discussion of ethical proof in the first chapter when we suggested that a speaker makes himself known in two ways: with what he brings to the speech (his character, reputation) and with what he says in the speech (the judgments and commitments he makes through his choice of means and ends, through his statements of fact and opinion as well as of value).

Many times, before the speaker begins to speak, the audience will already know something about him, about his integrity, his intelligence, his good will. As Isocrates admonished "... the man who wishes to persuade people will not be negligent as to the matter of character ... for who does not know that words carry greater conviction when spoken by men of good repute. ..." [1]

A person's reputation may change *as* he speaks. On a very simple level, think of how we "offer" ethical proof almost constantly. Mary Jones may have borrowed her roommate's sweater. If she returned it clean and intact, she may simply say, "May I borrow your blue sweater again this week?" because she has already established her reliability in borrowing sweaters. On the other hand, if she ripped the sweater, Mary may have to say, "If I can borrow your blue sweater this week, I promise to take better care of it." Mary has attempted to establish her reliability by or through the "speech" itself.

So, if a speaker is not known—or is known but wants to further establish his reliability—he reminds the audience about his credentials and makes them stronger. He offers ethical proof in the speech by the choices he makes, choices made from the very outset of the rhetorical act, from the selection of subject to the actual delivery of the speech itself. He has:

[1] Isocrates, *Antidosis,* trans. George Norlin, The Loeb Classical Library (London: William Heinemann, Ltd., 1929), 278.

(1) included certain details, certain facts, and omitted others
(2) drawn certain relationships between ideas
(3) emphasized some ideas and not others
(4) at each stage, made a series of value judgments.

This last point cannot be emphasized too strongly, for surely when a speaker makes a public statement, he is making a public commitment.

It is difficult to find many distinguished speakers who have told audiences what they themselves have not believed. The distinguished speakers of the past have rarely spoken on subjects to which they were indifferent. To do so is, in effect, to be what Senator Albert Beveridge in 1924 called "a public liar." [2] No speaker ever has the right to try to influence the behavior of other people until, as a result of careful thought and study, he decides his point of view is worthwhile.

In the following speeches, each speaker has manifested integrity, presented ethical proof (*ethos*): (1) through attempting to convey directly to the audience a favorable impression of his good will and character; and (2) through allowing the audience to form an impression through the total of the value judgments implied by his statements.

An example of the first type is this speech by Daniel Webster, speaking for the prosecution to the jury in the White murder case:

> I am little accustomed, Gentlemen, to the part which I am now attempting to perform. Hardly more than once or twice has it happened to me to be concerned on the side of government in any criminal prosecution whatever; and never, until the present occasion, in any case affecting life.
>
> But I very much regret that it should have been thought necessary to suggest to you that I am brought here to "hurry you against the law and beyond the evidence." I hope I have too much regard for justice, and too much respect for my own character, to attempt either; and were I to make such attempt, I am sure that in this court nothing can be carried against the law, and that gentlemen, intelligent and just as you are, are not, by any power, to be hurried beyond the evidence. Though I could well have wished to shun this occasion, I have not felt at liberty to withhold my professional assistance, when it is supposed that I may be in some degree useful in investigating and discovering the truth respecting this most extraordinary

2 Albert J. Beveridge, *The Art of Public Speaking* (Boston: Houghton Mifflin Company, 1924), p. 20.

murder. It has seemed to be a duty incumbent on me, as on every other citizen, to do my best and my utmost to bring to light the perpetrators of this crime. Against the prisoner at the bar, as an individual, I cannot have the slightest prejudice. I would not do him the smallest injury or injustice. But I do not affect to be indifferent to the discovery and the punishment of this deep guilt. I cheerfully share in the opprobrium, how great soever it may be, which is cast on those who feel and manifest an anxious concern that all who had a part in planning, or a hand in executing, this deed of midnight assassination, may be brought to answer for their enormous crime at the bar of public justice.[3]

An example of the second may be found in the "First Inaugural Address" of Thomas Jefferson. After saying that ". . . it is proper that you should understand what I deem the essential principles of our government. . . ."[4] Jefferson lists eleven clearly stated principles to which he commits himself. Why? The presidential campaign of 1800 was an unusually bitter one between the Federalists and the Republicans. In addition, the two Republican candidates both polled the same number of votes. The election was thrown into the House of Representatives. Thus, the whole speech is an attempt to manifest an *ethos,* to say, "Here is the manner of man I am." So, throughout, he is very explicit: ". . . though the will of the majority is in all cases to prevail, that will, to be rightful, must be reasonable; that the minority possess their equal rights, which equal laws must protect, and to violate which would be oppression."[5]

It is not enough, however, for the speaker to be sincere. He has an obligation to be informed. Rhetoric measures not only the sincerity of the man but also the accuracy of what he says. Good intentions are meaningless unless the speaker has checked carefully to make sure that his materials are accurate and that his sources are reliable. A mistake in statistics, a misquoted authority, whether motivated by ill will or by an honest mistake, are in either case false and misleading. The use of an unrepresentative example, because the speaker is intent on trickery or because he has not read widely enough to know that the example is unrepresentative, is unethical. The character of the speaker cannot, in the end, be separated from the integrity of his materials.

Although it is difficult to know exactly how ethical proof operates,

[3] Wayland Maxfield Parrish and Marie Hochmuth, eds., *American Speeches* (New York: Longmans, Green and Co., 1954), pp. 122–23.

[4] *Ibid.,* p. 98.

[5] *Ibid.,* p. 96.

a large number of experimental studies support the position that the speaker's prestige significantly influences the persuasive outcome of a speech.[6] One study used a single tape-recorded speech and prepared two introductions to it. One version of the introduction employed techniques to build the speaker's prestige and the other did not. The audience hearing the speech with the favorable introduction changed their opinion more than did those who heard either no introduction or a poor one.[7]

In another experiment, the same tape-recorded speech was presented to three different groups. The speech was variously attributed to a Northwestern University sophomore, to the Secretary of the Communist Party in America and to the Surgeon General of the United States. Not only was the Surgeon General rated as significantly more competent than the other two supposed speakers, but his speech was also more effective in changing attitude than was either of the other speeches.[8]

Still another experiment attributed a taped speech, in one instance, to a political science professor and in another, to a college student. For women listeners there was no large difference in the effects of the "two" speeches, but among male listeners the proportion of those shifting opinion was larger in the group which thought it had been addressed by the professor.[9]

As pointed out earlier, not only may *ethos* be related to the position or reputation of the sources, but the internal message may vary in ethical elements. In an experiment which included or excluded quotations by authorities in two versions of the same speech, experimenters found that both versions caused a significant shift in attitude with a slight trend to favor the inclusion of authorities.[10]

High correlations have also been found between evaluations of authors and later judgments of passages to which authors' names

[6] See Kenneth Andersen and Theodore Clevenger, Jr., "A Summary of Experimental Research in Ethos," *Speech Monographs* (June, 1963), pp. 59–78.

[7] Barbara Kersten, "An Experimental Study to Determine the Effect of a Speech of Introduction upon the Persuasive Speech that Followed," as cited in Andersen and Clevenger, pp. 69–70.

[8] Franklyn Haiman, "An Experimental Study of the Effects of Ethos in Public Speaking," *Speech Monographs* (September, 1949), pp. 190–202.   –

[9] Stanley F. Paulson, "The Effects of the Prestige of the Speaker and Acknowledgment of Opposing Arguments on Audience Retention and Shift of Opinion," *Speech Monographs* (November, 1954), pp. 267–71.

[10] Howard Gilkinson, Stanley F. Paulson, and Donald Sikkink, "Effects of Order and Authority in an Argumentative Speech," *Quarterly Journal of Speech* (April, 1954), pp. 183–92.

were randomly attached. Thus, the author's name seemed to influence the ratings of passages.[11] Judgments of art seem to be somewhat similar. One study cites results which indicated that recognition of the artist's name had some favorable effect on the evaluation of pictures.[12]

But although there have been a large number of studies trying to relate *ethos* to the impact of a message, the concept of ethical proof is such that the results are not yet sufficiently numerous and sophisticated to permit definitive conclusions about how *ethos* operates. However, almost all of the studies have suggested that the *ethos* of the speaker is in some way related to the impact of his message on an audience.

Logical Proof

Supporting materials may be presented in two ways: verbally or visually. Both types of supports may be cast into different forms. The most common types of verbal support are: (1) events: historical and present, (2) statistics, (3) examples, (4) comparisons and contrasts, (5) definitions, and (6) testimony. The most common types of visual supports are: (1) actual objects or models, (2) diagrams and graphs, and (3) maps and charts. We shall discuss each type and then suggest some tests to determine whether or not your supporting materials do, in fact, operate as evidence to help prove the points you want to make.

EVENTS: HISTORICAL
AND PRESENT

A "fact" is material which may be verified independently of the speaker. There is no question about its existence and its nature. It is not disputable. It operates independently of interpretation and evaluation. One of the most useful kind of "facts" for the speaker is a statement about an event or groups of events, either from the past or from contemporary life, such as:

(1) On December 20, 1606, the *Susan Constant, Godspeed* and the *Discovery* set sail from London for Virginia under the command of Captain Christopher Newport.

[11] Muzafer Sherif, "An Experimental Study of Stereotypes," *Journal of Abnormal and Social Psychology* (1935), pp. 371–75.
[12] Paul Farnsworth and Issei Misumi, "Further Data on Suggestion in Pictures," *American Journal of Psychology* (1931), p. 632.

(2) Talleyrand was born in Paris on February 2, 1754.

(3) Dylan Thomas was twenty years old when his first book of poems was published in 1934.

(4) There àre 751 in this year's freshman class.

All these statements are easily checked and verified by each member of the class. Since the speaker says them, we assume he is accurate; that is, that Talleyrand *was* born in 1754 and not in 1753. If any of these statements is being disputed, the speaker should say so.

STATISTICS

The word "statistics" in common usage is synonymous with data; for example, the statistics of a football game or statistics relating to automobile accidents. They denote description recorded in numerical form such as this description of the percentage of total unemployment according to certain types of job classifications: [13]

	Per Cent
Operatives and kindred workers	7.7
Service workers	6.4
Farm laborers	5.5
Private household workers	5.3
Craftsmen, foremen, and so forth	4.8
Sales workers	4.3
Clerical workers	4.1

Since statistics are often badly abused, the audience may well ask: "How do we know these figures are accurate?" "What makes them acceptable?" The question can be forestalled and answered in advance by naming the source. The statistical material concerning unemployment was taken from *The 1964 Manpower Report of the President* prepared by his Council of Economic Advisers. It can also, of course, be verified in a variety of reference works. Several sources that can be very helpful are: *The Statistical Abstract of the United States, World Almanac, Information Please Almanac, Statistical Yearbook of the United Nations,* and *Demographic Yearbook of the United Nations.* The publications of various bodies concerned chiefly with statistics are also helpful: for example, The United Nations Statistical Office, The United States Bureau of the Census, and The United States Bureau of Labor Statistics.

When necessary, the *method* used for arriving at the statistics should be indicated. For example, in comparing the per capita Gross

[13] (Washington, D.C.: Government Printing Office, 1964), p. 25.

National Product of the United States with the per capita Gross National Products of the European Common Market countries, it would be necessary to note two things: (1) that the dollar aggregates have (or have not) been divided by converting national aggregates into dollars at official exchange rate; that is, that you are actually comparing the same things; and (2) that European currencies have a larger domestic purchasing power than is indicated by exchange rate conversion. Consequently, the total when compared with the United States will be understated. In short, the speaker should tell the audience what it needs to know to guarantee accuracy of information and to make the material more meaningful. Although it was impossible in these examples to round off the numbers, it is generally better to do so, unless small differences are crucially important, since round numbers are usually easier for an audience to assimilate.

EXAMPLES

An example is the use of one particular instance, to clarify or vivify a more general statement. Examples may well be the best remembered expression of the ideas in a speech. To illustrate: A speaker may be explaining the concept that languages have "signals" which give clues as to whether or not an object is animate or inanimate, large or small. He may choose to cite either: (1) an *instance* (a short, undetailed example), or (2) an *illustration* (a longer, more detailed example):

(1) *Instance:* In the Algonquin language, small animals are often assigned to the class of inanimate objects, while particularly important plants are assigned to the animate class.

(2) *Illustration:* In Liberia's Gola language, a noun which normally takes another prefix, takes the o-prefix of humans and animals if it is particularly large, valuable, or outstanding in some way. These qualities put it in the class of living creatures. Instead of *kesie*, oil palm, one would say *osie*, which characterizes this palm as one of the most important trees; or *kekul*, tree, but *okul*, a particularly large and beautiful tree; or *ebu*, field, but *obuo*, a very beautiful and luxuriant field.

One determines the length of an example by raising the question, "Is my example complete enough to be clear?" "Is it long enough to be meaningful to my audience?" The speaker may also use hypothetical examples. A hypothetical example is an attempt to explain ideas which cannot be exemplified by referring to an actual experience. Although they may occasionally dramatize the speaker's point more effectively than a real example, they nevertheless remain grounded in imagination rather than in empirical (observed) evidence.

A speech should not be overburdened with examples but have a sufficient number of them to illustrate the point. Cicero, in one of his orations against the tyrant Verres, could have revealed the latter's despicable character by giving two, three, or even five or six examples of the crimes he had committed; but after Cicero had listed six or seven dozen, the listener probably was too tired to be impressed by anything.

COMPARISON AND CONTRAST

These two types of supporting material are based on the same process—putting two or more things together and studying them both to see how they are alike (comparison) and how they are unlike (contrast). The speaker is calling attention to certain aspects of one object, one event, one person, through the copresence of another object, event, or person.

Analogy. One important type of comparison is the *analogy.* Analogy is especially useful in showing a similarity or resemblance of relations in two or more objects. It is this notion of relationship which is the mark of an analogy. For example, whenever we draw a diagram, such as the map of a given area, we are drawing a "logical picture" of something. This relationship of the map to the actual location is one of analogy. The black dots on the map are not really like actual cities; the lines on the map are not tall like actual mountains nor are they wet like actual rivers. However, the structure of a good map corresponds to the structure of the actual country it represents. The shapes of the actual states are like the shapes on the map and the relative distances between the dark dots on the map are like the relative distances between the actual cities. In each analogy the speaker must indicate in what respects and to what extent the objects are analogous, similar. In the comparison cited, the structure of the map and the structure of the landscape are similar. Suppose a speaker wants to compare the cost of the Louisiana Purchase with something today. He might say: "Though $15,000,000 would not even buy one aircraft carrier today, the sum was more than double the $7,000,000 it cost to run the entire government (including the Army and Navy) in 1800." Obviously the comparison here involves only cost. But let us take a more complicated comparison. The speaker wants to compare two poems: Dylan Thomas' "The Force that through the Green Fuse" and Gerard Manley Hopkin's "Spring and Fall: to a Young Child." From the outset the speaker should make clear that the one similarity they share is central theme. They are unlike in tone and in method. Here again the speaker has acknowledged the *area* of similarity (and the scope of difference).

Suppose that a speaker suggests a solution to a problem and states that because it has solved a similar problem in City A it will solve one in City B. Here the speaker infers that the two cities are more *alike* than they are different. We suppose that they are alike in size, government, functioning, location, social groupings, and so forth, *and* that the two problems were initiated by similar causes and exhibit similar symptoms. If there are serious differences in any of these characteristics, differences serious enough to interfere with the solution, then the speaker should acknowledge and clarify the conditions under which his analogy (in this case, his proposed solution) could not hold true. Every analogy must break down at some point since the objects, events, and other elements are only similar and not identical.

Of great importance then is *fairness of sampling*. Are there more similarities than dissimilarities? Have I acknowledged the conditions under which the analogy would not hold true? The soundness of an analogy depends both upon the number of positive characteristics as compared to the number of negative characteristics and upon the relative essentialness of the resemblances. Obviously the number of dissimilarities between the particulars must not be more numerous nor more significant than the similarities.

One of the results of faulty analogy is *stereotyping*, which occurs when we group people, objects, events together and treat them as a unit simply because they may share one or a few properties in common. Lippmann defines a stereotype as "an ordered, more or less consistent picture of the world, to which our habits, our tastes, our capacities, our comforts and our hopes have adjusted themselves. They may not be a complete picture of the world, but they are a picture of a possible world to which we are adapted. In that world, people and things have their well-known places, and do certain things. . . . There we find the charm of the familiar, the normal, the dependable; its grooves and shapes are where we are accustomed to find them." [14]

The stereotype we have of hillbillies, Southerners, mid-Westerners, jazz musicians, psychiatrists are to a large extent based on faulty analogies.

Metaphors and Similes. Short compressed comparisons are called *metaphors* and *similes*. These have often been thought to be the semi-exclusive property of creative literature, but they are an important and effective tool of the speaker. Let us recall several examples:

(1) Jonathan Edwards: "The sovereign pleasure of God, for the present, stays his rough wind; otherwise it would come with fury, and your destruction would come like a whirlwind, and you would be like the chaff of the summer threshing floor." [15]

(2) Patrick Henry: "Has Great Britain any enemy, in this quarter of the world, to call for all this accumulation of navies and armies? No, sir, she has none. They are meant for us: they can be meant for no other. They are sent over to bind and rivet upon us those chains which the British ministry have been so long forging." [16]

(3) Wendell Phillips speaking of the Russian press: "Dead silence, like that which reigns at the summit of Mont Blanc, freezes the whole empire...." [17]

Here, as in the literal analogy, credulity should not be stretched. A good *test* of the figurative analogy is to break it down into a ratio with four terms. Here the relationship can be checked more easily, more directly for an *equality* of ratios, for example, "My experience [as an Apprentice Seaman] thus provided me with a very special view—what could be called a worm's-eye view—of the service." [18] The ratio would then be—worm's-eye view: world:: apprentice seaman's view: service. We shall discuss metaphor and simile at length in Chapter VII.

DEFINITION

Since the speaker assumes responsibility for the audience's understanding, definition is especially important. The speaker asks him-

[14] Walter Lippmann, *Public Opinion* (New York: The Macmillan Company, 1922), p. 95.

[15] Parrish and Hochmuth, eds., *American Speeches*, p. 81.

[16] *Ibid.*, p. 93.

[17] *Ibid.*, p. 355.

[18] From *Major Campaign Speeches of Adlai E. Stevenson, 1952.* Copyright 1953 by Random House, Inc. Reprinted by permission. p. 17.

self: Am I using words which are new, unfamiliar to my audience? Am I using words with vague and/or ambiguous meanings? Am I using a familiar word in a somewhat new, unique way?

Good definitions include all that is necessary for clarity and interest. A definition is an inquiry into the nature of a thing. In effect, it answers the question, "What does it mean to say that something is government, that something is Socialism, that something is matter?" The answer should describe the basic characteristics and not the accidental or irrelevant properties. When we give a word meaning, when we have circumscribed its uniqueness, we have defined it.

There are numerous methods of defining, but perhaps the soundest scheme is suggested by Ehninger and Brockriede: (1) definition by classification; (2) definition by necessary conditions; and (3) definition by operational description.[19]

Definition by classification consists of placing a term within a class of similar phenomena and showing how it differs from others in the same class. This may be done by: (1) straightforward classification and differentiation; (2) placing a term in a continuum; (3) comparison and contrast; (4) through negation; and (5) by etymology.

When Aristotle defined "Rhetoric" as "the faculty for observing, in any given case, all the available means of persuasion,"[20] he placed Rhetoric in a class (faculty) which is differentiated from other faculties in that it has a different function: It observes (not necessarily uses) all available means of persuasion. It is still further differentiated from all the processes which observe means of persuasion, by adding, "in any given (particular) case;" that is, with reference to time, to place, and to audience. When we suggest that chartreuse is "yellow-green" we have placed it in a continuum—in this case the color spectrum.

Bertrand Russell's definition of "matter" illustrates defining by comparison and contrast: "We commonly mean by 'matter' something that is opposed to 'mind', something which we think of as occupying space and as radically incapable of any sort of thought or consciousness."[21]

[19] Douglas Ehninger and Wayne Brockriede, *Decision by Debate* (New York: Dodd, Mead and Co., 1963).

[20] Aristotle, *Rhetoric*, trans. W. Rhys Roberts (New York: Random House, Inc., 1954), 1355b 26–27.

[21] Bertrand Russell, *The Problems of Philosophy* (New York: Oxford University Press, 1959), p. 13. Originally published in 1912.

Definition by negation uses contrast to indicate clearly what a term does not mean. *De facto* recognition of a government is not the same as *de jure* recognition. *De jure* recognition carries with it the implication of approval, whereas, *de facto* recognition does not. It implies only the awareness that a given government is *in fact* controlling the affairs of the state.

We have already used the method of definition by etymology when we defined the terms "communication" and "proof." The critic Sainte-Beuve uses this method in his essay "What is a Classic?" He points out:

> A classic, according to the usual definition, is an old author canonised by admiration, and an authority in his particular style. The word *classic* was first used in this sense by the Romans. With them not all the citizens of the different classes were properly called *classici*, but only those of the chief class, those who possessed an income of a certain fixed sum. Those who possessed a smaller income were described by the term *infra classem*, below the pre-eminent class. The word *classicus* was used in a figurative sense . . . and applied to writers: a writer of worth and distinction, *classicus assiduusque scriptor*, a writer who is of account. . . ." [22]

The definition by necessary conditions, as the name implies, is an enumeration of the conditions that must be met before the term can be used properly. For example, a monopoly exists only if there is exclusive control (however obtained) of the supply of any given commodity in any given market.

Lincoln in his "First Inaugural Address" used the definition by necessary condition to meet the contention of the secessionists that the Constitution nowhere authorized the federal government to take forcible measures against the withdrawing states. "Perpetuity is implied, if not expressed, in the fundamental law of all national governments;" [23] that is, it is a fundamental feature of, condition to, "national governments." Lincoln thus suggests that whatever is recognized as a "government" has the obligation to defend itself from without and from within.

Winston Churchill, distinguishing between "Liberalism" and "Socialism," demonstrated operational definition by pointing out how

[22] C. A. Sainte-Beuve, "What is a Classic?" in *Great Essays*, ed., Houston Peterson (New York: Pocket Books, Inc., 1954), p. 228.
[23] Parrish and Hochmuth, eds., *American Speeches*, p. 36.

they function. In this example, operational description is set in the context of comparison and contrast:

> Socialism seeks to pull down wealth; Liberalism seeks to raise up poverty. Socialism would destroy private interests; Liberalism would preserve private interests in the only way in which they can be safely and justly preserved, namely, by reconciling them with public right. Socialism would kill enterprise; Liberalism would rescue enterprise from the trammels of privilege and preference. Socialism assails the pre-eminence of the individual; Liberalism seeks, and shall seek more in the future, to build up a minimum standard for the mass. Socialism exalts the rule; Liberalism exalts the man. Socialism attacks capital; Liberalism attacks monopoly.[24]

In addition to these kinds of definitions, there are definition by example and authoritative definition. Both could probably be used in defining a term by any of the methods discussed above.

TESTIMONY

Testimony is support drawn from the authority of someone other than the speaker. In form, it may contain solely an interpretation or it may contain factual material of all kinds with interpretation or judgment by an "expert," someone whose relationship with the facts makes him particularly qualified to interpret them.

For an example of testimony which includes statistics and contrast, consider the statement of H. P. Miller, Special Assistant in the U.S. Bureau of the Census:

> Between 1947 and 1961, the real output of the private economy in the United States increased by 59 per cent, but man-hours rose by only 3 per cent. In other words, a tremendous increase in output was achieved with a slight rise in employment.[25]

Or observe how a speaker could use an authority within an authority; for example, Catherine Bowen's reflections about an event which gives insight into another historian, Bernard DeVoto:

> Bernard DeVoto lived with history, read history at night and in the morning, talked history, and was restless when other people did not want to talk history. When I began to write about John Adams, I asked DeVoto if I should buy the *Dictionary of American Biography*. . . . There are twenty-one volumes and it is not cheap. DeVoto was

[24] *The Eloquence of Winston Churchill,* ed., F. B. Czarnomski (New York: The New American Library of World Literature, Inc., 1957), p. 16.
[25] *Employment Service Review* (July, 1964), p. 20.

surprised at my question and surprised that I did not already own the volumes. "Of course, buy it," he said. "It's good to read in bed at night before you go to sleep." [26]

The most obvious point one could make about the use of testimony and authority is that the authority should be an authority. He should have wide knowledge of the facts, wide experience in correlating them, interpreting them, evaluating them. He should be unbiased in his handling of them. In the actual presentation of the speech, enough should be said about the expert to establish his credentials for the audience.

VISUAL AIDS

One of the criteria for selecting all the materials for a speech should be potential interest and attention value. Change generally helps maintain attention, change in terms of variety among types of verbal supporting materials and change from presenting supporting material verbally to presenting such material through visual aids. Visual aids in a speech add interest chiefly because they *do* involve a change from one activity (hearing) to another (seeing).

The other basic difference between visual and verbal support is this: Words are discursive, they are temporal in nature and are heard one at a time, with the complete meaning withheld until the entire sentence, paragraph, or even the whole speech has been delivered. Visual symbols, on the other hand, are presentational; their complete meaning is presented all at once.

Many people are more "eye-minded" than "ear-minded." One study reports that 85 per cent of learning is gained through the eyes. Their subjects learned one-third faster through visual instruction than through aural instruction only, and the material that was seen was remembered 55 per cent better than material that was only heard. So visual aids not only have attention value, but they strengthen understanding as well since they serve to promote clearness. It is hard to compare more than two numbers when hearing them, but when they are presented in a graph or chart, it is easy to understand the interrelationships of many numbers.[27]

[26] Catherine Drinker Bowen, "The Historian," in *Four Portraits and One Subject: Bernard DeVoto* (Boston: Houghton Mifflin Company, 1963), p. 23.
[27] Reported in Robert T. Oliver, Harold P. Zelko, and Paul D. Holtzman, *Communicative Speech*, 3rd ed. (New York: Holt, Rinehart and Winston, Inc., 1962), p. 250.

Some students discovered these two effective uses of visual aids in a classroom speech. For example, when discussing the campaigns of General Washington, one student made the speech more meaningful and more vivid by pointing out the campaigns on a large, multicolored map. Another student, when discussing the plight of slum children evoked much more feeling and compassion and a clearer belief in the need for action by showing photographs taken from a weekly news magazine.

Whether you are using models, diagrams, charts, maps, graphs, or objects, there are two major criteria for selecting them: (1) Are they easy to use? To handle? To explain? and (2) Are they large enough to be seen by everyone in the audience? Unless your aids meet both criteria, they are more hindrance than help and will distract attention from your speech rather than attract it. Visual aids are, as the name implies, aids which supplement not supplant the spoken word.

If the visual aid hinders the speaker's direct relationship with his audience, if the speaker talks to the diagram instead of to his audience, his actions detract from the speech rather than help it. Practice with the aid will help the speaker use it efficiently without giving it his complete attention at the audience's expense.

TESTS OF EFFECTIVE
SUPPORTING MATERIAL

The speaker should raise certain questions about each of the supports he uses to test their effectiveness. Basically, he should ask:

(1) Is my material relevant to my speech?
(2) Is my material accurate? Does it come from a reliable source?
(3) Is my material recent enough?
(4) Is my material fairly stated? Are my examples typical? Is my information sufficient in scope to present an accurate picture?
(5) Is my material appropriate to this particular audience? Will it be meaningful to them?
(6) Is my material interesting and vivid?

If the supporting materials meet the first five requirements, it will be acceptable as rhetorical proof. If it also meets the sixth, it will have still a better chance of actually being accepted by the audience.

INFERENCE

An inference is that which is derived by *implication*. Inferences are often drawn when the speaker wants to go beyond empirical evidence. In this case, the types of supporting material which we have just discussed become the basis of an inductive generalization, an inference. Let us illustrate by showing how statistics can be used as the basis of inference. For example, a newspaper reporter questions twenty-five people in a town about their opinions of proposed legislation. Twenty of them are in favor of it, and five are opposed. If the reporter records that twenty out of twenty-five people were in favor of the legislation, he is only describing what he has observed. But if his story records that 80 per cent of the town's people favor the legislation, he is *inferring* that the percentage of the population favoring the legislation is basically the same as in his small sample. The question then becomes: Is the sample large enough in scope to allow the inference? In this case, probably not.

The reporter could have said: "Since twenty of the twenty-five people I sampled were in favor of the legislation, I can be 95 per cent confident that the proportion of the citizens in favor of it is somewhere between 54 per cent and 91 per cent." This may not be as dramatic, but is more accurate. As soon as the speaker makes an inductive generalization, saying in effect that because this is true (that which can be empirically proven) then this is probably also true (that which cannot be empirically proven), the speaker is no longer describing—he is drawing an inference.

The most important thing for the beginning speaker to remember when drawing an inference is to limit his claim to the scope of the supporting material or evidence from which he has made his inference. Inferences, by definition, are limited in such ways as "much of the time," "most of the time," "80 per cent of the time," "possibly," "there is a high degree of probability that what I say is in fact likely to hold true." So the speaker must be sure that when he is moving from observed or known facts to a "prediction" (that which is unable at the moment to be observed or known), his claim is appropriate to the amount of supporting materials or evidence available.

AMPLIFICATION

When necessary, both for clarity and for interest value, the speaker may need to enlarge upon the bare statement of support.

Instead of merely saying that the Louisiana Purchase consisted of 872,987 square miles, one student added that through this purchase the United States doubled the size of the nation and that the area was eventually divided into six states—Arkansas, Missouri, Iowa, Nebraska, Oklahoma, Kansas, and parts of eleven other states—North and South Dakota, Montana, Wyoming, Colorado, New Mexico, Minnesota, Mississippi, Alabama, Texas, and Louisiana. Through amplification, the speaker clarified the concept of area, and impressed very vividly upon the listeners just how large and how important the Louisiana Purchase actually was.

Another student, giving the reasons she had enjoyed a recent trip to Ireland, said that it cost her comparatively little to stay there, about ten dollars a day. She added that her hotel cost about $4.00 a day; a lunch cost about $1.00; dinner, $1.50; a theater ticket, $1.00; and transportation around $1.50. For those in the audience accustomed to paying considerably more for theater tickets in New York and Boston than $1.00 or those who had driven across the country to pay from $7 to $15 at a motel, the speaker's point was more vivid through amplification of her original statement. She did not add the cost of occasional cups of coffee, cigarettes, or post cards because it would have added little to the point which she had already made. Thus, tell all that needs to be said to make your point clear and vivid, and no more. That is the key to the effective use of amplification.

Emotional Proof

We earlier discussed the concept of functional selectivity: Objects that are important to the listener, which serve some immediate purpose to him, are naturally perceived first. This selectivity, then, is governed to a very large degree by the needs of the hearer, by his motives and emotions.

These needs are both physiological and intellectual. We worry about safety and welfare, about belonging, about the good opinion of our friends, about feeling a sense of adjustment and of creativity. These personal desires are greatly influenced by group pressures: emphasis on the appropriate, on material well-being, on progress, on status, and so forth.

From the earliest known rhetoricians to advertising's motivational researcher, those interested in communication have been trying to find out what impelling motives are and to develop methods of appealing to them. In fact, the mass psychoanalysis which guides television persuasion campaigns has already become the basis for a large industry. Professional persuaders continually rely upon it as they seek to sell us refrigerators or images of public men. Note the great variety of emotional appeals utilized in campaigns to sell the public everything from soap powder to political candidates.

The speaker can develop emotional proof: (1) by using words which refer the hearers to specific emotions; or (2) by describing and/or suggesting the emotions, moods, and feelings he wishes his audience to feel. Lincoln, for example, in his "First Inaugural Address" changed the word "Union" to "fabric" and added "with all its benefits, its memories and its hopes." [28] Here he sought to suggest attitudes which were conducive to heightening the feelings of his audience.

Note further how Samuel Adams, Robert Ingersoll, and Henry Grady appeal to the emotion of their audiences:

Samuel Adams, in a speech in Philadelphia at the State House on August 1, 1776:

> Our union is now complete; our constitution is composed, established and approved. You are now the guardians of your own liberties. . . .
>
> You have now in the field armies sufficient to repel the whole force of your enemies and their base and mercenary auxiliaries. The hearts of your soldiers beat high with the spirit of freedom; they are animated with the justice of their cause, and while they grasp their swords can look up to Heaven for assistance. Your adversaries are composed of wretches who laugh at the rights of humanity, who turn religion into derision, and would, for higher wages, direct their swords against their leaders or their country. Go on, then, in your generous enterprise, with gratitude to Heaven for past success, and confidence of it in the future. For my own part, I ask no greater blessing than to share with you the common danger and common glory. If I have a wish dearer to my soul than that my ashes may be mingled with those of a Warren and a Montgomery, it is that these American States may never cease to be free and independent.[29]

Robert Ingersoll in a speech nominating James G. Blaine for President at the Republican National Convention in Cincinnati on June 15, 1876:

[28] Parrish and Hochmuth, eds., *American Speeches,* p. 63.
[29] From *The World's Great Speeches,* Lewis Copeland and Lawrence Lamm, eds., 2nd rev. ed. (New York: Dover Publications, Inc., 1958), p. 235.

This is a grand year; a year filled with the recollections of the Revolution, filled with proud and tender memories of the past, with the sacred legends of liberty; a year in which the sons of freedom will drink from the fountains of enthusiasm; a year in which the people call for a man who has preserved in Congress what our soldiers won upon the field; a year in which we call for a man who has torn from the throat of treason the tongue of slander—for the man who has snatched the mask of Democracy from the hideous face of Rebellion —for the man who, like an intellectual athlete, has stood in the arena of debate and challenged all comers, and who, up to the present moment, is a total stranger to defeat.

Like an armed warrior, like a plumed knight, James G. Blaine marched down the halls of the American Congress and threw his shining lance full and fair against the brazen foreheads of the defamers of his country and the maligners of his honor.[30]

Henry Grady, the journalist, in a speech before the New England Society of New York in 1886. His point is: There is a new South, not through protest against the old, but because of new conditions, new adjustments, because of new ideas and aspirations:

Dr. Talmage has drawn for you, with a master's hand, the picture of your returning armies. He has told you how, in the pomp and circumstance of war, they came back to you, marching with proud and victorious tread, reading their glory in a nation's eyes! Will you bear with me while I tell you of another army that sought its home at the close of the late war—an army that marched home in defeat and not in victory—in pathos and not in splendor, but in glory that equaled yours, and to hearts as loving as ever welcomed heroes home. Let me picture to you the footsore Confederate soldier, as, buttoning up in his faded gray jacket the parole which was to bear testimony to his children of his fidelity and faith, he turned his face southward from Appomattox in April, 1865. Think of him as ragged, half-starved, heavy-hearted, enfeebled by want and wounds; having fought to exhaustion, he surrenders his gun, wrings the hands of his comrades in silence, and, lifting his tear-stained and pallid face for the last time to the graves that dot the old Virginia hills, pulls his gray cap over his brow and begins the slow and painful journey. What does he find—let me ask you, who went to your homes eager to find in the welcome you had justly earned, full payment for four years' sacrifice—what does he find when, having followed the battle-stained cross against overwhelming odds, dreading death not half so much as surrender, he reaches the home he left so prosperous and beautiful? He finds his house in ruins, his farm devastated, his slaves free, his stock killed, his barns empty, his trade destroyed, his

[30] *Ibid.*, pp. 323–24.

money worthless; his social system, feudal in its magnificence, swept
away; his people without law or legal status, his comrades slain, and
the burdens of others heavy on his shoulders.[31]

While these three examples may be overstated for contemporary
tastes, they nevertheless serve to point out the basic feature of well-
used emotional proof. We accept them as genuine, not synthetic
emotions. Cicero comments:

> Nor is it possible that the judge should feel concern, or hate, or
> envy, or fear in any degree, or that he should be moved to com-
> passion and tears, unless all those sensations which the orator would
> awaken in the judge shall appear to be deeply felt and experienced
> by the orator himself.[32]

So the emotion expressed must be genuine. But more than sincerity
is involved. The speaker places a value judgment on each statement
he makes. He, in effect, endorses the motive, the emotion he attempts
to arouse. A "value" is a fundamental significance which we attach
to what we are and through which we orient ourselves. The emotion,
the motives appealed to by Adams—freedom, justice, independence;
by Ingersoll—preservation of peace, honest actions initiated by courage; by Grady—compassion, all call for preexisting value judgment;
that is, the speakers judged them to be *useful* values.

Value also implies permanence and choice. We generally distinguish a lasting value from the kind of significance which we attach
to passing sensation or to immediate, practical means. In short,
values imply a reasonable basis for appealing to motives or emotions.
Herein lies the legitimate use of emotional proof—as a mover to
action which is guided by reason. When there is no worthwhile
guide, when irrational behavior is exploited, then demagoguery and
exploitation set in.

There may be some truth in Cicero's comment that "... mankind
makes far more determinations through hatred, or love, or desire, or
anger, or grief, or joy, or hope, or fear, or error, or some other affection of mind, than from regard to truth, or any settled maxim, or
principle of right, or judicial form, or adherence to the laws." [33]
But the speaker must never knowingly use means which impede

[31] Parrish and Hochmuth, eds., *American Speeches*, p. 454.
[32] Cicero, *On Oratory*, trans. J. S. Watson, The Bonn Classical Library
(London: H. G. Bonn, 1855), II, 45.
[33] *Ibid.*, 42.

man's ever-continuing struggle to make *responsible* choices and judgments. If he in any way contributes to the fulfillment of the Orwellian prediction of "Group think" and the picture of man as a "cheerful robot," then he has forgotten that rhetoric reserves the right to check the *quality* of the premises which a speaker makes.

The speaker and the exploiters know equally well that there are "hidden needs" in all men, but there is one great difference in the ways this knowledge is used. The responsible speaker knows that emotional security is to be found in deep and lasting relationships and not in home freezers; that reassurance of worth is to be found in one's own judgments and the judgments of those in whom we place trust and not in the length of the tail fin on one's automobile; the responsible speaker knows that "ego-gratification" is to be found in tasks well done and not in the shiniest new electric egg beater on the block; that creative outlets are to be found in facing problems and solving them and not in choosing the cake mix to which one can add an egg; that a sense of roots is found in understanding and participating in the institutions he values and not in slogans such as "The good old days—the home-sweet-home wine—the wine that grandma used to make."

The idea of "merchandising" emotional proof via the spoken word does not stop at toothpaste and haircream and electric razors, but carries over into "selling" political candidates, government policies, and outlooks on life. Herein lies the ultimate indignity to the democratic process and to man himself.

The speaker should have a firm grasp of the available materials concerning the emotions and he must surely consider how these materials are relevant to his particular speech. He might however recall the words of Gladstone when he said:

> Let him [the speaker] not suppose that he is to deviate one step from the course which Love of Truth would prescribe: but he is to learn that the truth is not necessarily loved when seen: that she is not necessarily seen when shown: that she is not necessarily shown, when intended and honestly attempted to be set forth through the imperfect medium of language, and by faculties in a still more imperfect state of self possession: in short, let him be guided by the love of truth, to adopt for his law and principle, the desire of making truth effective: for his object, the giving to that desire a maximum of effect.[34]

[34] Loren Reid, ed., "Gladstone's Essay on Public Speaking," *Quarterly Journal of Speech* (October, 1953), p. 267.

The responsible public speaker always draws a distinction between appealing to the sentiments in his hearers and appealing to the best sentiments in them.

Summary

Rhetorical invention concerns the content of a speech. It includes the selection of subject, the selection of purpose, and all the materials which the speaker uses to fulfill his purpose. He may say, "Listen to me because of who I am," "Listen to me because of what I know," "Listen to me because I share certain motives, certain values, and emotions with you." Most often he will say all three because they are in the final analysis inseparable. When a speaker says "Listen to me because of who I am," he is after all saying, "Listen to me because of what I know." And, any time one person speaks to another, he is in the very act of trying to establish a "commonness" with others, saying, "Listen to me because I share basic motives and emotions with you."

All the speaker's materials, his proofs, are his way of establishing the fact that he has a right to speak on his topic; that is, that he knows something about it and that what he says is worthy of being accepted by those who hear him speak.

There are tests of evidence which both the speaker and the audience can use to see whether or not his credentials are in fact acceptable. If they are acceptable then he can use them as the basis for inference, for moving beyond them to speculation and interpretation. The worth of the inference is limited by the kind and the scope of evidence on which it is based. The worth of both evidence and inferences determines the *acceptability* of the speaker's proof.

Rhetorical Exercises

(1) Give an eight to ten minute speech in which you support your thesis with a wide variety of kinds of logical proof. Then give a speech on the same topic including emotional and ethical proof. If you would like help on the use of notes, you might like to read the section concerning notes in Chapter IX.

(2) Listen to a speech or a debate. What kinds of supporting materials were offered? Were they acceptable as proof? Why or why not?

(3) What effect is ethical proof likely to have on evidence? Can you point to specific examples to support your answer?

(4) Find some examples of emotional proof. Is there any evidence that they were successful or not? What kinds of limitations should be placed on the use of emotional proof?

(5) Read one of the articles listed in the collateral reading list. Report on it to the class. Most of them will provoke discussion. Perhaps you would like to see if one of the experiments yields the same results in your class.

(6) Check the *Quarterly Journal of Speech, Speech Monographs,* and other journals which your teacher can recommend for some other interesting work done experimentally with the kinds of proof used in a speech.

Collateral Readings

Andersen, Kenneth, and Theodore Clevenger, Jr., "A Summary of Experimental Research in Ethos," *Speech Monographs* (June, 1963), pp. 59–78.

Bormann, E. G., "An Empirical Approach to Certain Concepts of Logical Proof," *Central States Speech Journal* (1961), pp. 85–91.

Ehninger, Douglas, and Wayne Brockriede, "The Unit of Proof and its Structure," *Decision by Debate.* New York: Dodd, Mead and Co., 1963, pp. 98–109.

Haiman, Franklyn, "Democratic Ethics and the Hidden Persuaders," *Quarterly Journal of Speech* (December, 1958), pp. 385–92.

Hovland, Carl I., and Walter Weiss, "The Influence of Source Credibility on Communication Effectiveness," *Public Opinion Quarterly* (1951), pp. 635–50.

Hovland, Carl I., Irving L. Janis, and Harold H. Kelley, "Credibility of the Communicator," in *Communication and Persuasion.* New Haven: Yale University Press, 1953. Chapter Two.

McKeon, Richard, "Communication, Truth and Society," *Ethics* (January, 1957), pp. 89–99.

Pence, Orville L., "Emotionally Loaded Argument: Its Effectiveness in Stimulating Recall," *QJS* (October, 1954), pp. 272–76.

Rogge, Edward, "Evaluating the Ethics of a Speaker in a Democracy, *QJS* (December, 1959), pp. 419–25.

Ruechelle, Randall C., "An Experimental Study of Audience Recognition of Emotional and Intellectual Appeals in Persuasion," *SM* (March, 1958), pp. 49–58.

Utterback, William E., and Harold F. Harding, "Some Factors Conditioning Response to Argument," *SM* (November, 1955), pp. 303–308.

Wallace, Karl R., "An Ethical Basis of Communication," *Speech Teacher* (January, 1955), pp. 1–9.

Wieman, Henry Nelson, and Otis M. Walter, "Toward an Analysis of Ethics for Rhetoric," *QJS* (October, 1957), pp. 266–70.

*... every discourse is put together like a living creature—it has
a kind of body of its own—and hence lacks neither head nor
foot, but has both middle and extremities all composed in
such sort that they suit each other and the whole.*

PLATO

V   Before beginning our discussion of how the speaker decides to arrange and proportion his materials, let us recall something rather basic about the nature of cognition. Man is naturally an organizing animal. He does not attempt to collect all the facts before he organizes them. As soon as he collects two or more facts, he begins to perceive them as organized into some kind of meaningful whole. So, in a sense, when the speaker began the selection of his topic and the selection of his proofs, he began the process of disposition. He may have eliminated some ideas, added others. The very attempt to arrange materials on any one subject may suggest other materials, new lines of thinking. It is the process of arrangement that gives the speaker a complete view of the subject.

The closeness between the invention process and the arrangement process cannot be overemphasized. The process of invention has proceeded from a result of thinking according to one kind of method or another, both good and bad. Often just in seeking the best method, pertinent and useful materials are suggested to the speaker. Skill in disposition lies in the capacity to see facts and ideas not as isolated and random, but in combination with other facts and ideas.

ARRANGEMENT
OF MATERIALS

Speech Organization

A speech, informative or persuasive, is generally divided into three parts: Introduction, Discussion and Conclusion. Each of these parts has a distinct function. The advice sometimes given to young men going into the clergy is useful to recall: "Tell the audience what you're going to say. Say it. Then, remind them of what you've said." Time and considerable skill are needed to construct a clear but interesting speech which has maximum chance of fulfilling its intended purpose. All parts of the speech are governed, in the final analysis, by what the speaker knows about the specific occasion and his specific audience.

Arrangement of materials for a speech consists of more steps than a simple determination of what materials will go in an introduction, a discussion, and a conclusion. It also consists of the arrangement of main points, of sequencing supporting materials under each main point, and of proportioning the material for proper emphasis. We shall discuss each one of these aspects of arrangement.

INTRODUCTION

The introduction serves to: (1) gain attention; (2) give useful materials which the audience may need to start thinking about the subject, materials which allow the listener to become oriented to the subject; (3) present a clear statement of purpose which permits the audience to see what the speaker hopes to accomplish; (4) provide a thesis which suggests the main point of the speech; (5) indicate the approach to the subject through a partition or division of the materials.

Although each speaker must learn to adapt this method for opening a speech to his own particular situation, the reasons for, and basic order of, all introductions remain very much the same. We shall discuss the reasons for this by explaining in some detail how each portion of an introduction functions.

Attention-Getter. Persuasion begins by gaining attention. The speaker cannot under any conceivable circumstance influence an audience unless he has first captured their attention. The speaker can attempt to get attention by means of a striking fact which most people are not aware of, by means of a question; for example, "How many of you know a copepodologist?", and by a variety of other means. The nature of the topic, the speaker's ingenuity, plus recognition of the importance of an attention-getter should provide such a device for a speaker.

A good attention getter must be stimulating enough to make an audience focus its attention on the speech and not on some other aspect of its environment. To do this, it must somehow provide a contrast with what the members of an audience have been thinking about before the speech. A good attention-getter attempts to involve the audience. It lets the audience participate directly in the speech. The audience ought to be able to say about the attention-getter: "I never thought of that before!" or "That's happened to me too." or "How interesting that is (to me)!" How much time the speaker spends in considering the problem of getting attention and how much freshness and vitality he brings to his subject determines how much attention he will get or, indeed, if he gets any at all. Although an attention-getting device is necessary at first, the speaker should remember that he must work throughout the speech to get and to maintain attention.

Orientation. Next, the speaker should recall the implication of the temporal nature of the speaking act. Time must be given for the intellect to deal with what is being said and to deal with it vigorously. At the beginning of his speech, the speaker must provide his audience with:

(1) a clear statement of purpose
(2) a direct assertion, a thesis, a subject sentence which in effect summarizes the whole speech in one sentence
(3) a clear suggestion of the structural progression to be followed in the speech development.

Let us take an example. Suppose the speaker has chosen as his topic "An Introduction to Alaska." His thinking might proceed along these lines:

Attention-getter and orientation to his topic: If you had lived at the beginning of the eighteenth century, one of the questions which might have kept you guessing was this one: "Are America and Asia one continent or two?" To answer the question, Tsar Peter the Great sent Danish born Vitus Bering east to Kamchatka in Siberia with orders to explore the waters off its coast. At that time, the North Pacific lay shrouded in mystery. In 1728 Bering sailed through the fogbound strait that was to bear his name and proved that Asia and America were separate. Russia's claim to Alaska rested in Bering's discoveries. In the 1860's, Tsarist Russia, considering Alaska a financial and strategic liability, offered it to the United States. Secretary of State William H. Seward snapped at the $7,200,000 bargain; but the Senate ratified the purchase with reluctance, and wits called the deal "Seward's Folly" and the new possession his "ice box."

Statement of purpose: Today, I'd like to tell you why Seward's "ice box" is one of the best buys the United States has ever made. Subject Sentence: Alaska, with her tremendous natural resources and her strategic location, has a very great value as a state for the U.S.

Specific statement of purpose. We have already considered the formulation of purpose under the heading of invention. After the speaker has selected one of the three general reasons for speaking (informing, entertaining, persuading), he needs to think more in terms of a specific statement of purpose in relationship to the specific aim of his speech. Suppose you had chosen the general topic "Alaska" for a speech. Do you want to describe the "discovery and exploration" of Alaska? Do you want to discuss its economic potential? Do you want to describe its geography and climate? Do you want to recount tales of a trip to Alaska? After you have answered this kind of question, your answer will become an explicit statement of purpose—your audience will know exactly what aspect of Alaska you are going to talk about and will have its first specific clue about the direction of your speech. Then they will know what sort of information, ideas, judgments to expect. It is not always necessary that a speaker explicitly state his purpose, especially when speaking to an unfriendly audience. He must, of course, state his purpose in his own analysis.

The thesis sentence. The audience's expectation should be fulfilled as soon as possible or evidence offered that its expectations will be fulfilled. That is the function of the subject sentence. The purpose sentence tells the audience what you're going to do; the subject sentence does it. It is in effect a one-sentence summary, the one statement in your speech which all others support, either directly or indirectly.

The subject sentence is the assertion of an idea or an opinion. Let us consider the basic nature of an assertion. When some one coughs, you may suppose that he has a cold. You may feel sorry for him and you may even say, "It's too bad you're catching a cold." But you would not say, "That's true." His cough shows that he has a cold.

It does not say it. If he had said, "I am catching a cold," you could agree or disagree with him—but not with his cough. This cough is, in a way, similar to three types of sentences: interrogative, imperative, and exclamatory. You can not judge any of them true or false.

A declarative sentence, on the other hand, is either true or false: "The temperature today is 45 degrees." "If I study harder, I may be able to improve my grades." "Deficit spending is a wise policy." In short, these sentences make assertions. If the assertions are debatable, if their truth or falsity is questionable, as: "The Federal Government should guarantee an opportunity for higher education to all qualified high school graduates," then they are termed opinions. If the statements can be tested by direct observation, they are said to be facts; for example, "There are more students in this year's freshman class than in last year's class." Beardsley defines assertion in this way:

> When someone . . . utters or writes a statement in such a way (that is, with such a tone of voice, or in such circumstances) that he appears to believe what he is saying, and appears to invite others to believe it as well, we shall say that he is *asserting* the statement, or making an assertion.[1]

The subject or thesis sentence is the statement of your case, that is, the point you intend to prove, the opinion you hope will be accepted, the particular policy you are asking your audience to adopt. All other statements in the speech are directed essentially at proving the thesis. They will show why your opinion is right or valuable or wise. They will show why the policy you are proposing is practicable or advantageous.

Partition. After the thesis sentence, the audience may want to know exactly *how* the speaker is going to handle his subject. Often this is a preview of the main heads. One student, in a speech about the contemporary French philosopher Gabriel Marcel, used this partition in his speech:

> First, I want to tell you *who* Gabriel Marcel is. Then, I want to tell you *what* he has to say. And lastly, I want to tell you *why* I think everyone in this class should become familiar with his writings.

Often the partition is implicit in the statement of the thesis sentence itself. Consider this example: "In learning to play tennis, the begin-

---

[1] Monroe C. Beardsley, *Thinking Straight: Principles of Reasoning for Readers and Writers,* 2nd ed. (Englewood Cliffs, N.J.: Prentice-Hall, Inc., 1956), p. 10. This discussion follows that of Prof. Beardsley's from pp. 8–12.

ner should concentrate on developing three basic strokes: the fore-hand, the backhand, and the serve." Whether the partition, or division of the subject, is included in the thesis sentence or stated separately, it provides the audience with insight into what to expect.

Identification. In order to persuade a person, the speaker needs to identify his opinion or the course of action he is suggesting, with one or more of the opinions or customary courses of action of his audience. Often the speaker first attempts identification at some point in the introduction. Murphy describes Theodore Roosevelt's sense of identification in this way:

> Everywhere he went he found things in common with his audience: some of his Rough Riders had come from the district, he had close friends in the area, he had read the history of the locality. He told an audience of Presbyterians that he often attended their services because they were so much like those of his own church, the Dutch Reformed.... He reminded the legislature in Texas that he had been a legislator.... At the Sorbonne, he interjected extemporaneous sentences in French to make meanings clear.[2]

This is not meant to suggest that the speaker compromise his own integrity, that he be subservient completely to his audience, but it does mean that people listen more directly, more easily when they see the common ground they share with the speaker. An audience needs to feel itself directly involved in the speaker's topic. So, he should speak *with* them, not merely before them.

One of the most striking opening statements made by a student in a classroom speech urged the other members of the class to support a volunteer service program at one of the local mental hospitals:

> It has been estimated that one out of every ten people in the United States will, during the course of his lifetime, receive help of some kind for mental illness. If these figures are correct, and we have every reason to believe they are, that means three people in this room may some day suffer from one kind of emotional disturbance or another. So, the problem of caring for the mentally ill is a problem which you and I must face very seriously. It is *our* problem.

> Now, the first question which probably comes to your mind is this: How can I help care for the mentally ill? I am not a psychologist or a psychiatrist. I am not a trained orderly. The answer to this question is one which dozens of students answer every Thursday night

<hr>

2 Richard Murphy, "Theodore Roosevelt," in *A History and Criticism of American Public Address*, ed. Marie Kathryn Hochmuth (New York: Longmans, Green and Co., 1955), III, 338–39.

between the hours of seven-thirty and nine-thirty when they perform volunteer services at one of the local mental hospitals.

Today I'd like to tell you about our volunteer program, some of the things we have accomplished, and some of the things we can accomplish with your help.

This speaker, in seeking a link between himself, his topic, and his audience, found a very direct and attention-getting one. He established that the problem was not just his problem, or the problem of other people, but "our" problem. Thus the audience became a direct participant in his speech. He kept the audience participating in the speech until the last portion when he dealt with "some of the things which the volunteer services program can accomplish with *your* help." This speaker knew that the task of identification does not end with the opening remarks, that the common ground between the speaker and the listener must continually be established throughout the speech.

Observe a political speaker, campaigning across the country, establishing three different links with three different audiences: [3]

(1) In Minnesota: "I am grateful for the opportunity to talk with you about national farm policies. I won't waste your time this afternoon telling you . . . all about how I am myself a farmer. I own farm land in Illinois, and I come from a family that has lived in the heart of the Corn Belt for over a hundred years. . . . My first venture into public service was in Washington in the old Agricultural Adjustment Administration. . . ."

(2) In Virginia: "Here in Richmond tonight, in Virginia, rich both in history and in the knowledge of its history, I am moved to talk for a few minutes of the past. . . . The South is a good place to take our bearings, because in no part of the country does the past —a past of great nobility and great tragedy—more sharply etch the present than in the South."

(3) In Massachusetts: "I don't know why it is that an American, no matter where he was born or where he lives, has a feeling in New England of coming home. Perhaps it is because this country of yours looks so homelike; perhaps it is because the people and their welcome are always friendly; perhaps it is because so much of what we are as Americans came out of these valleys and these hills—our habit, for example, of making up our own minds in our own way, and saying what we think—our habit of respect for each other, and for ourselves—our habit, if you please, of freedom."

[3] From *Major Campaign Speeches of Adlai E. Stevenson, 1952.* Copyright 1953 by Random House, Inc. Reprinted by permission, pp. 64, 149, 140.

THE DISCUSSION:

OUTLINING FOR A

MOTIVATIONAL SITUATION

In Chapter III we discussed the notion of lines of argument as they are derived from six motivational situations: the information situation, the difficulty situation, the goal-oriented situation, the barrier situation, the threat situation, and the identification situation. The outline forms for speeches are determined primarily by the motivational situation. In each of the motivational situations, a series of questions is indicated in an attempt to discover what sorts of materials you must offer to have your thesis accepted. Those questions necessary for the acceptance of your speech are called issues.

Let us suggest a basic approach to each of the situations in which you might be giving a speech. In each case we shall present a general outline and then a specific example.

The information situation. The need for information exists:

(A) The first major portion of information is . . . .
(B) The second major portion of information is . . . .
(C) The third major portion of information is . . . .

Thesis sentence: To become a good debater you must possess five basic skills.

   I. You must be able to analyze the topic for debate, searching out the basic areas of controversy.
  II. You must be able to support your position with adequate, well-documented materials.
 III. You must be able to organize materials clearly and efficiently.
 IV. You must be able to demonstrate skill in refuting what your opponents say.
  V. You must be able to present your materials fluently and with ease.

The problem situation. A problem exists:

(A) The nature of the problem
(B) Scope and magnitude of the problem
(C) Cause of the problem.

Thesis sentence: A very serious problem exists in higher education today.

I. Abut half of the top 24 per cent of high school graduates do not enter college.

II. The problem is serious both to the students themselves and to the nation as a whole.

III. The reasons for failing to enter college vary, but the primary one seems to be that prospective students cannot obtain the necessary finances.

The solution situation. This solution should be accepted:

(A) Other solutions have been tried and have failed.

(B) This solution does meet the problem.

(C) It is practicable.

(D) There are other advantages.

Thesis sentence: The Federal Government should guarantee an opportunity for higher education to all qualified high school graduates by means of a federally underwritten loan system.

I. The solutions which have been tried in the past have not succeeded in diminishing the percentage of above average students who cannot attend college because of lack of finances.

II. Under the proposed plan students could borrow at low rates of interest and thereby finance their college education.

III. A federally underwritten loan program could be carried out by already existing governmental departments at no extra cost to the Federal Government.

IV. There are two major advantages to such a program.

The barrier situation. Although such a solution may be difficult to achieve, it is necessary:

(A) Its outcomes are worth achieving.

(B) The objections to such a plan are not serious.

(C) The objections can be met.

Thesis sentence: Although there may be objections to a federal loan system, it is vitally necessary.

I. The outcome would be beneficial to both the well-being of the individual and of the nation.

II. The objections to such a plan are based on misconceptions.

III. The objections can be met and fear of federal control allayed.

The threat situation. A threat exists:

(A) It is serious.
(B) It is inherent in the present structure.
(C) It is immediate.

Thesis sentence: The potential loss of this talent represents a serious threat of loss in terms of new ideas and economic gain.

    I. The talent loss represents a potential of $177,000 in earnings to the persons who cannot attend college; it represents untold loss in human creativity.

    II. This talent loss is due in large part to our current conception of the proper methods of providing means for needy students to go to college.

    III. The nation can not afford such a loss at a time when it is competing very directly with communist countries.

The identification situation. Group A should help Group B:

(A) They are related.
(B) Group B should be helped.
(C) Only Group A can do it.

Thesis sentence: The Federal Government should provide financial aid to students who can not otherwise afford to go to college.

    I. The quality and quantity of national output depends on education.

    II. Higher education is a worthwhile cause to support as it allows the individual to fulfill his potential for growth.

    III. Since other resources have failed, the Federal Government must try.

By this time you have probably devised other lines of argument and ways to develop them. What are they? How did you arrive at them?

THE DISCUSSION:

OTHER TYPES OF OUTLINES

In addition to ordering material according to the motivational situation, it is also possible to outline according to the kinds of relationships that the speaker is trying to draw between ideas. Is it essentially a time relationship? A spatial relationship? A topical relationship? A cause-effect relationship? A problem-solution relationship? Let us explore a few examples:

Time pattern. Thesis sentence: The history of trade unions in the United States is a long and interesting one.

I. The National Labor Union was formed in 1836.
II. The Knights of Labor was formed in 1869.
III. The American Federation of Labor was formed in 1886.
IV. The Congress of Industrial Organizations was formed in 1935.
V. The A.F. of L. and C.I.O. memberships merged in 1955.

Space pattern. Thesis sentence: The plan of our campus is like a wheel.

I. The administrative offices are at the center of the campus.
II. The classroom buildings are circled around the administrative offices.
III. The dormitories are circled around the classroom buildings.

Topic pattern. Thesis sentence: Berdyaev, in his attempt to explore Dostoevsky's "world-vision," points to the main themes of his novels.

I. Dostoevsky's first concern is the nature of spirit.
II. Dostoevsky's second concern is the nature of man.
III. Dostoevsky's third concern is the nature of freedom.
IV. Dostoevsky's fourth concern is the nature of evil.
V. Dostoevsky's fifth concern is the nature of love.

Causal pattern. Thesis sentence: A problem exists in the financing of higher education.

I. The problem originated from lack of interest in co-ordinated effort.
II. The lack of interest resulted in lack of funds.
III. The lack of funds is also partially due to past ways of deciding who should pay for higher education.

Problem-solution pattern. Thesis sentence: A problem exists in the financing of higher education.

I. We must first realize the seriousness of the problem.
II. Then, we must consider possible solutions.
III. From the possible solutions we must select the best one.

Whatever type of pattern the speaker selects, there is one point which should be remembered about each main heading within the pattern: It should directly support the subject sentence. A good test of directness of support is to see if the main heads can be joined to the subject sentence by such connectives as: for, because, in that. For example: Subject sentence: John Smith is a better instructor than Bill Brown: (for)

I. He has greater enthusiasm and interest in his subject.
II. He reflects greater understanding of student needs.

Sample Outline One

Here is an example of an outline by a student facing a "Difficulty Situation." [4] He proceeds primarily by the use of examples to point out some problems which he sees in the policies of labor unions which would call for firm federal legislation.

THESIS STATEMENT: I would like to tell you why I think *there is a need for the federal government to substantially increase its regulation of labor unions.*

I. A study of the activities and policies of labor unions reveals serious problems in both their internal and external activities.   (because)

   A.   There are serious internal problems.   (because)
      1.   There are problems in admission policies.   (because)
         a.
         b.
         c.
      2.   There are problems arising from compulsory membership.   (because)
         a.
         b.
      3.   Problems exist concerning the voting rights of union members.   (because)
         a.
         b.
      4.   Problems are created by denial or evasion of union members' rights to protest.   (because)
         a.
         b.
         c.

[4] The material in these two sample outlines has been adapted from a brief prepared by students and faculty participants in The Eighth Annual Illinois Summer Debaters Workshop held at the University of Illinois, Urbana.

      5. There is evidence of criminal activity in the administration of union funds. (because)
        a.
        b.
      6. There are problems in the trusteeship system. (because)
        a.
        b.

  B. There are serious problems arising from the external activities of unions. (because)
     1. Collective bargaining procedures and policies constitute a serious threat to effective unions. (because)
       a.
       b.
       c.
     2. Procedures for handling grievances of employees create serious problems. (because)
       a.
       b.
     3. The mishandling of welfare and pension funds is a serious problem. (because)
       a.
       b.
     4. Serious problems are present in union political activities. (because)
       a.
       b.

II. Problems in the internal and external affairs of labor unions are national in scope. (because)

  A. Union activities are widespread in geographical scope.

  B. Union activities affect a major portion of the economy. (because)
     1.
     2.

III. Problems of unions' internal and external affairs are inherent in the present extent of federal regulation. (because)

  A. The problems will remain even if unions undertake self-regulation. (because)
     1.
     2.

  B. State regulation cannot solve the problem. (because)
     1.
     2.

C. The problem will remain even if the federal government "slightly" increases its regulation of labor unions. (because)
1.
2.

SAMPLE OUTLINE TWO

Here is a sample of an outline by a student facing a "Goal-Oriented Situation." Rather than refute directly the previous speaker, he has decided to talk about the disadvantages of increased federal legislation over labor unions.

THESIS STATEMENT: I believe that *a substantial increase in federal regulation of labor unions cannot be instituted without incurring four serious disadvantages.*

I. Such a policy would have the disadvantageous effect of weakening the powers of states to regulate unions. (because)

   A. The states' power to regulate unions *would* be weakened. (because)
      1. Federal legislation may tend to discourage some states from acting because of an over-reliance upon the federal government.
      2. The Supreme Court has made it clear that it will not permit state deviation from federal policy. (because)
         a. An example occurred in the case of Bethlehem Steel Co. vs. New York Labor Board.
         b. An example occurred in the case of La Crosse Telephone Corporation vs. Wisconsin Labor Board.

   B. If the states' power to regulate labor unions is weakened, this would constitute a serious disadvantage. (because)
      1. Multiform state legislation tests various proposals and provides experiments to guide in evolving solutions.
      2. A mistaken remedy at the federal level could have drastic repercussions on the entire labor movement.

II. Such a policy would have the disadvantageous effect of weakening the power of labor unions. (because)

   A. Such a policy would have the disadvantageous effect of threatening the stability and strength of union membership. (because)
      1. Such legislation may well hamper the organizing and operating of unions.
      2. If the strength and stability of union membership is threatened, this would constitute a serious disadvantage. (because)

    a.
    b.
    c.

B. Such a policy would have the disadvantageous effect of weakening the power of labor unions in effective collective bargaining. (because)
1. If such a policy is adopted, the power of labor unions to bargain collectively effectively *would* be weakened. (because)
    a. Authoritative testimony says it will.
      (1)
      (2)
    b. Centralized collective bargaining calls for authority by the national officers to enforce their commitments in labor-management negotiations without hindrance by governmental interference.
2. If the power of labor unions to bargain collectively effectively is weakened, this would constitute a serious disadvantage. (because)
    a. Unless a union is strong it has little bargaining power and without strong bargaining power unions could not have made all of the favorable advances they have in the past.
    b. Labor unions must have substantial economic, political, and social power if they are to assume the social responsibilities that modern society has placed upon them.

C. Such a policy would have the disadvantageous effect of preventing the maintenance of stable industrial relations. (because)
1. If such a policy is adopted, the maintenance of stable industrial relations *is* prevented. (because)
    a. Authoritative testimony says it is.
      (1)
      (2)
    b. Without a strong union shop agreement, many businesses would not enjoy the stable labor relations which have been conducive to their prosperity in the past.
2. If the maintenance of stable industrial relations is prevented, this would constitute a serious disadvantage. (because)
    a.
    b.
    c.

III. Such a policy would have the disadvantageous effect of creating economic dislocation and competition among the various states. (because)

A. If such a policy is adopted, economic dislocation and competition among the various states *is* created. (because)

      1. An example occurred in Kansas.

      2. An example occurred in Indiana.

  B. If economic dislocation and competition is created among the various states, this would constitute a serious disadvantage. (because)

      1.

      2.

      3.

IV. Such a policy would have the disadvantageous effect of giving the federal government excessive power in labor-management relations. (because)

  A. Authoritative testimony says so.

      1.

      2.

  B. There is no compelling national need at this time which overrides the basic value of federalism and justifies preferring national legislation over state legislation. (because)

      1.

      2.

      3.

TRANSITIONS

As the speaker moves from one idea to another, the audience must see how he makes the movement; that is, what relationships exist between one idea and another. Transitions fulfill this function. They serve to make evident the pattern of ideas. How they are phrased depends on what kind of outline pattern the speaker is using. You may want to use one of the following methods: (1) the flash-back-preview device; for example, "not only" (what you have said previously), "but also" (what you are going to say); (2) conjunctive adverbs: "also," "in addition," "however"; (3) sign posts: "first," "second," "third," "finally."

CONCLUSIONS

An effective conclusion generally consists of two parts: (a) a summary; and (b) a direct indication of how the speech may be used; that is, how it is the basis for further discussion. Because of the temporal nature of a speech, a summary is necessary to recount the main points of the speech and to remind the audience about the basic relationship which the speaker has drawn between his main ideas. The key here is repetition with variation. If the repetition of the main ideas is so unvaried as to be boring, the summary may do more harm than good.

The speaker should state his conclusions specifically and positively. It is most often an ineffective practice to "let the facts speak for themselves." They may or may not. Or, they may "speak," but say one thing to the speaker and another to his audience. Thus, the speaker should directly interpret his facts for the audience and explain why his is a reasonable and valuable interpretation. A good speech should have more "life" to it than the three or fifteen minutes it takes the speaker to deliver it. The specific implications for its use after the audience has left the room should be indicated. One especially useful fact concerning the statement of the final appeal is that the positive statement is more likely to be heeded than the negatively worded conclusion; that is, "Please be on time" is more likely to meet with success than "Don't be late."

The degree of emotional appeal in the conclusion must also be carefully considered. This is determined primarily by the nature of your topic, and of course by the particular audience. The most interesting research in the area of emotional appeal has concerned "threat appeal." Generally speaking, if a strong appeal is made, the threat itself is remembered; if a weak appeal is made, the source and explanation of the threat is remembered. Thus, the strength of the appeal is determined by the specific response the speaker hopes to elicit from his audience.

Sequencing Materials

There is yet another kind of order to be mentioned—that which has to do with the sequencing of materials according to strength. There are three basic methods of sequencing ideas:

(1) climax order—from the weakest to the strongest
(2) anti-climax order—from the strongest to the weakest
(3) pyramidal order—weak-strong-weak-strong

Experimental studies have resulted in apparently contradictory conclusions about which method is best. Some indicate that in attitude change, climax order was found to be superior, some favor anticlimax and some, pyramidal order.[5] Most can find no great difference, but

[5] Halbert E. Gulley and David K. Berlo, "Effects of Intercellular and Intracellular Speech Structure on Attitude Change and Learning," *Speech Monographs* (August, 1956), p. 296.

there is a slight tendency to favor the climax order. And, in most cases, few if any differences in learning were observed. If the audience is interested in the subject and favorable to it, climax order is probably best. If the audience is not interested or is unfavorable, anticlimax order is probably best. The pattern that best fits the topic and audience should be used. However, a speaker should try different patterns to see which one seems most effective. The speaker must carefully mold the organization of his materials to achieve the desired response and make sure that the pattern is clear enough (without being obtrusive) for the audience to grasp easily and follow the direction of the speech.

Proportion

After the speaker has determined the direction and arrangement of his materials, he must proportion his material. Here the speaker chooses the amount of time he will devote to each point. There are several questions he might raise: (1) What ideas are most important and therefore need to be emphasized? (2) What ideas are most complicated and therefore need to be explained in more detail? (3) Which ideas are most readily accepted by the audience and therefore will need less time?

Direct Suggestion

If the speech is predominantly an attitude-modifying communication, the speaker must decide where his suggestion for a change should occur in the speech. If he introduces the suggestion too early, many in the audience may not yet have been convinced and he will lose a portion of their attention. If he has not prepared the way for the suggestion rather carefully, his chances of success will be diminished considerably. To decide on the best place the speaker must recall what he knows about audiences in general and his audience in particular. He must also know something about the nature of suggestion as it effects attitude change. Schramm suggests the following basic facts about suggestion and attitude change: [6]

(1) *"To accomplish attitude change, a suggestion for change must first be received and accepted."* This fact gives the speaker the first

[6] Wilbur Schramm, ed., *The Process and Effects of Mass Communication* (Urbana: University of Illinois Press, 1954), pp. 210–12.

clue about where to place his most direct suggestion for change. It is generally accepted that people will try to avoid any communication which is unsympathetic to their existing attitudes. They tend to forget an unsympathetic communication or they attempt to recast it to fit the existing frame of reference. So if the suggestion comes too soon in a speech, it will likely meet one of these fates. Where the direct suggestion occurs within a speech depends basically on the attitudes of the audience toward the direction of the change and how strongly the audience feels about the objects, ideas, or emotions involved in the change.

(2) *"The suggestion will be more likely to be accepted if it meets existing personality needs and drives."* Generally this is self-explanatory. It should be noted however that some people are more suggestible than others and that some attitudes are more easily changed than others. The speaker should allow the members of the audience time to clarify their own thinking so that they are fully aware of their attitudes on the topic. He should also point out that a shift in attitude will be to their favor; that is, that it will fulfill their needs. The degree of change involved and the force of existing attitudes help determine where the suggestion for change should occur.

(3) *"The suggestion will be more likely to be accepted if it is in harmony with valued group norms and loyalties."* Almost every study on the subject stresses the importance of group relationships to individual attitude change. Members of a group will more quickly reject standards opposed to group norms than those opposed to their individual norms. The speaker must consider which set of norms he is "attacking" and determine which needs more time to prepare the way for his suggestion for change.

(4) *"The suggestion is more likely to be accepted if the source is perceived as trustworthy or expert."* We have already discussed the influence of ethical proof on evidence. Here the question the speaker must ask is, "How long will it take me to establish my 'trustworthiness,' my 'expertness,' concerning my topic?" One feature of attitude change is important to note: "When group norms are in conflict with expert opinion, they may win out, unless the matter is very technical or the expert unusually prestigeful or the matter relatively unrelated to the group norms." The speaker should consider this feature of attitude change in determining where direct suggestion should occur.

Summary

To separate the act of arrangement from the act of invention is misleading. As the speaker selects his material, as he eliminates some materials, he is shaping his materials. As he explains one point, expands it, reconstructs it, he is proportioning material. When he explores the associations which exist between his ideas, he is beginning to determine the way in which they can be ordered for his audience. In short, he is already performing the first stages of arrangement.

As the materials and proofs are selected, they may suggest in themselves the order and proportion to fit a particular audience. The speaker's most important task is to make sure that he molds the organization of his speech; otherwise the audience may mold its own and it may or may not coincide with the speaker's way of handling his topic. Worse yet, the audience may perceive no direction at all. For complete understanding, the audience must be able to apprehend the speaker's method of thinking, his method of searching for the most pertinent and useful thoughts about his subject.

The importance of arrangement to the success of a speech can best be emphasized by relating a story of two of the greatest political antagonists of all times, Demosthenes and Aeschines, as they debated whether or not Demosthenes should receive an award from the Athenian Assembly. Aeschines, in his speech opposing the award urged the judges to require Demosthenes to follow the same order in the reply to the charges which Aeschines had leveled against him. Demosthenes turned the tables very neatly with the following approach. He asked the judges to give him an impartial hearing and to demonstrate their openmindedness by permitting him to use whatever arrangement of arguments he thought best for his defense. Demosthenes then chose a very different arrangement from that of Aeschines, because he knew as well as his antagonist that the arrangement of materials which is appropriate for fulfilling one speaker's purpose may not be appropriate for another's purpose. This story also illustrates one very basic point for the beginning speaker to keep in mind. Arrangement, when efficiently performed, becomes a means of persuasion as surely as are the speaker's proofs.

Rhetorical Exercises

(1) Deliver a ten to fifteen minute speech from a complete sentence outline. In this speech analyze the cause(s) of some international or national problem.

(2) Below is a rhetorical jigsaw puzzle—a dissected speech. Can you reassemble and label the parts of this speech?
Directions: Each paragraph below is a separate unit of a speech. When put together in the right order, the units make up a complete speech. Put the parts together to make the best possible speech.

Finally, think of the ordinary door-to-door salesman.

Have you ever noticed how easy it is to do something else when the TV announcer is droning out his commercial? But what happens when he stills that golden tongue? You know that the set is on, but you don't hear the announcer's voice extolling the virtues of "lavish Camay Soap." So what do you do? You look at the TV screen, of course, to see what is going on.

Well, one way is by a brief interval of silence before and after the name of the product or sponsor.

The next time someone says to you, "Silence is golden," just smile and think to yourself, "Brother, you don't know how right you are."

Secondly, let us consider television.

Are you aware of the methods radio announcers use to call attention to their sponsor or product?

Such a salesman is one who has learned that silence is golden.

So you see, people in the field of selling are indeed aware that silence is golden, for they know it can mean dollars and cents in radio, in TV, and even in door-to-door selling.

As you see, the announcer puts a parenthesis of silence around the name of the product in order to catch your attention.

Silence is golden. That's an old cliché which you have heard many times, especially when your parents wanted to impress upon you another cliché—namely, that children should be seen and not heard.

First of all, take radio selling.

Thus you can see that the TV salesman has also discovered that silence can be golden.

The announcer doesn't say: Women-all-over-the-world-are-learning-that-delicious-Wrigley-spearmint-gum-is-a-grand-wholesome-family-treat. Instead he says: Women—all over the world—are learning that delicious—Wrigley's Spearmint gum—is a grand—wholesome—family treat.

I contend, however, that silence really IS golden.

If he's really good, he knows better than to just reel off his pitch—he knows how to listen to you.

And I would like to present three instances in the field of selling to prove my contention.

If you doubt the effectiveness of silence in TV, you just try not looking at the picture and notice how irresistibly your eyes will be pulled to the screen by a few moments of silence.

He is willing, if necessary, to listen to all of your troubles. If you want to raise a question, he will be quiet while you do. He will ask you a question, then be silent while you answer.

(The "jigsaw puzzle" was printed in *The Speech Teacher,* March, 1963 in an article "A Rhetorical Jigsaw Puzzle: A Device for Teaching Certain Aspects of Speech Composition" by Theodore Clevenger, Jr. By permission of The Speech Association of America and the author.)
Construct similar jigsaw puzzles for use in class.

(3) Listen carefully to the other speeches in class. Try to outline them. Can you easily perceive the speaker's purpose? Is the subject sentence a direct assertion? Is there a clear suggestion of structural progression to be followed in the speech development? Are the main ideas and subdivisions cast in a definite pattern and made evident through the use of transitions? Were the main ideas summarized and used as the basis for a future line of discussion?

(4) Select a topic and outline it according to different patterns. Which one do you think is best? Why?

(5) Outline the following speeches. First inquire into the speech situation for which each was designated. Then, evaluate the appropriateness of each organizational pattern:

(1) Abraham Lincoln's "Address at Cooper Union";
(2) Thomas Jefferson's "First Inaugural Address"; and
(3) Abraham Lincoln's "First Inaugural Address."

Collateral Readings

Bryant, Donald C., and Karl R. Wallace, *Fundamentals of Public Speaking,* 3rd rev. ed. New York: Appleton-Century-Crofts, Inc., 1956. Chapter 12, "Outlining"; Chapter 13, "Introductions, Conclusions, and Transitions."

Gilkinson, Howard, Stanley F. Paulson, and Donald E. Sikkink, "Effects of Order and Authority in an Argumentative Speech," *Quarterly Journal of Speech* (April, 1954), pp. 183–92.

Gulley, Halbert E., and David K. Berlo, "Effect of Intercellular and Intracellular Speech Structure on Attitude Change and Learning," *Speech Monographs* (August, 1956), pp. 288–97.

Hovland, Carl I., ed., *The Order of Presentation in Persuasion*. New Haven: Yale University Press, 1957.

Hovland, Carl I., Irving L. Janis, and Harold H. Kelley, *Communication and Persuasion*. New Haven: Yale University Press, 1953. Chapter Four, "Organization of Persuasive Arguments."

Krech, David, and Richard S. Crutchfield, "Perceiving the World," in *The Process and Effects of Mass Communication*, ed., Wilbur Schramm. Urbana: University of Illinois, 1954, pp. 116–37.

Smith, Raymond G., "An Experimental Study of the Effects of Speech Organization upon the Attitudes of College Students," *SM* (November, 1951), pp. 292–301.

Sponberg, Harold, "The Relative Effectiveness of Climax and Anti-Climax Order in an Argumentative Speech," *SM*, No. 1 (1946), pp. 35–44.

Language most shews a man: speak
that I may judge thee.

SENECA

VI When Bergen and Cornelia Evans prepared their
Dictionary of Contemporary American Usage, they
stated that most people say, "None of them are coming,"
rather than saying, "None of them is coming." The *Chicago
Tribune* saw fit to honor the Evanses with no fewer than ten
attacks concerning this usage. Even though the Evanses had
not said either one was right, the *Tribune* remained in-
censed with this license taken with "the language." Finally,
Evans wrote a letter pointing out that Shakespeare had used
"none" with the plural and that, in fact, God used "none"
with the plural in the First Commandment as found in
Deuteronomy 5:5.[1] History does not record whether the
Tribune was impressed with such authority. The point of
this story is not whether "none is" is more acceptable than
"none are," but that usage often reveals a good many things
about the person who is speaking, his occupation, and often
his relationship with his audience. For example, the use of
"pad," "cool," and "far out" provokes visions of a very definite sort of person. The use of such terms as "median,"

[1] Bergen Evans recounts this story in "Editor's Choise—You Couldn't
Do Woise," a speech reprinted in pamphlet form by the G. and C.
Merriam Company.

STYLE: SOME THEORETICAL
CONSIDERATIONS

"mean," "frequency polygon," and "asymmetrical distributions" indicates that the man speaking is a statistician and the use of such terms as "ozone," "endothermic compounds," and "dicyanocetylenes" indicates that the man who is speaking is a specific kind of scientist.

Language in Use

Usage often reveals the nature of the interpersonal relationship between the speaker and the one he is speaking to. For example, in French, a speaker may select "tu" or "vous"; in Spanish, he may select "tu" or "usted." In English, usage often reveals whether or not the one addressed is older than the speaker, whether or not the one addressed is the parent of the speaker or his employer, whether the speaker and his audience share the same profession, attend the same schools, have the same parents. For example, a father says "Jim" to his son, but doesn't ordinarily expect to be called "Jack" in reply. On a college campus, what the student refers to as "the libe" to other students, becomes "the library" when he is speaking to someone not connected with the college, what is "the P.O." becomes "the post office," "sike" and "sosh" become "psychology" and "sociology," a "bluebook" becomes "an hour exam." The terms "phoneme," "taxeme," "morpheme," "allotax," "allograph" generally indicate not only that the speaker is a linguist but also that he is speaking to another linguist.

Only in church, for example, would we hear this kind of language:

> Eternal God, Who dost call all men into unity with Thy Son, Jesus Christ our Lord, we pray Thee to pour Thy spirit upon the students of all nations, that they may consecrate themselves to Thy service; that being joined together by their common faith and obedience, they may come more perfectly to love and understand one another, that the world may know that Thou didst send Thy Son to be the Saviour and the Lord of all men; through the same Jesus Christ our Lord Who with Thee and the Holy Spirit liveth and reigneth one God world without end. Amen.[2]

Stylistically, what has happened in this passage which makes it different from ordinary everyday speech? Without going into a detailed analysis, we might easily note these features: The use of direct address employing adjective plus noun is almost entirely restricted

[2] Randolph Quirk, *The Use of English* (New York: St. Martin's Press, 1962), p. 156.

to religious usage, although occasionally in a formal letter one might say, "My dear Sir." In this passage, the noun is postmodified by a relative clause "Who dost call." It would be unusual to find this construction elsewhere. Probably the most apparent characteristic is the speaker's use of the distinctive second person pronoun "Thee" and its adjectival form "Thy" together with the distinctive second and third person singular verb forms "dost," "didst," and "reigneth." Occasionally we find such passages in poetry and in a few dialects but rarely in standard American English.

The following selection is one part of a bill designed to authorize the Secretary of Agriculture to permit certain properties to be used for forestry work:

> *Be it enacted by the Senate and House of Representatives of the United States of America in Congress assembled,* That the Congress recognize that for many years the United States and certain States have cooperated in the production of tree planting stock for use in the reforestation of the public and private lands of the Nation; that the program of production of tree planting stock which was initiated and pursued under the Soil Bank Act (7 U.S.C. 1801 et seq.) was carried on under written agreements which provided for (a) cooperation between the Forest Service, on behalf of the United States, and the States which participated in the program, (b) payments to said States for costs and expenses incurred in the development of nursery facilities, (c) the holding of such funds by the States in trust for the purpose of carrying out the provisions of said agreements, and (d) restoration to the trust fund of an amount equal to the residual value of any supplies, materials, equipment, or improvements acquired or constructed with trust funds and transferred to State forestry work other than the soil bank program; that such program under said Soil Bank Act has been discontinued, but the need for trees continues to be great; that the States and Federal Government are cooperating in the procurement, production, and distribution of forest-tree seeds and plants under section 4 of the Clarke-McNary Act of June 7, 1924 (16 U.S.C. 567), and in the reforestation of lands under title IV of the Agricultural Act of 1956 (16 U.S.C. 568e–g); and that said supplies, materials, equipment, or improvements for use in connection with their respective forestry programs, and it is in the public interest to permit these States to use said property without the requirement that payment be made for the residual value thereof.[3]

[3] *United States Statutes at Large, 1962* (Washington, D.C.: Government Printing Office, 1963), p. 107.

Government language, like legal language, needs to weave the stipulations of bills into unbroken chains of grammatical constructions to lessen the probability of deliberate misinterpretation or the occurrence of some kind of fraudulent manipulation. Like the language of the law, business language, scientific language, or journalistic language, it contains certain characteristics which set it apart from the other uses of language. In all these instances, the word choice and the syntax reveal important features of the professions which use them and about the audience for which they are intended.

The Users of Language

Just as the various professional styles reveal something about the profession, so the style of an individual tells us something about that individual. Before beginning our discussion of style, it would be useful to distinguish between two types of style. The features of the English language that everyone shares may be termed the "style of the language"; the way in which one man uniquely uses the resources of the English language may be termed the "style of the individual." Thus, style can be characterized in terms of a contrast between the variable and the constant, and a speaker's style may be said to be his unique relationship with the language. Contrast these two versions of the "Gettysburg Address": [4]

> (1) I haven't checked these figures but eighty-seven years ago, I think it was, a number of individuals organized a governmental setup here in this country, I believe it covered certain eastern areas, with this idea they were following up, based on a sort of national independence arrangement and the program that every individual is just as good as every other individual.
>
> Well, now of course we are dealing with this big difference of opinion, civil disturbance you might say, although I don't like to appear to take sides or name any individuals, and the point is naturally to check up, by actual experience in the field—see whether any governmental setup with a basis like the one I was mentioning has any validity—whether that dedication, you might say, by those early individuals has any lasting values.

[4] Version One is printed by permission of the author and copyright owner, Oliver Jensen, *American Heritage.* Version Two, the Lincoln text, is taken from *American Speeches*, eds., Wayland Maxfield Parrish and Marie Hochmuth (New York: Longmans, Green and Co., 1954), pp. 306–7.

Well, here we are, you might put it that way, all together at the scene where one of these disturbances between different sides got going. We want to pay our tribute to those loved ones, those departed individuals who made the supreme sacrifice here on the basis of their opinions about how this setup ought to be handled. It is absolutely in order and 100 percent O.K. to do this.

But if you look at the overall picture of this, we can't pay any tribute—we can't sanctify this area—we can't hallow, according to whatever individual creeds or faiths or sort of religious outlooks are involved, like I said about this particular area. It was those individuals themselves, including the enlisted men—very brave individuals—who have given this religious character to the area. The way I see it, the rest of the world will not remember any statements issued here, but it will never forget how these men put their shoulders to the wheel and carried this idea down the fairway.

Our job, the living individuals' job here is to pick up the burden and sink the putt they made these big efforts here for. It is our job to get on with the assignment and from these deceased, fine individuals to take extra inspiration, you could call it, for the same theories about which they did such a lot.

We have to make up our minds right here and now as I see it, they didn't put out all that blood, perspiration and—well—that they didn't just make a dry run here, that all of us, under God, that is, the God of our choice, shall beef up this idea about freedom and liberty and those kind of arrangements, and that government of all individuals, by all individuals, and for all individuals shall not pass out of the world picture.

(2) Four score and seven years ago our fathers brought forth on this continent, a new nation, conceived in Liberty, and dedicated to the proposition that all men are created equal.

Now we are engaged in a great civil war, testing whether that nation, or any nation so conceived and so dedicated, can long endure. We are met on a great battle-field of that war. We have come to dedicate a portion of that field, as a final resting place for those who here gave their lives that that nation might live. It is altogether fitting and proper that we should do this.

But, in a larger sense, we can not dedicate—we can not consecrate—we can not hallow—this ground. The brave men, living and dead, who struggled here, have consecrated it, far above our poor power to add or detract. The world will little note, nor long remember what we say here, but it can never forget what they did here. It is for us the living, rather, to be dedicated here to the unfinished work which they who fought here have thus far so nobly advanced. It is rather for us to be here dedicated to the great task remaining before us—that from these honored dead we take increased devotion

to that cause for which they gave the last full measure of devotion—
that we here highly resolve that these dead shall not have died in
vain—that this nation, under God, shall have a new birth of freedom
—and that government of the people, by the people, for the people,
shall not perish from the earth.

You may well want to analyze these two versions of the "Gettysburg
Address" carefully, trying to point to differences in them. But let us
briefly notice certain *dimensions* of style:

Impersonal/Personal
  1. A number of individuals organized a governmental setup
  2. Our fathers brought forth on this continent

Colloquial/Formal
  1. I haven't checked these figures but eighty-seven years ago I
     think it was
  2. Four score and seven years ago

Emphasis on Speaker/ on Audience
  1. The way *I* see it, the rest of the world will not remember any
     statement issued here
  2. The *world* will little note, nor long remember what we say here

Prosaic/Poetic
  1. to see whether any governmental set up with a basis like I
     was mentioning has any validity
  2. testing whether that nation, or any nation so conceived, and
     so dedicated, can long endure

Non-rhythmic/Rhythmic
  1. shall beef up this idea about freedom and liberty and those
     kinds of arrangements, and that government of all individuals
     by all individuals and for all individuals, shall not pass out
     of the world picture
  2. that we here highly resolve that these dead shall not have died
     in vain—that this nation, under God, shall have a new birth
     of freedom—and that government of the people, by the peo-
     ple, for the people, shall not perish from the earth.

Loose Parallel Structure/Stricter Parallel Structure
  1. if you look at the overall picture of this, we can't pay any
     tribute—we can't sanctify this area—we can't hallow, according
     to whatever individual creeds or Faiths or sort of religious out-
     looks are involved,
  2. But, in a larger sense, we can not dedicate—we can not con-
     secrate—we can not hallow—this ground.

In fact, when read carefully, these versions are not only different in
style, but in a very real sense, they do not say the same things. For

example, Lincoln asks the audience to be "dedicated to the great task remaining before [them]." "Great task" is replaced in the other version by "big effort." The point of the Address is that the living must finish the work the dead had started, the work which they had, in effect, handed on to the living. "Task" suggests something that is imposed on one by duty; the other phrases do not. "Great" means not only "big" but it also suggests "eminent" and "noble." *In short, style and content are inextricably associated and to talk about one is to talk about the other.*

The speaker's task as he starts developing his own style is not an easy one. First, he must be fully aware of the resources of language before he can learn to manipulate them as a means of persuasion. Consequently, we shall divide our discussion of style into two chapters, one in which we shall explore the resources of language, another in which we shall discuss the characteristics of effective oral style.

The Meaning of Meaning

Language may be defined as *systematic verbal symbolism.* Thus, we may say that language has to do with verbal symbolism (words), that language has to do with system (pattern and order), and that oral language has to do with sound. When someone speaks he uses symbols, system, and sound to say something, to convey some *meaning.* To say that language has "meaning" causes some confusion, for even the term "meaning" has a number of meanings. Consider the various uses of the word illustrated by the following sentences:

(1) He doesn't exactly understand what you mean when you use that term.

(2) I saw a flash of lightning. That usually means rain.

(3) Winning that game means a lot to the team.

(4) "S" as the end of a noun usually means that the noun is plural.

(5) In tone languages such as Chinese, pitch serves to distinguish the difference in meaning between four or five forms which would otherwise be identical.

The meaning of the term "meaning" in these sentences may be defined in these ways:

(1) He doesn't know exactly what object or event you are referring to when you use that term.

(2) Lightning is a sign which usually indicates that it is going to rain.

STYLE: SOME THEORETICAL CONSIDERATIONS

(3) Winning that game has a certain value to the team.
(4) The *formal* meaning of an "s" on the end of a noun is "plural."
(5) Pitch (a characteristic of *sound*) helps us to distinguish between four or five forms which are otherwise the same.

In these sentences then, "meaning" has at least three different aspects: (1) meaning *signifies* something (an object, an event, a value); (2) form has meaning; and (3) sound has meaning. To say that language has meaning is to suggest that there are three basic resources of language: (1) semantic (significant) meaning; (2) formal meaning; and (3) sound (as it operates conjointly with semantic and significant meaning) meaning.

Semantic Meaning

Words, as such, are merely scratches on a piece of paper or acoustic phenomena. Where, then, does their meaning come from? Meaning resides in the *relationship* between a word and the object (event or value) which it represents or re-presents. It also resides in the associations we have for those objects, events and values.

Why does "table" represent what we think of as table and not what we think of as chair? There is nothing in the nature of a table which makes it a "table"; somebody labeled it "table," and *by agreement* it became "table." The arbitrary nature of meaning requires us to consider carefully the ways in which semantic meaning is developed: (1) through denotation; (2) through connotation; and (3) through context.

DENOTATION

The relationship between the word and the object it stands for is called the word's *denotative meaning*. Words come to represent the objects and events in our environment in much the same way as the pictures of objects in a mail order catalogue do. Just as there is a very real difference between the pictures (visual symbols) in the catalogue and the objects they represent, so there is a difference between words (verbal symbols) and things. Words represent things because they produce some replica of our actual behavior toward them.[5] But to think about a thing is not the same as to "see" it and

[5] Charles E. Osgood, *Method and Theory in Experimental Psychology* (New York, Oxford University Press, 1953), p. 695.

to react overtly toward it. So a word does not directly represent a thing, but our conception of that thing.

The denotative, or *literal*, meaning a word has is purely informative. For example, consider the language of the following passage:

> The hardness of metal can be measured in one of two ways, either by denting the metal with a ball of steel dropped from a known height or by using a diamond point, held in a testing machine to scratch the metal. Both the size of the scratch and the size of the dent can be examined with the aid of a microscope.[6]

This kind of language ideally would "move" a person no more than the simple equation "two plus two equals four." Here, language serves only to assert, to state an objective fact, to convey information.

The scientist especially makes use of predominantly informative, referential "meanings." He works carefully to eliminate all emotional colorings, associations, and implications of judgment. Denotative meanings would not be described in terms of aesthetic adjectives such as "pretty," "lovely," and so on. Denotative meanings do not elicit emotions such as anger, fear, or joy. In fact, the scientist is trying *not to influence* the hearer's attitude toward what he is saying.

CONNOTATION

It cannot be too strongly stressed that total context (the situation, the person involved) finally determines the point at which a meaning is no longer purely denotative, but connotative as well. Almost any word can have personal meanings as well as strictly denotative or referential ones. On a very elementary level, the sentence "Look! There is a spider!" can illustrate this point. To the scientist used to dealing everyday in an impersonal, objective way with arachnids, the word "spider" holds no emotive connotations. To the young child who has been frightened by a spider prankishly put on his bed, "spider" becomes an emotive word, carrying with it a fear response. Thus, although denotative meaning resides in the relationship between the object and the word which represents it, *connotative meaning* resides in the relationship between the object, the words, and the speaker/listener.

Recall our discussion of how communication takes place. If the experiences of the speaker do not at least partially coincide with

[6] F. A. Philbrick, *Language and the Law* (New York: The Macmillan Co., 1949), p. 5.

those of his listener, then communication is very difficult, if not altogether impossible. Mr. A (the speaker) views each word in the
context of all the psychophysiological events which he associates
with it. So does Mr. B (the listener). These may be referred to as
each one's personal or connotative meanings. Where these associations overlap, communicated meaning occurs. Although it is relatively easy to agree on denotative meaning, it is much more difficult
to agree on a word's connotative meaning.

One class constructed the following Semantic Differential to test
the likenesses and differences found in a word's meaning by the
members of the class:

	Very		Slightly	Neutral	Slightly		Very	
Good								Bad
Beautiful								Ugly
Soft								Hard
Strong								Weak
Quick								Slow
Pleasant								Unpleasant
Masculine								Feminine
Active								Passive
Large								Small
Positive								Negative
Honest								Dishonest
Tall								Short
Happy								Unhappy
Fast								Slow
Hot								Cold
Young								Old
Peace								War
Love								Hate
Straight								Crooked
White								Black
Sweet								Sour
Moving								Still

Charles E. Osgood and his associates have designed a way to
check how well we agree on, how well we are able to share, the
meaning of any one word. He calls this method the Semantic Differ-

ential.[7] The Semantic Differential consists of a scale which permits people to indicate the meaning they attach to a word by making a series of binary decisions: It is beautiful (not ugly), soft (not hard), quick (not slow), and so forth. If asked to rate the word "tornado" on a seven point scale from slow $\longrightarrow$ fast, a person would probably rate it "extremely fast." On the other hand, someone rating the same word in terms of honest $\longrightarrow$ dishonest would probably be neutral. Osgood and his colleagues determined that there were three dominant factors or dimensions: (1) a Potency Factor (represented by scales such as: strong $\longrightarrow$ weak, heavy $\longrightarrow$ light, hard $\longrightarrow$ soft); (2) an Evaluation Factor (represented by scales such as good $\longrightarrow$ bad, pleasant $\longrightarrow$ un-pleasant, positive $\longrightarrow$ negative); and (3) an Activity Factor (represented by such scales as fast $\longrightarrow$ slow, active $\longrightarrow$ passive, excitable $\longrightarrow$ calm). Of course, some words have a greater variety of connotative meanings than others and words often prove to have slightly variable referential meanings as well.

CONTEXT

Single words do not comprise the bulk of our communication or literature. Rather, most communication consists of groups of words such as phrases, clauses, sentences. Placing a word in context stabilizes meaning somewhat. For example, the word "Robert" might not have any meaning for a person because too many meanings are possible. The word could refer to any one of many Roberts. On the other hand, if "Robert E. Lee" or "Robert Burns" were specified, who Robert is—that is, what the word "Robert" means—becomes more obvious.

The street address of a person in New York City is not enough "context" to identify such a person for the post office. "Joan Hollins, Sellersburg, Indiana," may be sufficient for an address, or "Mary Dodd, 22220 Grand Concourse, Apartment 2C, Chicago, Illinois," may be necessary. With enough additions to the context, however, one person can be identified among several billion people. The same kind of consideration must be given to "identifying" a word's meaning. Abstract words generally need more context to establish their meanings than concrete ones do.

[7] Charles E. Osgood, George J. Suci, and Percy Tannenbaum, *The Measurement of Meaning* (Urbana: University of Illinois Press, 1957).

Structural Meaning

Vocabulary comes and goes. New words are invented; for example, "sputnik," "beatnik," "fallout," and old words acquire new meanings; for example, "clean" now refers to air free from radioactivity and "cool" to something that is unusually nice. Vocabulary and vocabulary meanings are the least stable elements of language; structure is the most stable.

SIGNALS

Spoken language may be viewed as a series of physical or acoustical events. When they are intelligible, these events are not random; rather, they succeed each other in characteristic sequences and within strictly limited possibilities. These patterns of the English language are often complex, but because they are recurring, they are at least partially predictable. To help the listener predict what is coming next in a message, all languages are full of *signals*. A signal is something in one word that tells us something about another one. Consider the following four sentences:

> *The* children go home.
> *Die* Kinder gehen nach Hause.
> *Les* enfants vont chez eux.
> *Los* chicos van a casa.

Although the languages are different and contain different signals, the articles maintain a certain relationship with the nouns. In French, for example, the article tells us the number of the noun; and, if it is in the singular, also the gender.

In English, the verb "sing" reflects the *number* ("sings" would tell us that the subject of the sentence was singular), the *tense* of the action ("sang" would tell us the action was past). The verb also reflects the *voice,* active or passive ("is sung" would tell us that the verb is passive) and the *mood* ("that the children sing" would tell us that the mood is subjunctive).

To further illustrate how form tells us something—that structure has meaning—let us consider the following sentence: [8]

> Most zaps have lak.

[8] This treatment follows one suggested by David K. Berlo, *The Process of Communication* (New York: Holt, Rinehart and Winston, Inc., 1960), pp. 196–206.

Do we know what the word "zaps" means? Or the word "lak"? Yet not knowing what these two terms refer to does not mean that the sentence has no meaning. Where, then, does the meaning reside? To discover that, we shall have to compare two more sentences with the first one:

> One zaps have lak.

and

> Most zap has lak.

Both sentences make us uncomfortable. Why? For several reasons. First of all, when we say "one" we usually say "has" rather than "have" and when we say "most" we say "have" rather than "has." Plural noun forms are generally followed by plural verb forms. Also, nouns which end in "s" rarely follow the adjective "one," just as the adjective "most" is rarely followed by a noun without an "s" ending. Thus, the form or structure of language sequences means something, not in the semantic sense—it does not *denote* anything, refer us to any object—but it does help us to communicate more efficiently. Signals help reduce uncertainty for the listener.

WORD-WORD RELATIONSHIPS

Note how the relationship between words changes the meaning of these two sentences:

> The football coach said, "The halfback is stupid."
> "The football coach," said the halfback, "is stupid."

Here, the same words were used; the same semantic meanings involved. The word ⟶ object relationships (denotative meaning of each word) remained stable but the word ⟶ word relationships were changed and thus the meaning of the sentences also changed.

TIME ORDER

To change word order is also to change sentence meaning. Consider these two sentences:

> John hit Bill.
> Bill hit John.

The same words are used and the same semantic meanings are employed. But the order is different and thus the meaning is also different.

Sound Meaning

Perhaps much of your past thinking about language has been almost exclusively concerned with written English. In reality, written language is a reflection of spoken language and it is perhaps inevitable that, as a copy of actual speech, it should be imperfect and incomplete. Note, for example, the different overtones of meanings this sentence can have depending upon emphasis:

> *What* do you think?   What *do* you think?
> What do *you* think?   What do you *think*?

Although printed language can use varying type faces and different sizes and colors of types, it has not yet duplicated the speaker's tone of voice or the subtleties of inflection and rate which give us clues to his feelings.

Now let us discuss certain ways in which sound is organically related to sense and the way in which, at the same time, sound operates as an independent aspect of language separable from sense.

CHARACTERISTICS OF SOUND

All vocal sounds have four fundamental attributes: loudness, pitch, duration, and quality. The neuromuscular controls of the human vocal mechanism are subtle and complex enough to allow a wide range of variation for each sound attribute. Although we shall consider each of them separately, they operate simultaneously.

Loudness. We shall assume that the speaker has no problem in making himself heard and is now concerned with the use of loudness or force to give color and meaning to what he is saying. Force is the way in English by which we establish syllable stress in polysyllabic words. Differences in the meaning of words occur when the syllable stress is shifted from one syllable to the other. Consider, for example:

> ob*ject*   *ob*ject
> con*vict*   *con*vict
> *con*duct   con*duct*

When we change the stress from one word in the sentence to another, the emphasis in the sentence shifts and so, to some extent, do the various shades of meaning. Change the stress from the first word of these sentences to the succeeding words and you will agree:

> Mary can do anything.
> You and I must go.

Or try to change the stress emphasis in this line of a Churchill speech:

> Never in the field of human conflict was so much owed by so many to so few.

Or, in Patrick Henry's:

> I know not what course others may take; but as for me, give me liberty or give me death.

Pitch. Although changes of pitch in speaking are not so wide or so distinct as they can be in singing, nevertheless pitch often reveals subtleties of meaning. We often associate a rise in pitch with anger, fear, or excitement. Variations in pitch in English are most closely associated with conventions that have arisen concerning sentence types and formations. For example, we generally use a downward or falling inflection to indicate that we have completed our thought. The upward or rising inflection we associate with uncertainty or incompleteness. In between these two inflections we would somehow have to account for the vast spectrum of inflections which express sarcasm, cynicism, innuendo, irony, and so forth. Although most of us would employ one of the three circumflex inflections (down-up, up-down, or down-up-down), each individual use is likely to call for more subtle differences than we can chart here. Consider the variety of inflections one would normally use when saying "Yes" to indicate absolute certainty, some doubt, real indecision, or a bit of sarcasm. Or, the way in which one says, "No" to indicate "Absolutely not"; "Well, perhaps"; "I'm a bit surprised to hear that"; "That certainly annoys me"; and, "I am glad to hear that."

Duration. Changes in both the time intervals between words and phrases and the time involved in the production of speech sounds allow us to emphasize or subordinate meanings and to express our feelings more vividly. The simple fact is that some sounds take longer than others to articulate. Quite often sorrow or sadness are expressed by a slow rate of utterance and joy and gladness by a faster rate.

One way of emphasizing key words in a sentence is by slowing the rate. *Pause,* or silence, however, is the feature which requires the most discussion. Occasionally we must stop to ask whether a friend has said he will meet us on East Eighth Street or East State

Street. One of the differences between the two is where the silence occurs. Just so, silence indicates the end of structural units such as sentences or phrases. Silence in speech often operates much as the pause or rest in a musical composition. It is an integral part of the meaning. In fact, we often talk about the "meaningful pause." When the speaker pauses, the listener must wait and, while waiting, he tends to fill the silence with the last bit of information he has heard. This kind of inner repetition of what the speaker has said emphasizes the idea, makes it more vivid. Franklin D. Roosevelt quite often used the pause in this way:

> We Americans of today, together with our allies, are passing through a period of supreme test.//It is a test of our courage// of our resolve// of our wisdom// of our essential decency.//
>
> If we meet that test// successfully and honorably//we shall perform a service of historic importance which men and women and children will honor throughout all time.//
>
> As I stand here today, having taken the solemn oath of office in the presence of my fellow countrymen// in the presence of our God// I know that it is America's purpose that we shall not fail.// [9]

Consider Dwight D. Eisenhower's use of the pause in his "Second Inaugural Address":

> May we pursue the right//without self-righteousness.//May we know unity//without conformity.//May we grow in strength// without pride of self.// [10]

Quality. Here, we are not concerned with quality in terms of breathiness or nasality, but rather with quality as related to the speaker's feeling or mood. There is no real way to capture the quality of a speaker's voice in written language. The best way to study voice quality is to listen to records of distinguished speakers giving speeches on a variety of topics and under different circumstances. The quality of Franklin Roosevelt's voice as he delivered the United States' declaration of war in 1941 is very much different from the voice quality of campaigner Roosevelt delivering a cutting attack

[9] In *A History and Criticism of American Public Address,* III, ed., Marie Kathryn Hochmuth (New York: Longmans, Green and Co., 1955), p. 510. Parallel lines are those of this author.

[10] In Ernest J. Wrage and Barnet Baskerville, eds., *Contemporary Forum: American Speeches on Twentieth-Century Issues* (Harper and Row, Publishers, 1962), p. 314. Parallel lines are those of this author.

against a political opponent or the President talking about domestic matters in one of his fireside chats. Churchill managed to convey by voice quality, as well as by what he said, his deep and abiding hatred of Hitler and Mussolini. Contrast with this the quality of his voice when he spoke of his beloved Britain.

ELEMENTARY SOUND DEVICES

On a somewhat different level, the speaker must consider other sound devices of language which affect meaning. Here, we shall discuss onomatopoeia and specific speech sounds which are often somehow related to various emotions and moods.

Onomatopoeia. Onomatopoeia means quite literally "name-making." Onomatopoeic words are words that are imitative of their own literal meanings; onomatopoeia refers to the use of words to suggest, by their sounds, the objects they represent. It has even occasioned a theory of the way language originated. While such a theory is open to much question, the sounds of such words as "crash," "buzz," "swish," "whiz," "roar," "rumble," "flop," "sniffle," "flash," and "thump" are highly suggestive of their meanings. Onomatopoeic effects are most likely to occur in either descriptions or narrative passages to intensify the actions being talked about.

Sound suggestion. Although onomatopoeia depends upon direct imitation, vowel and consonant sounds can be related to meaning in a more sophisticated way. Here, sound does not imitate but suggests. Review for a minute the sounds of the English language: Some are harsh and short, some are long and fluid. We often associate harsh sounds with harsh meanings. Winston Churchill, for example, called Mussolini a "jackal" and Hitler a "bloodthirsty guttersnipe." "Jackal" and "guttersnipe" are both ugly-sounding words.

Although a speaker need not analyze speech sounds in detail, certain elementary facts are directly helpful to him. Let us first consider some of the vowels as they progress along a continuum, from those placed high and toward the front of the mouth to those pronounced high and toward the back of the mouth. One writer [11] has suggested that this progression is from "thin, bright, shrill" vowels to "richer, darker, more resonant" ones:

[11] This follows a treatment by Chad Walsh, *Doors into Poetry* (Englewood Cliffs, N.J.: Prentice-Hall, Inc., 1962), pp. 87–88.

eat	hot
it	law
ate [12]	home
met	good
cat	food
art	

He suggests that there are four more with a "muffled" quality:

cut	father
hurt	sofa

There are also diphthongs or combinations of two vowels. Because they are composite sounds, the pace with which they are said tends to be slowed:

right	there
boy	dear
out	poor
use	

Consonant sounds may be either voiced or voiceless. A consonant is voiced when the vocal cords vibrate; a voiced consonant tends to have a fuller sound than a voiceless one. One group of consonants is the stop plosives, those consonants made by abruptly stopping the flow of air from the mouth. They tend to have "an explosive, staccato effect":

unvoiced	*voiced*
p	b
t	d
k	g

Another group of consonants are called fricatives, or sounds made with only a partial closure of the articulating organs. They are characterized, as the name indicates, by the sound of friction:

unvoiced	*voiced*
f	v
s	z
th(in)	th(en)
sh	zh
h	

[12]This sound may be pronounced either as a vowel [e] or as a diphthong [ei].

Another group of consonants are smoother in sound. They are all voiced:

l   n
r   ng (single sound)
m

And, lastly, two consonants are often termed "semi-vowels." Speak them and you will see why: w, y.

One can suggest certain general effects with certain sounds. For example, we associate an effect of heaviness with the sonority of the long back vowel sounds such as oh, ah, aw, oo. A good way to appreciate how sound helps convey an idea is to list words designed to describe the emotions. Recall Atlanta newspaperman Henry Grady's speech in 1886, describing the Confederate soldier after the Civil War. He pictures the soldier as making a "slow" and "painful" journey home. The long *o* and *a* sounds help to emphasize the point the speaker was trying to make. One ought to note, however, that this kind of relationship between sound and meaning holds true only when sound operates in conjunction with the other resources of language.

SOUND REPETITION

Now, let us consider how the speaker may organize sounds, especially through repetition, to achieve certain effects. We shall discuss three devices varying in complexity from the relatively simple forms of repetition known as alliteration and assonance to the highly complex level of organization known as rhythm.

Alliteration. The repetition of consonant sounds beginning neighboring words or accented syllables is perhaps one of the best known "sound effects" of oral language. Notice how Lincoln used alliteration very simply but very effectively in his "Farewell Address" to the citizens of Springfield, Illinois, as he left there to assume the Presidency:

> No one, not in my situation, can appreciate my feeling of sadness at this parting. To this place, and the kindness of these people, I owe everything. Here I have lived a quarter of a century, and have passed from a young to an old man. Here my children have been born, and one is buried.[13]

[13] Parrish and Hochmuth, eds., *American Speeches*, p. 305.

There are whole chains of alliterated words: "appreciate . . . parting . . . place . . . people . . . passed." Especially effective is the alliteration in "been born . . . buried."

Effective alliteration does not call attention to itself. Recall the effects manifested in the opening words of the "Gettysburg Address": "Four score and seven years ago our fathers brought forth. . . ."

Assonance. Assonance can be defined as the repetition of the same stressed vowel sound; for example, dream . . . beach. Again recall examples from the "Gettysburg Address":

[f]our	score
in	liberty
testing	whether
final	lives
on	continent
not	consecrate
our	power
so	nobly
will	little

Rhythm. There are varying degrees of formality in rhythm between ordinary prose and strict verse forms such as the sonnet. Any language, however prosaic or poetic, is capable of possessing rhythm. Rhythm may be defined as a regularity in the occurrence of accents. It possesses a far more highly developed level of organization than alliteration and assonance do. We can think of rhythm in terms of repetition and expectancy. It is this very combination of repetition and expectancy which allows rhythm to animate and bring emphasis to ideas. Consider this line from Edmund Burke's "Speech on Conciliation," urging England to attempt to reconcile the breach between herself and her American colonies:

It will take / its perpet / ual ten / or, it

will receive / its fi / nal impress / sion, from the

stamp of this very hour.[14]

<hr>

[14] For a discussion of prose rhythm see: Wayland Maxfield Parrish, "The Rhythm of Oratorical Prose," in *Studies in Rhetoric and Public Speaking in Honor of James Albert Winans*, reprint edition (New York: Russell and Russell, Inc., 1962), pp. 217–32.

Basically there are three kinds of rhythm: (1) the metrical rhythm of verse, in regular feet. Although sometimes used in prose, this is rarely used for more than three or four continuous feet. (2) syllabic stress-rhythm. Here the syllables which are most heavily stressed occur at regular time-intervals, generally with a varying number of either unstressed or lightly stressed syllables in between. (3) rhythm of grammatical units. Here, the recurring phrase patterns or sentence-patterns give the effect of regularity. Note how this speech by Churchill before the House of Commons on June 18, 1940, combines all three of these rhythmic types (primarily the first two):

> The Battle of Britain is about to begin. On this battle depends the survival of Christian civilization.
>
> Upon it depends our own British life and the long continuity of our institutions and our empire. The whole fury and might of the enemy must very soon be turned upon us. Hitler knows he will have to break us in this island or lose the war.
>
> If we can stand up to him all Europe may be freed and the life of the world may move forward into broad sunlit uplands; but if we fail, the whole world, including the United States, and all that we have known and cared for, will sink into the abyss of a new dark age made more sinister and perhaps more prolonged by the lights of a perverted science.
>
> Let us therefore brace ourselves to our duty and so bear ourselves that if the British Commonwealth and Empire last for a thousand years, men will still say "This was their finest hour." [15]

Just as alliteration and assonance do not operate fully by themselves, rhythm cannot produce its total effect without meaning and form. Ultimately then, language is not composed only of semantic meanings or of structural meanings or of sound effects. Rather, language = semantic meanings + structural meanings + sound.

Summary

All the resources of language are available to the speaker. Every speech is a *selection* from the English language. Just as the speaker has selected his topic, his proofs, his pattern of organization, so he selects from all possible resources of the language those which compose the style of his speech. Therefore, he must first become aware

[15] From *The World's Great Speeches*, eds., Lewis Copeland and Lawrence Lamm, 2nd rev. ed. (New York: Dover Publications, 1958), p. 446.

of the vast array of potentialities which language holds for him: semantic meaning, structural meaning, and sound. As Weaver puts it: "Using a language may be compared to riding a horse; much of one's success depends upon an understanding of what it *can* and *will* do." [16] To know the resources of language is to find "an inexhaustible abundance of manifold treasures." We have mentioned only a few of them. As "the instrument with which man forms thought and feeling, mood, aspiration, will and act," and as "the instrument by whose means he influences and is influenced," language and its resources may surely be said to be "the ultimate and deepest foundation of human society." [17]

Rhetorical Exercises

(1) Write a ten to fifteen minute speech and deliver it from manuscript. Thus, you will be able to "polish" the language of your speech more carefully.

(2) Design your own Semantic Differential to test how well your own class agrees on the meaning of words they often use. Discuss the points of disagreement to see why they have arisen.

(3) Find examples where the context of a word helps stabilize word meaning. What kinds of words need more of a context for their meanings to be clear?

(4) Select a prose passage and look for all of the possible structural "signals" or meanings which you can find. How did you go about discovering these "signals"?

(5) Select passages to read aloud which you feel illustrate the close relationship between sound and meaning.

Collateral Readings

Berlo, David K., *The Process of Communication: An Introduction to Theory and Practice.* New York: Holt, Rinehart and Winston, Inc., 1960. See especially Chapter Seven, "Meaning and Communication," and Chapter Eight, "Dimensions of Meaning."

Black, Max, ed., *The Importance of Language.* Englewood Cliffs, N.J.: Prentice-Hall, Inc., 1962. See especially "Words and their Meanings" by Aldous Huxley.

Langer, Suzanne K., *Philosophy in a New Key.* Cambridge: Harvard University Press, 1942. See especially Chapter Five, "Language."

[16] Richard Weaver, *The Ethics of Rhetoric* (Chicago: Henry Regnery Co., 1953), p. 117.

[17] Louis Hjelmslev, *Prolegomena to a Theory of Language,* rev. Eng. ed., trans. Francis J. Whitfield (Madison: The University of Wisconsin Press, 1963), p. 3.

Osgood, Charles E., George J. Suci, and Percy Tannenbaum, *The Measurement of Meaning*. Urbana: University of Illinois Press, 1957.

Quirk, Randolph, *The Use of English*. New York: St. Martin's Press, 1962. See especially Chapter Ten, "Looking at English in Use."

Richards, I. A., *The Philosophy of Rhetoric*. New York: Oxford University Press, 1936. See especially "The Interinanimation of Words" and "Metaphor."

Whatmough, Joshua, *Language: A Modern Synthesis*. New York: New American Library, 1957.

> *Style, in its finest sense, is the last*
> *acquirement of the educated mind;*
> *it is also the most useful.*
>
> ALFRED NORTH WHITEHEAD

VII   Effective oral style is not magic. The decisions the speaker makes about what to say, as well as how to say it, determine his style. Both reflect the speaker's way of viewing objects, events, and people, so that the most general of his attitudes and the most general of his ideas find expression as characteristically in his style as they have in the content of his speech. The beginning speaker cannot immediately become a William Pitt or a Winston Churchill, an Adlai Stevenson or a John Kennedy, but he can recognize, as they have, that our language is capable of stating ideas with vitality and drama, that it is capable of conveying information concisely and accurately, and that it is capable of sensitively conveying attitudes and relationships. Basically, there are three steps in becoming an effective stylist: (1) The speaker must determine what the qualities of effective style are; (2) he must learn how to achieve them; and (3) he must practice constantly to use them at every opportunity.

Aristotle described three qualities of effective style,[1] and

[1] Aristotle, *Rhetoric*, trans. W. Rhys Roberts (New York: Random House, Inc., 1954). Book Three, Chapters 2, 6, and 7.

STYLE:
SOME PRACTICAL APPLICATIONS

while many other authors have since divided those qualities into lists of eight or ten or twenty-five qualities, they generally can still be placed under a three-fold division. To be effective, style should be clear, appropriate, and vivid. We shall consider each of these three qualities briefly, suggesting how you may achieve them.

Clarity

The first prerequisite of effective oral style is clarity. Without clarity of statement, there is no meaning or the meaning is ambiguous and perhaps misleading.[2] For example, when Calvin Coolidge announced "I do not choose to run," one might have questioned, "Do you mean that you do not intend to run under any circumstance; that is, that you *will* not run? Or, do you mean that you do not really want to run, though duty may require it; that is, that you will bow to pressure for you to run?" "Choose," in the Coolidge statement, is an ambiguous word. An ambiguous word is any word whose meaning is obscure or uncertain, a word which is capable of being understood in either of two or more possible ways. From time to time, ambiguity may be semi-humorous, as in the following example:

Professor: When you turn in your mid-term papers, I shall lose no time in reading them.

Students: (to themselves, of course): Good, then we shall lose no time in writing them.

However, in the language of diplomacy or of "political concealment," ambiguity may have far-reaching consequences.

The word "run" according to one dictionary has over two hundred fifty verbal meanings. The meanings are clearly distinguishable only if they are given a context. Often, then, ambiguity can be avoided by giving a word enough context to clarify its intended meaning. From the statement, "Max rented the house yesterday," a listener would not know whether Max rented the house *to* somebody or *from* somebody. Here, the context is not complete enough to give the listener an accurate picture of what "rented" means.

Because of the difficulty in defining them, certain words are in and of themselves ambiguous. They are meaningless, not in the

2 See Monroe C. Beardsley's discussion of ambiguity in *Thinking Straight: Principles of Reasoning for Readers and Writers*, 2nd ed. (Englewood Cliffs, N.J.: Prentice-Hall, Inc., 1956), pp. 151–59.

sense that they have no meaning, but in the sense that they may have a great variety of subtly different meanings. For example, the "truth" of a scientific principle is a very different "truth" from a Biblical one. The meaning of "believe" in the sentence, "I don't believe in coddling children," is not the same "believe" as in the sentence, "I don't believe in sea monsters." Even a word such as "case" in the sentence, "I was reading an interesting police case in the newspaper this morning," is a very different "case" from the one used in the sentence, "I think we should buy a case of cokes for the party."

Ambiguity may also arise when the parts of a phrase or of a clause are not clearly related as in "A moment after Miss Baker christened the ship, the S.S. Goldenrod, she was afloat in the river." Or, "The diamond pin was a present for Mrs. Donahue, when she married Mr. Donahue in 1964, at a cost of $50,000." We will consider syntactical ambiguity after we have completed our discussion of clarity in word choice. Words are said to be clear when they are accurate, when they are concrete, and when they are familiar. Let us discuss each of these qualities briefly.

ACCURACY

In one of the two versions of the "Gettysburg Address" discussed earlier, Lincoln asked his audience "to be dedicated to the great task remaining before [them]." The other version used "big effort." It is not really synonymous with "great task" because, to be accurate, it simply does not mean the same thing.

Accuracy comes from the Latin *ad-cura,* to care. Note the care which Thomas DeQuincey, the nineteenth-century English essayist, once wrote in "On Knocking at the Gate of *Macbeth*": ". . . I had always felt a great perplexity on one point in *Macbeth*." [3] Why is "perplexity" a better word than "interest" or "curiosity" or "bewilderment" or "confusion"? It is better because "interest" and "curiosity" convey only one portion of DeQuincey's feeling; so would "bewilderment" and "confusion." "Perplexity," however, suggests that DeQuincey's interest was aroused and that he was puzzled as well; thus, "perplexity" accurately states his mood.

Each person has three vocabularies: (1) the vocabulary of his

[3] Thomas DeQuincey, "On Knocking at the Gate in *Macbeth*," in *Handbook of Rhetorical Analysis: Studies in Style and Invention* by John F. Genung (Boston: Ginn and Company, Publishers, 1892), p. 8.

ordinary conversation; (2) the vocabulary of his more formal conversation and of his writings; and (3) his recognition vocabulary of the words he reads or hears. The beginning speaker must constantly and systematically work to unite his speaking vocabulary and his recognition vocabulary. Although a large vocabulary does not mean that a speaker will be good, it does provide him with a larger choice of words and more materials with which to be precise.

The use of specific rather than general words helps the speaker achieve accuracy. "Our old black cat" carries more meaning than "an animal we once owned." Specific words name individual objects or events. For example, "move" is a general verb; "stride," "amble," "glide," "run," "trot," are specific verbs and give a more accurate picture of the kind of movement involved. General words are, of course, a very important part of the language, but too frequent and unnecessary use of them risky. How old is a "middle-aged" man? What is the temperature when it is "cold" outside? How rich is a "rich" man? In each case, the wide variety of answers would make the key words in those sentences all but useless. No one could tell with any degree of accuracy what the speaker meant.

CONCRETENESS

Accuracy and concreteness are closely related. For example, Joe X meets Bill Y on the street and says: "I've just come from a good lecture!" Here, the word "good" may mean that the lecture was instructive. It may mean that the lecture was witty or stimulating or eloquent. The lack of accuracy here is compounded by the use of the word "good," which on an abstract ⟶ concrete continuum tends to be abstract.

Concrete words tend to yield more "information" than do abstract ones. A concrete word stands for an observable thing, for something perceived through the senses; for example, "tree," "robin," "coffee aroma," "noise."

FAMILIARITY

Unless a word is familiar (or made familiar through definition) it contains no "information" at all. If a zoologist says to his non-zoologist friend, "I met a very interesting copepodologist today," the non-zoologist probably would not understand whom his friend had met.

Audiences are critical of a speaker who uses words they don't understand. During one class session five students were asked to write a critique of another student who gave a speech on the Latin poet, Virgil. Here are some of the comments: "I don't think you paid enough attention to whether or not anybody in the class knew what you were talking about. Many words without definitions." "You tended to throw around names without telling us who they were." "What *is* an eclogue?" "Audience interest was rather good considering we often did not know what you were talking about." "You used a lot of terms unknown to the listeners. Why?" Still another student gave a speech using the terms familiar to a debater but not to a class of non-debaters: "flow sheet," "prima facie case," "canned rebuttal," and "causal warrants." Both speakers might just as well have been speaking Russian or Serbo-Croatian.

SYNTACTICAL AMBIGUITY

After the speaker decides that his words are accurate, concrete, and familiar, he must remember not to destroy the clearness of his message by the improper *arrangement* of words. Here, we shall discuss some of the typical kinds of syntactic ambiguity and show how they may be corrected.

Modifiers. There are two simple "rules" to remember when using modifiers: (1) Place all modifiers, whether they are words, phrases, or clauses, as close as possible to the words they modify; and (2) Do not place these elements close to other words they might be taken to modify.

Clauses:

Unclear:	When you were young do you remember all the good times you had? (The clause could refer to "remember" or "good times you had.")
Clear:	Do you remember all the good times you had when you were young?

Phrases:

Unclear:	Mary began to lose her desire to finish the project after a time. (The phrase could refer to "to finish" or "began to lose.")
Clear:	After a time Mary began to lose her desire to finish the project.

Words:

| Unclear: | She merely goes because she has nothing else to do. |
| Clear: | She goes merely because she has nothing else to do. |

Squinting modifiers (modifiers placed so they could be understood with either the following or the preceding words):

| Unclear: | As Jack and Bill walked along occasionally they slipped on the ice. (The speaker could place a long pause after "along," but that may not eliminate the confusion.) |
| Clear: | As Jack and Bill walked along, they occasionally slipped on the ice. |

It is also good practice not to separate words that usually belong close together, such as subject and verb.

| Unclear: | The scientists had after many years of work and a number of setbacks successfully completed their experiment. |
| Clear: | After many years of work and a number of setbacks, the scientists successfully completed their experiment. |

Correlatives. Remember to use correlatives such as "both . . . and," "not only . . . but also," "whether . . . or," "either . . . or," "neither . . . nor," only before sentence elements that actually are parallel in form.

| Incorrect: | You are either wrong or I am. |
| Correct: | Either you are wrong or I am. |

Parallels. Avoid parallel structure, when, in fact, your ideas are not parallel.

| Unclear: | Joan has brown hair, grey eyes and is very tanned. |
| Clear: | Joan has brown hair, grey eyes, and tanned skin. |

Shift in point of view. Avoid any unnecessary shift in point of view.

In subject:

| Unclear: | Jack was a good scholar, but athletics were not his strong point. |
| Clear: | Jack was a good scholar but a poor athlete. |

In pronoun person and number:

| Unclear: | If one's ears pop while driving in high altitudes, chew a stick of gum. |
| Clear: | One should chew a stick of gum, if his ears pop when driving in high altitudes. |

In verb tense:

Unclear: Terry asked the teacher about his mistakes, but gets little help.

Clear: Terry asked the teacher about his mistakes, but got little help.

In verb voice:

Unclear: We dusted our room meticulously, and the floors were also swept.

Clear: We meticulously dusted the room and swept the floors.

Pronoun references. Avoid letting a pronoun refer to an antecedent that is remote or vague.

Unclear: I can recall that Mary and I spoke with many people that day, but I did not enjoy it at all.

Clear: I can recall that Mary and I spoke with many people that day, but I did not enjoy speaking with any of them.

Transitions. When it is possible, use transitions to connect thoughts within a sentence or in a group of sentences. You might:

Use conjunctions and transitional expressions:

at the same time	in addition
for example	on the other hand
conversely	next
in particular	to sum up
of course	finally
moreover	indeed
after all	on the contrary

Repeat key words:

Four score and seven years ago our fathers brought forth on this continent, a new *nation, conceived* in Liberty, and *dedicated* to the proposition that all men are created equal.

Now we are engaged in a *great* civil *war*, testing whether that *nation,* or any *nation* so *conceived* and so *dedicated,* can long endure. We are met on a *great* battle-*field* of that *war.* We have come to *dedicate* a portion of that *field. . . .*[4]

[4] *American Speeches,* eds. Wayland Maxfield Parrish and Marie Hochmuth (New York: Longmans, Green and Co., 1954), p. .306. This author's underlining.

Use parallel structure and repetition of key words conjointly:

> Our Constitution, the foundation of our Republic forbids it [depriving "millions" of the "blessings of liberty"]. The principles of our freedom forbid it. Morality forbids it. And the Law I will sign tonight forbids it. (President Lyndon Johnson on the Civil Rights Bill) [5]

Length. Now that we have suggested some ways to achieve syntactical clarity, we might consider how many words are necessary for clarity. The answer is, of course, "As many as it takes to accomplish whatever purpose the speaker has in mind." Let us again proceed through examples. One critic said about the novelist Thomas Wolfe: "For a moment, but a moment only, there is a sudden release of compassion. . . . Then the moment passes, and compassion fails." [6] He could have said this in fewer words and still have retained the clarity of the sentence, but not without limiting the effect. Instead of saying: "For a moment, but a moment only," he could have said, "For only a moment," hence deleting three words. Why is the first more effective than the second? Because it better emphasizes the point the critic is trying to make—the fleeting nature, the momentariness of the compassion.

Length, however, is no guarantee of clearness nor of effectiveness. Lincoln used five words to say, "all men are created equal" and another version of the "Gettysburg Address" used ten words to say, "every individual is just as good as every other individual." Repeating "every individual" twice really gains nothing and tends to be boring.

Rather than talking about sentence length in absolute terms, the speaker should consider: How many words are necessary for the adequate expression of my thoughts? Why are the words being used: that is, for what effect? How can I best achieve my specific purpose? Nikos Kazantzakis, author of *The Odyssey—A Modern Sequel,* was once criticized for using too many adjectives with each noun. He replied:

> I love adjectives but not simply as decoration. I feel the necessity of expressing my emotion from all sides, spherically; and because my emotion is never simple, never positive or negative only, but both together and something even more. . . . One such adjective, what-

[5] *New York Times,* July 3, 1964.
[6] As cited in Maurice Natanson, "The Privileged Moment: A Study in the Rhetoric of Thomas Wolfe," *Quarterly Journal of Speech* (April, 1957), p. 148.

ever it might be, would cripple my emotion, and I am obliged, in order to remain faithful to my emotion and not betray it, to invite another adjective, often opposed to the previous one, always with a different meaning, in order that I may see the noun from its other equally lawful and existent side.[7]

In short, he used as many as he thought necessary to accomplish his purpose.

Length, as such, is not wordiness. The speaker should use only as many words as he needs. He should make sure every word is doing its job and never hesitate to eliminate all the "loafers." Economy should not be achieved at the expense of clarity and effect. Fuzziness often results not so much from long sentences as from awkward, confused, and illogical sentence structure, which often just reflect carelessness and/or lazy thinking.

Appropriateness

Effective style is not only clear, it must also be appropriate to the speaker, his audience, the topic, and the occasion. A speech that is clear to the audience is most likely to be appropriate. As previously suggested, the speaker should use words which are familiar to his audience or he risks having them misunderstood or not understood at all. The speaker would do well to remember these words from Shakespeare's *Richard II:* "Uncle ... speak comfortable words!" [8] The audience must feel "at home" with the language they hear in the speech, either because they know the words and precisely how they are meant in the particular speech, or because they are explained to them during the speech itself.

The language of the speech should be appropriate not only to the audience, but also to the speaker. The speaker should avoid the use of unfamiliar technical terms and infrequently used "grand" words. Bergen Evans in his book, *Comfortable Words,* argues against the use of elegant words by a speaker who is not really used to them:

> The cheapest form of decoration is the unfamiliar word, which the speaker thinks must be elegant merely because it is unfamiliar to him. But since no one can use a word effectively unless he is so fa-

[7] Nikos Kazantzakis, *The Odyssey: A Modern Sequel,* trans. Kimon Friar (New York: Simon and Schuster, 1958), p. xxxii.
[8] *The Complete Plays and Poems of William Shakespeare,* eds. William A. Neilson and Charles J. Hill (New York: Houghton Mifflin Company, 1942), p. 611.

miliar with it that he has no awareness of its being strange or in any way unusual, the *un*familiarity is the thing that stands out.[9]

One cannot make a poor choice of words better by decorating it with unnecessarily complex or elegant adornment. Ornament, as such, is a fairly tricky business in any field and if the ornament is wrongly used, the result may be disastrous.

The language of the speech should also be appropriate to the topic and to the occasion. Just as you do not attend a formal dinner in jeans, sweater, and sneakers, but appropriate formal clothes, so a speaker's good sense is his best gauge in degree of formality. For example, colloquialisms are not wrong in themselves. They may be correct in informal speeches or in conversation but they are not appropriate to a more formal speech. On the other hand, the speaker should avoid, at all times, stiff, formal language that is not natural to him.

The language of formal speech is not measured by the number of syllables per word, but by choice of words and sentence structure. Let us examine three examples: (1) the formal language of a presidential inaugural; (2) the less formal language of a public man bidding farewell to the public at the end of his tenure of office; and (3) the informal language of an everyday conversation.

Formal language is marked by its lack of colloquial style. It is direct, but it is not chatty. Here is an excerpt from the "Inaugural Address" John F. Kennedy delivered on January 20, 1961:

> So let us begin anew—remembering on both sides that civility is not a sign of weakness, and sincerity is always subject to proof. Let us never negotiate out of fear. But let us never fear to negotiate.
>
> Let both sides explore what problems unite us instead of belaboring those problems which divide us.
>
> Let both sides, for the first time, formulate serious and precise proposals for the inspection and control of arms—and bring the absolute power to destroy other nations under the absolute control of all nations.
>
> Let both sides seek to invoke the wonders of science instead of its terrors. Together let us explore the stars, conquer the deserts, eradicate disease, tap the ocean depths and encourage the arts and commerce.

[9] Bergen Evans, *Comfortable Words* (New York: Random House, Inc., 1962), pp. 8–9.

> Let both sides unite to heed in all corners of the earth the command of Isaiah—to "undo the heavy burdens ... (and) let the oppressed go free." [10]

Now let us consider a somewhat less formal, but nevertheless not casual passage from President Harry Truman's "Valedictory," a radio broadcast at the end of his Presidency:

> I suppose that history will remember my term in office as the years when the "cold war" began to overshadow our lives. I have had hardly a day in office that has not been dominated by this all-embracing struggle—this conflict between those who love freedom and those who would lead the world back into slavery and darkness. And always in the background there has been the atomic bomb.

> But when history says that my term of office saw the beginning of the "cold war," it will also say that in those eight years we have set the course that can win it. We have succeeded in carving out a new set of policies to attain peace—positive policies, policies of world leadership, policies that express faith in other free people.[11]

The "I suppose that history will," is measurably more informal than "History will." "I have had hardly a day in office" is measurably more personal even than "Hardly a day in office." And yet, phrases such as "this conflict between those who love freedom and those who would lead the world back into slavery and darkness" mark the speech as something other than casual conversation.

Consider this example of conversation between two students:

> I don't know if I should use a term like "marginal propensity" in my speech on inflation. Of course, I could just not use it, but then the speech might be pretty superficial. I suppose if I clarified it, it might be all right. Still, it would probably take too much of my time to explain it. Ten minutes is not a lot of time to get anything said in. I'll probably just end up changing my subject.

To be really accurate, we would probably have to consider the same conversation, this time between student and teacher:

> I'm not sure if it is possible to deal with a topic like inflation in a ten minute speech. So many terms such as "marginal propensity" would have to be explained that it might be best to select another subject. I find it very difficult to get much said in a ten minute speech.

[10] *Contemporary Forum: American Speeches on Twentieth Century Issues,* eds. Ernest J. Wrage and Barnet Baskerville (New York: Harper and Row, Publishers, 1962), p. 319.
[11] *Ibid.,* p. 308.

So, even within our conversational style, there are varying degrees of formality. Contrast "just end up changing my subject" with "might be best to select another subject." In all four examples, the speakers have let the occasion and the audience determine the *appropriate* style.

Impressiveness

Style should not only be clear and appropriate, it should also be vivid, impressive. Impressive language depends on a frame of mind. It depends on a fresh, incisive way of viewing the objects one is speaking about. New relationships are seen and explored, made clear and vivid. One critic suggests that image-making (one of the elements of impressiveness which we shall discuss in detail later) is synonymous with imagination. Imagination may be the key to all the elements of impressiveness. Two examples serve to demonstrate this point. They are both from Wendell Phillips' speech "The Scholar in a Republic" delivered in 1881.[12] At one point he mentions Ralph Waldo Emerson. He suggests that Emerson's characteristically quiet words were powerful explosives against the prejudices of his time. He terms Emerson "[t]hat earthquake scholar at Concord, whose serene word, like a whisper among the avalanches, topples down superstitions and prejudices. . . ." We are a bit startled by two such disparate objects as an earthquake and a scholar placed side by side. We are impressed with the newness of the comparison.

Consider Phillips' fresh way of viewing the naturalness of the growth and development of the American Republic and the great power inherent in that naturalness:

> English common-sense and those municipal institutions born of the common law, and which had saved and sheltered it, grew inevitably too large for the eggshell of English dependence, and allowed it to drop off as naturally as the chick does when she is ready. There was no change of law, no thing that could properly be called revolution, only noiseless growth, the seed bursting into flower, infancy becoming manhood. It was life, in its omnipotence, rending whatever dead matter confined it. So have I seen the tiny weeds of a luxuriant Italian spring upheave the colossal foundations of Caesars' palace, and leave it a mass of ruins.

[12] Parrish and Hochmuth, eds., *American Speeches*, pp. 349, 335.

Impressiveness of word choice may be obtained through the use of: (1) concrete language; (2) imagery; and (3) metaphor and simile.

CONCRETE LANGUAGE

Concreteness is closely linked to accuracy. Specific verbs, rather than general ones, not only name an action, but they describe concretely the manner of the action; *e.g.*, "spoke" is a general verb, "whispered," "shouted," "muttered," "mumbled" are more specific. When possible, it is effective to use a verb that carries within itself the force of a descriptive, adverbial modifier; for example, instead of "ran quickly," say "fled," "rushed," "sprinted."

Concrete nouns tend to evoke a more specific image: for example, "bird" is general; "robin," "crow," "sparrow" are specific. They tend to present a definite picture to the listener's mind. Concrete adjectives function in the same way. Precise adjectives such as "friendly," "generous," and "sympathetic" are more effective than "nice." The more "clues" the speaker can give his audience about exactly what he means, the greater his chance of making his point.

IMAGERY

Imagery may be defined as the use of words designed to make the listener respond with his sensory apparatus as he would if he were actually around the objects the speaker refers to. As we noted earlier, the word "imagined" contains the central key to the term "image," for the response to an image is a *replica* of an actual sense impression. For example, check your responses to the following images: "cold as ice," "quick as lightning," "smooth as silk."

Through verbal images we can capture the representation of seven general types of sense impressions: (1) those we see (visual); (2) those we hear (auditory); (3) those we smell (olfactory); (4) those we taste (gustatory); (5) those we feel through the sense of touch (tactile); (6) those we feel through bodily movements (motor); and, (7) those we feel through muscle sense (kinesthetic).

Not only the speaker but the listener participates in the use of imagery. The listener's understanding of what the speaker says is strengthened by his own activity in *responding* to the image. The speaker is creative when he uses an image and asks the listener to be creative also, to be an active participant in the speech. Consider these images: [13]

(1) We will not be stampeded into the dark night of tyranny.

(2) ... our political parties must never founder on the rocks of moral equivocation.

(3) ... we must take care not to burn down the barn to kill the rats.

(4) The road we travel is long, but at the end lies the grail of peace. And in the valley of peace we see the faint outlines of a new world, fertile and strong. It is odd that one of the keys of abundance should have been handed to civilization on a platter of destruction.

(5) No nation can longer be a fortress, lone and strong and safe. And any people, seeking such shelter for themselves, can now build only their own prison.

(6) From Stettin in the Baltic to Trieste in the Adriatic, an iron curtain has descended across the Continent.

What happens when you read these passages? Let us consider only the first example. "Dark night" suggests primarily a visual image although one would also have to account for all other associations the hearer might have. "Stampede" suggests a visual image (running cattle), an auditory image (sounds of pounding hoofs), an olfactory image (the smells associated with running cattle, dust), and a sense of movement. And, in fact, "dark night" and "stampede" operate together, not as separate images; for example, a stampede in the daytime would not have precisely the same associations.

METAPHORS AND SIMILES

Imagery and metaphor are closely related in that both are creative forces in language. Imagery seeks to *re*-create, or to *create a replica*, of a sense impression. Metaphor, on the other hand, *creates* a new idea by finding a similarity in two essentially disparate ideas or objects. For example, let us consider some relatively simple metaphors: [14]

My roots are deep in our prairies

this portal to the Golden Age

we want no shackles on the mind or the spirit

[13] The first four examples are from *The Major Campaign Speeches of Adlai E. Stevenson, 1952* (New York: Random House, Inc., 1953), pp. 226, 104, 20, 22. By permission. The fifth example is from *Contemporary Forum*, p. 316. The last example is from *The World's Great Speeches*, eds. Lewis Copeland and Lawrence Lamm, 2nd rev. ed. (New York: Dover Publications, Inc., 1958), p. 615.

[14] From *The Major Campaign Speeches of Adlai E. Stevenson, 1952*, pp. 14, 10, 3. By permission.

The first metaphor involves a comparison of a plant's roots with a person's basic beliefs: Both bring nourishment and sustain. The second metaphor involves a comparison of an impressive, grand doorway with a way of entering into a historical period of great promise and fulfillment: Each is an entry way. The third compares physical chains which bind man with ideological restraints which limit man's potential: Both are restrictions. Yet it is difficult to say that the meaning of each of these metaphors comes from either of the things compared. Rather, the metaphor's meaning is a result of the *interaction of both.*

Metaphor is not some "happy extra trick with words" but rather a basic animating force of the language. Its animating power comes from the interaction just described. Our everyday language is deeply metaphorical: "the sun is trying to come out" "a snow-capped mountain" "table leg" "party platform" "jump on the bandwagon" "tied up in knots" "don't try to pin me down to an exact meaning." Metaphors which have become so common are often called dead metaphors because the implied comparison no longer offers new ideas.

A metaphor consists of two parts as we have already suggested: the underlying idea, termed *the tenor,* and the figure of speech, called *the vehicle.* The principle on which metaphor is founded is the formal principle of analogy. A metaphor is often called a compressed comparison. One way of checking the soundness of a metaphor can also be used to check the soundness of an analogy: to break it down into a ratio of at least four terms which could be stated much in the same way as 2:4::6:12. If the relationship between the two sets of terms is the same, the analogy or the metaphor is correct. How can we apply this system to language? Recall the example we gave earlier by Wendell Phillips:

> English common-sense and those municipal institutions born of the common law, and which had saved and sheltered it, grew inevitably too large for the eggshell of English dependence, and allowed it to drop off as naturally as the chick does when she is ready.

It can be broken down into the following ratio:

> sustenance which the chick draws from within the eggshell : growth and independence of the chick as she emerges from the shell :: sustenance which the early United States drew from her British heritage of laws and institutions : the growth and emergence of the new nation as an independent force.

Patrick Henry's cry: "Our chains are forged! Their clanking may be heard on the plains of Boston!" [15] can be broken down into the following ratio:

> chains : individual for whom they are forged :: tax on tea and housing militia in private homes : colonies

In metaphor, the comparison is implied; in a simile, the comparison is expressed; for example, "She is an angel" is a metaphor but "She is like an angel" is a simile. Consider these examples of similes:

> [Ralph Flanders speaking of the Army-McCarthy hearings] There are new synthetic and irrelevant mysteries served up each day, like the baker's breakfast buns, delivered to the door hot out of the oven.[16]

> [Jonathan Edwards, the great Puritan preacher, exhorting his colonial parishioners] They [the efforts of man to help himself] are as great heaps of light chaff before the whirlwind; or large quantities of dry stubble before devouring flames.[17]

Similes may be tested for soundness much in the same way as metaphors. Like metaphors, they are among the most basic forces animating the language.

STRUCTURAL IMPRESSIVENESS

We have already suggested that order gives meaning and that through order we see the relationships the speaker draws between his words. Now, let us discuss some of the ways a speaker can develop an impressive effect through the manipulation of order. We shall discuss briefly the techniques of emphasis, contrast and antithesis, suspense, and variety.

Emphasis. If the speaker wants to emphasize a word, he often places it either toward the beginning of a sentence or at the end. He may construct a sentence involving a hierarchy of clauses, or he may invert the usual order of construction. Consider G. Lowes Dickinson's summary of the Greek view of life: "The beauty, the singleness, and the freedom which attracts us in the consciousness of the Greek was the result of a poetical view of the world...."[18] Why didn't he say: "In the consciousness of the Greeks, the beauty,

---

[15] Parrish and Hochmuth, eds., *American Speeches*, p. 94.
[16] Wrage and Baskerville, eds., *Contemporary Forum*, p. 303.
[17] Parrish and Hochmuth, eds., *American Speeches*, p. 75.
[18] G. Lowes Dickinson, *The Greek View of Life* (Ann Arbor: The University of Michigan Press, 1958), p. 67.

the singleness, the freedom . . . ?" Because here, the key words are "the beauty, the singleness, the freedom"; that is, the qualities of the Greek view constitute the most important piece of information. They come before the prepositional phrase for emphasis.

Not only *position* helps determine emphasis—parallel structure is also a key means for emphasizing, especially through repetition. A good example comes from Franklin D. Roosevelt's 1937 speech on the urgency of domestic problems:

> Here is one-third of a Nation ill-nourished, ill-clad, ill-housed—NOW!
>
> Here are thousands upon thousands of farmers wondering whether next year's prices will meet their mortage interest—NOW!
>
> Here are thousands upon thousands of men and women laboring for long hours in factories for inadequate pay—NOW!
>
> Here are thousands upon thousands of children who should be at school, working in mines and mills—NOW!
>
> Here are strikes more far-reaching than we have ever known, costing millions of dollars—NOW!
>
> Here are Spring floods threatening to roll again down our river valleys—NOW!
>
> Here is the Dust Bowl beginning to blow again—NOW!
>
> If we would keep faith with those who had faith in us, if we would make democracy succeed, I say we must act—NOW! [19]

Here both the same word and the same type of construction are repeated for maximum effect.

Contrast and antithesis. To stress the contrast between two ideas, objects, the speaker might place them close together by means of antithesis. Technically speaking, antithesis may be defined as an opposition of ideas which is brought out by means of a parallelism in expression. Edmund Burke, in his speech "On Conciliation with America" says at one point: ". . . a great empire and little minds go ill together." [20] How much more effective it is than "a great empire does not go well with little minds." Another case in point is La Bruyère's comment on the court of Louis XIV: ". . . its joys are visible, but artificial, and its sorrows hidden, but real." [21] Or G. Lowes

[19] Cited in *A History and Criticism of American Public Address,* III, ed. Marie K. Hochmuth (New York: Longmans, Green and Co., 1955), p. 511.
[20] Chauncey A. Goodrich, *Select British Eloquence,* photo offset edition (Indianapolis: The Bobbs-Merrill Company Inc., 1963), p. 291.
[21] As quoted in Adlai E. Stevenson, *Putting First Things First* (New York: Random House, Inc., 1960), p. 35.

Dickinson's, "The eating of the tree of knowledge drove the Greeks from their paradise; but the vision of that Eden continues to haunt the mind of man. . . ." [22] In each example, the opposition of ideas is brought out more clearly by placing the ideas close together.

Suspense. Notice the suspense that is involved when the key ideas are placed at the end of a sentence. Churchill, in speaking to the House of Commons in 1955, said: "It may well be that we shall by a process of sublime irony have reached a stage in this story where safety will be the sturdy child of terror, and survival the twin brother of annihilation." [23]

The speaker may also heighten suspense even more through the use of a somewhat longer and more complex periodic sentence structure. Notice how the audience has to wait for John Bright's full meaning until the end of this sentence.

> By adopting that course [negotiation] he would have the satisfaction of reflecting that, having obtained the object of his laudable ambition—having become the foremost subject of the Crown, the director of, it may be, the destinies of his country, and the presiding genius in her councils—he had achieved a still higher and nobler ambition: that he had restored the sword to the scabbard—that at his word torrents of blood had ceased to flow—that he had restored tranquility to Europe, and saved his country from the indescribable calamities of war.[24]

Variety. The "law of change" is one of the laws governing attention. Sentence variety, both in types and in length, appeals to attention. Recall the sentences of conversation. We simply do not always think in sentences of six words in length. Nor do we always think in declarative sentences. We question. We use imperatives. Note the variety in the length of the sentence in this passage from Adlai Stevenson's speech "Ordeal of the Mid-Century":

> History has not stood still for us. Instead it has moved faster than ever before, and with the development of the H-bomb and the ferment of revolution spreading from Asia to Africa, history's dizzy pace shows no signs of moderating.

*   *   *

[22] Dickinson, *The Greek View of Life,* p. 68.
[23] *The Eloquence of Winston Churchill,* ed., F. B. Czarnomski (New York: The New American Library of World Literature, Inc., 1957), p. 190.
[24] As cited in J. A. K. Thompson, *Classical Influences on English Prose* (New York: Collier Books, 1962), p. 122.

There was a time, and it was only yesterday, when the United States could and did stand aloof. In the days of our national youth Washington warned against "entangling alliances," John Adams spoke of that "system of neutrality and impartiality" which was to serve us long and well, and Jefferson enumerated among our blessings that we were "kindly separated by nature and a wide ocean from the exterminating havoc of one quarter of the globe." But those days are gone forever.[25]

For variety in both length and type, recall this portion of Daniel Webster's reply to Hayne. Hayne argued in 1829 that the states had a right to nullify acts of Congress that they deemed unconstitutional. Webster argued that, on the contrary, the Constitution established itself as the supreme law of the land:

> The Constitution has itself pointed out, ordained, and established that authority. How has it accomplished this great and essential end? By declaring, Sir, that *"the Constitution, and the laws of the United States made in pursuance thereof, shall be the supreme law of the land, any thing in the constitution or laws of any State to the contrary notwithstanding."*
>
> This, Sir, was the first great step. By this the supremacy of the Constitution and laws of the United States is declared. The people so will it. No State law is to be valid which comes into conflict with the Constitution, or any law of the United States passed in pursuance of it. But who shall decide this question of interference? To whom lies the last appeal? This, Sir, the Constitution itself decides also, by declaring, *"that the judicial power shall extend to all cases arising under the Constitution and laws of the United States."* These two provisions cover the whole ground. They are, in truth, the keystone of the arch! With these it is a government; without them it is a confederation.[26]

To separate style from thought here would be virtually impossible because thought is revealed through style.

Style and Purpose

Now that we have discussed the characteristics of effective oral style and have suggested ways by which the speaker can develop his own style, let us determine how style can be utilized as a means of persuasion through which the speaker can achieve his purpose. To

[25] Adlai E. Stevenson, *Call to Greatness* (New York: Harper and Row, Publishers, 1954), p. 3.
[26] Parrish and Hochmuth, eds., *American Speeches*, p. 221.

do that we must explore four interrelated aspects of language: sense, feeling, tone, and attitude.[27]

> *Sense.* The speaker speaks to say something.
> *Feeling.* The speaker has some attitude, some feeling for what he is saying.
> *Tone.* The speaker recognizes his relationship to his audience in what he says.
> *Intention.* The speaker sets up certain effects he is endeavoring to promote.

For the speaker, intention governs the other aspects. Notice the difference in intent evidenced in the word choice of what Cerf terms "conjugating irregular verbs": [28]

(a) I look younger.
    You are well preserved.
    She must have had her face lifted.

(b) I am stimulated by talking to successful people.
    You are a celebrity chaser.
    He is a snob.

Or, try the "conjugation": I am always firm. You are often obstinate. Bill is sometimes pig-headed.

Let us explore more closely three examples from the British philosopher, Bertrand Russell. Notice the tone and intention of the following passages:

(1) Here, he is discussing the philosophical tenet that there can be nothing real, or at any rate, nothing known to be real, except minds and their thoughts:

> Such an argument, in my opinion, is fallacious; and of course those who advance it do not put it so shortly or so crudely. But whether valid or not, the argument has been very widely advanced in one form or another; and very many philosophers, perhaps a majority, have held that there is nothing real except minds and their ideas. Such philosophers are called 'idealists.' When they come to explaining matter, they either say, like Berkeley, that matter is really nothing but a collection of ideas, or they say, like Leibnitz . . . that

---

[27] I. A. Richards, *Speculative Instruments* (Chicago: The University of Chicago Press, 1955).

[28] Bennett Cerf, "Trade Winds," *Saturday Review of Literature* (September 4, 1948), p. 4.

what appears as matter is really a collection of more or less rudimentary minds.[29]

(2) Here, he is reminiscing about a friend, the novelist Joseph Conrad. He is telling of their first meeting:

> At our very first meeting, we talked with continually increasing intimacy. We seemed to sink through layer after layer of what was superficial, till gradually both reached the central fire. It was an experience unlike any other that I have known. We looked into each other's eyes, half appalled and half intoxicated to find ourselves together in such a region. The emotion was as intense as passionate love, and at the same time all-embracing. I came away bewildered, and hardly able to find my way among ordinary affairs.[30]

(3) Here, he warns of the dangers of nuclear armaments:

> Is all this to end in trivial horror because so few are able to think of Man rather than of this or that group of men? Is our race so destitute of wisdom, so incapable of impartial love, so blind even to the simplest dictates of self-preservation, that the last proof of its silly cleverness is to be the extermination of all life on our planet? . . . I cannot believe that this is to be the end. I would have men forget their quarrels for a moment and reflect that, if they will allow themselves to survive, there is every reason to expect the triumphs of the future to exceed immeasurably the triumphs of the past. There lies before us, if we choose, continual progress in happiness, knowledge, and wisdom. Shall we, instead, choose death, because we cannot forget our quarrels? I appeal, as a human being to human beings: remember your humanity, and forget the rest. If you can do so, the way lies open to a new Paradise; if you cannot, nothing lies before you but universal death.[31]

About each passage let us ask a question: In the first, do we have a very elementary knowledge of one view of what is real? Yes, because the language *accurately* conveys that information. In the second, do we sense, feel the depth of the friendship between Russell and Conrad? Yes, because the language *sensitively* conveys Russell's attitude. In the third, do we grasp the importance of the decision we are urged to make? Yes, because the language states it with *vitality* and *force*. In each instance, we have a sense of fitness, of appropriateness

[29] Bertrand Russell, *The Problems of Philosophy* (New York: Oxford University Press, 1959), pp. 14–15. First Published 1912.

[30] Bertrand Russell, *Portraits from Memory* (New York: Simon and Schuster, Inc., 1956), p. 89. © 1951, 1952, 1953, 1956 by Bertrand Russell. By permission. Permission for rights outside the U.S. granted by George Allen & Unwin Ltd.

[31] *Ibid.*, p. 238.

of the language. Each statement has a different intention, a different purpose. To be sure, all three have the same basic function, to convey information. The first statement states the facts of the matter. The second statement not only states the facts of the matter but also demonstrates Russell's feeling toward the subject of his discourse. The third states a case, reveals what Russell thinks about what he says and, at the same time, indicates how the listener (or hearer) should respond.

To demonstrate more fully the relationship between purpose and style let us consider the "War Message" delivered by President Franklin D. Roosevelt on December 8, 1941. He was speaking to a joint session of Congress, asking for recognition of a state of war, when he said:

> To the Congress of the United States:
>
> Yesterday, December 7, 1941—a date which will live in infamy—the United States of America was suddenly and deliberately attacked by naval and air forces of the Empire of Japan.
>
> The United States was at peace with that nation and, at the solicitude of Japan, was still in conversation with its government and its Emperor looking toward the maintenance of peace in the Pacific. Indeed, one hour after Japanese air squadrons had commenced bombing in Oahu, the Japanese Ambassador to the United States and his colleague delivered to the Secretary of State a formal reply to a recent American message. While this reply stated that it seemed useless to continue the existing diplomatic negotiations, it contained no threat or hint of war or armed attack.
>
> It will be recorded that the distance of Hawaii from Japan makes it obvious that the attack was deliberately planned many days or even weeks ago. During the intervening time the Japanese government had deliberately sought to deceive the United States by false statements and expressions of hope for continued peace.
>
> The attack yesterday on the Hawaiian Islands has caused severe damage to American naval and military forces. Very many American lives have been lost. In addition American ships have been reported torpedoed on the high seas between San Francisco and Honolulu.
>
> Yesterday the Japanese government also launched an attack against Malaya.
>
> Last night Japanese forces attacked Hong Kong.
>
> Last night Japanese forces attacked Guam.
>
> Last night Japanese forces attacked the Philippine Islands.

Last night the Japanese attacked Wake Island.

This morning the Japanese attacked Midway Island.

Japan has, therefore, undertaken a surprise offensive extending throughout the Pacific area. The facts of yesterday speak for themselves. The people of the United States have already formed their opinions and well understand the implications to the very life and safety of our nation.

As Commander in Chief of the Army and Navy I have directed that all measures be taken for our defense.

Always will we remember the character of the onslaught against us.

No matter how long it may take us to overcome the premeditated invasion, the American people in their righteous might will win through to absolute victory.

I believe I interpret the will of the Congress and of the people when I assert that we will not only defend ourselves to the uttermost but will make very certain that this form of treachery shall never endanger us again.

Hostilities exist. There is no blinking at the fact that our people, our territory, and our interests are in grave danger.

With confidence in our armed forces—with the unbounded determination of our people—we will gain the inevitable triumph—so help us God.

I ask that the Congress declare that since the unprovoked and dastardly attack by Japan on Sunday, December 7, a state of war has existed between the United States and the Japanese Empire.[32]

Three "actors" emerge from the speech:

Japan (air squadrons, government, ambassador)
United States of America (we the people, our people, American ships, Congress of)
I (the President)

Notice how each one of the actors performs certain specific actions and in specific orders:

Japan squadrons had commenced bombing
        attacked (repeated six times)
United States *was* attacked, *was* (at peace), *was* (in conversation), and so on.
        (lives) *have been* lost
        will remember, *will* defend, *will* make very certain, *will* gain (the inevitable triumph)

[32] Parrish and Hochmuth, eds., *American Speeches*, pp. 507–9.

    I   believe
        assert
        ask
        declare

Note here especially the progression: the President believes, then asserts, stops to ask, and only then declares. What kinds of adverbs are used; that is, how is the action described?

Japanese actions	in infamy
	deliberately
	suddenly
United States actions	at peace
	in conversation
	always (will remember)
	very certainly
	well (understand)
	(have) already (formed)
President's action	(no adverbial modifiers)

The emphasis in this speech is on different kinds of action. Heavy reliance on adverbial modifiers lends significance to the precise nature of the action performed by each actor and tends to characterize two very sharply defined opposite groupings—exactly what the President needed to achieve when speaking to a nation suddenly and unexpectedly involved in war.

The key word is "attack." After picturing the United States in conversation, trying to negotiate, he reinforces his central idea (the key word) by constantly repeating it. Instead of saying "Last night Japanese forces attacked Hong Kong, Guam, the Philippine Islands, Wake Island, and Midway Island," he chooses to say:

Last night Japanese forces attacked Hong Kong.
Last night Japanese forces attacked Guam.
Last night Japanese forces attacked the Philippine Islands.
Last night the Japanese attacked Wake Island.
This morning the Japanese attacked Midway Island.

The repetition, the stylistic strategy helped Roosevelt make it abundantly clear that this declaration of war was necessitated by a widespread attack "extending throughout the Pacific Area." Reread the speech to determine the other ways in which the President prepared the nation for war, how he worked to fulfill his purpose in delivering the speech.

Let us discuss briefly one more example of the way in which a speaker worked to achieve his purpose. Abraham Lincoln, in the closing portion of his "First Inaugural Address" wanted to be concise, simple, and affectionate.[33] He wanted to be understood distinctly by all the people and to present himself as a peacemaker rather than a troublemaker, one who wanted to save the Union, not destroy it. Let us compare Secretary of State Seward's original suggestion with Lincoln's text of the speech as it was actually delivered. Through this comparison we can see more clearly how Lincoln directly tried, through word choice, to accomplish his purpose.

Secretary Seward's suggestion:

> "I close. We are not we must not be aliens or enemies but ~~countrym~~ fellow countrymen and brethren. Although passion has strained our bonds of affection too hardly they must not ~~be broken they will not~~ I am sure they will not be broken. The mystic chords of memory which proceeding from ~~every ba~~ so many battle fields and ~~patriot~~ so many patriot graves ~~br~~ pass through all the hearts and ~~hearths~~ all the hearths in this broad continent of ours will yet ~~harmo~~ again harmonize in their ancient music when ~~touched as they surely~~ breathed upon ~~again~~ by the ~~better angel~~ guardian angel of the nation." [34]

Lincoln's final draft:

> I am loath to close. We are not enemies, but friends. We must not be enemies. Though passion may have strained, it must not break our bonds of affection. The mystic chords of memory, stretching from every battle-field, and patriot grave, to every living heart and hearth-stone, all over this broad land, will yet swell the chorus of the Union, when again touched, as surely they will be, by the better angels of our nature.

"I close" is abrupt and states an obvious fact. "I am loath to close" reveals a frame of mind; he is sorry that he can not continue speaking with his audience. "We are not enemies, but friends" is positive, simple, direct and kind. "We are not, we must not be aliens or enemies but fellow countrymen" is more negative and "aliens" and "countrymen" less direct. "Though passion may have strained, it must not break the bonds of affection" places "strain" and "break" close together to heighten the contrast. The Seward version allows them to be further apart. Seward says "Passion has strained" but Lincoln tempers his language to "passion may have strained." Seward's "I am sure they will not be broken" interjects the speaker as an

[33] *Ibid.*, p. 69.
[34] *Ibid.* Facsimile of the original suggestion of Seward.

asserter; Lincoln is talking with, not at, his audience. "Every battle-field, and patriot grave" is stronger than "so many battlefields." Lincoln places "patriot grave" close to "every living heart and hearth-stone" to provide a more simple, a more direct contrast than Seward's "from ... so many battle-fields and ... so many patriot graves ... pass through all the hearts and all the hearths in this broad continent." The simple, more concise statement more directly links the living and the dead. "Will yet again harmonize" is a shade more negative than Lincoln's "will yet swell the chorus. ..." "[B]y the better angels of our nature" is much more personal than "by the ... guardian angel of the nation." And so Lincoln worked through personal tone, unifying imagery, word choice, and syntax to achieve directness, simplicity and warmth; that is, to fulfill his purpose.

Style and the Three Modes of Proof

One of the best ways the speaker can work to achieve his purpose through style is to become aware of the "dimensions" of language. In a sense, when we discussed connotative meaning and denotative meaning we began to discuss the dimensions of language. Recall our discussion of the relationship between words and things. Words act as a means of cataloguing the things, the events, and the processes in our environment. The key word is "catalogue." Or, as Leighton puts it: "Language is a means of categorizing experience." [35] The ways in which we categorize experience through language shape our ideas, our beliefs, our prejudices, and our aspirations. Roughly speaking, the ways we categorize experience correspond to the ways we offer proof. Just as, ultimately, one cannot separate the modes of proof one from the other, we cannot, in the end, separate the dimensions of language and response.

Because of the nature of human response, it is not accurate to say, "When I think, I think and when I feel, I feel." Human behavior is much more complex than that. We conceive of ideas, have feelings toward them, and pass value judgments on them—often all at the same time. Recognizing then the limitation of what we are about to say, let us discuss the ways in which the speaker works to choose

[35] Clyde Kluckhohn and Dorothea Leighton, "Language and the Categorizing of Experience," in *The Language of Wisdom and Folly*, ed. Irving J. Lee (New York: Harper and Row, Publishers, 1949), p. 266.

language suitable to the types of proof he uses by exploiting the logical, ethical, and emotional dimensions of language.

Before we look at some specific examples of referential words used in logical proof, it cannot be too strongly emphasized that total context (the situation, the persons involved, and so on) determines *how* a word functions; context determines, in the long run, the point at which a referential meaning becomes emotive. Recall the language used in the examples we gave of logical proof: "On December 20, 1606, the Susan Constant, Godspeed, and Discovery set sail from London for Virginia under the command of Captain Christopher Newport." Contrast that version with the following: "On December 20, 1606, that glorious year in American history, three gallant ships set sail from London filled with fearless men seeking new lives in Virginia under the command of that courageous seaman, Captain Christopher Newport." Or contrast, "Talleyrand was born at Paris on February 2, 1754 into a family well known in the court," with, "The clever and completely unscrupulous Talleyrand. . . ." or with, "Talleyrand was born on February 2, 1754 into a family who, for several generations, had been sound but undistinguished servants of the king." Or contrast "Dylan Thomas was twenty years old when he published his first book of poems," with "Dylan Thomas was only twenty years old when he published his first book . . . ," with "Dylan Thomas was twenty when he published what he termed 'the record of [his] individual struggle from darkness towards some measure of light.'" In each instance, we would label the first of the statements "logical proof" because they are predominantly referential in function. They refer the listener to rational experience.

Almost any word can be used to express our emotions, but we have, by convention, set certain words aside for that purpose. When the speaker deals with emotional proof he becomes concerned with this specific class of words. A good example of the emotive words is the speech by Marc Antony in Act Three of *Julius Caesar:*

> He was my friend, faithful and just to me;
> But Brutus says he was ambitious,
> And Brutus is an honourable man.
> He hath brought many captives home to Rome,
> Whose ransoms did the general coffers fill;
> Did this in Caesar seem ambitious?
> When that the poor have cried, Caesar hath wept;
> Ambition should be made of sterner stuff:

Yet Brutus says he was ambitious,
And Brutus is an honourable man.
You all did see that on the Lupercal
I thrice presented him a kingly crown,
Which he did thrice refuse. Was this ambition?
Yet Brutus says he was ambitious,
And, sure, he is an honourable man.
I speak not to disprove what Brutus spoke,
But here I am to speak what I do know.
You all did love him once, not without cause;
What cause witholds you then to mourn for him?
O judgement! thou art fled to brutish beasts,
And men have lost their reason. Bear with me;
My heart is in the coffin there with Caesar,
And I must pause till it come back to me.[36]

Emotive words are words deliberately used to excite feelings. Antony, here the persuasive speaker, appeals to the basic interests and instincts of his hearers. He appeals to the audience's indignation. Indignation is generally aroused when we think someone hasn't gotten "what's coming to him." Caesar, according to Antony, did not deserve to be killed. He was not "ambitious." He was "faithful" and "just" to his "friends." He "wept" for the "poor." Most of the words have rather specific emotive connotations.

Or, recall the words deliberately designed to excite feelings in Henry Grady's word picture of the Confederate soldier, returning to his home after the Civil War. Because of Grady's conscious effort, his audience, which was "Yankee" to the core and included Northern generals, was moved to make favorable responses:

Think of him as ragged, half-starved, heavy-hearted, enfeebled by want and wounds; having fought to exhaustion, he surrenders his gun, wrings the hands of his comrades in silence . . . and begins the slow and painful journey.[37]

Just as some words elicit specific emotions, some words, by convention, represent ethical values and judgment. It should be noted that although valuative words are often emotive, not all emotive words are valuative. Evaluative words generally claim a greater degree of objectivity than do emotive utterances. Recall the words of Henry Clay in 1850 when, as Nichols puts it, "he came out of

[36] Neilson and Hill, eds., *The Complete Plays and Poems of William Shakespeare*, p. 1031.
[37] Parrish and Hochmuth, eds., *American Speeches*, p. 454.

retirement to add his prestige and his wisdom to a cause more important than himself—and in minimizing man, he elevated him": [38]

> . . . what is an individual man? An atom, almost invisible without a magnifying glass—a mere speck upon the surface of the immense universe—not a second in time, compared to immeasurable, never-beginning, and never-ending eternity. . . . Shall a being so small . . . so fleeting, so evanescent, oppose itself to the onward march of a great nation, to subsist for ages and ages to come—oppose itself to that long line of posterity which, issuing from our loins, will endure during the existence of the world? Forbid it God! Let us look to our country and our cause, elevate ourselves to the dignity of pure and disinterested patriots, wise and enlightened statesmen, and save our country from all impending dangers. What if, in the march of this nation to greatness and power, we should be buried beneath the wheels that propel it onward. What are we—what is any man worth who is not ready and willing to sacrifice himself for the benefit of his country when it is necessary? [39]

As the speaker works to *clarify his reason for speaking,* he realizes that certain words help him achieve that purpose more directly and efficiently than others. As he becomes aware of the dimensions and resources of language as *means of persuasion,* he has progressed substantially toward acquiring an effective oral style.

Oral and Written Style

Generally when we have talked about style in this chapter we have specifically mentioned *oral* style and for a very good reason. When we are reading a book or an article, we may choose our own pace at which to read. If we find a word that we do not understand, we can stop, look it up in a dictionary, and then go on reading. If a whole passage is not clear, we can reread it a number of times until we more fully understand it. When we are listening, however, we cannot go back to rehear, we cannot hurry away to a dictionary and then come back to the speech. We can not pause at our own leisure to reflect on what the speaker is saying. Thus, although the writer need not be concerned with making his ideas *instantly intelligible,* the speaker must be vitally concerned with it.

Because of this necessity, several features of oral style make it

[38] Marie Hochmuth Nichols, *Rhetoric and Criticism* (Baton Rouge: Louisiana State University Press, 1963), p. 9.
[39] *Ibid.,* pp. 9–10.

somewhat different from written style. We shall discuss four: (1) Oral style must be quickly comprehensible; (2) It must be more direct than written style; (3) It must contain more restatement; and (4) It must be easily spoken. We have already suggested why oral style must be quickly comprehensible, mainly because of the temporal nature of the speech act. This is not to suggest that the speaker use only simple, monosyllabic words. What it does suggest, however, is that the speaker carefully analyze his audience to determine what words its members are likely to know. Then, if he thinks they may not be readily aware of a word's meanings, he must, either by context or by definition, work to ensure their understanding of it. Thus, there need be no difference between oral and written style in the selection of words. But, the speaker must, because his audience is listening rather than reading, doubly ensure that he is easily comprehended.

The speaker confronts his audience. Thus, quite often there is more direct reference to time, place, and occasion than there is in writing. He speaks directly to its members. They listen to him *while* he is speaking. He sees his audience most of the time unless he is speaking on radio or television and even then, an audience of some kind is often present; for example, the reporters at the Nixon-Kennedy debates of 1960, a small group of office workers, colleagues, and others when Franklin Roosevelt gave his fireside chats. Because the speaker is addressing his audience directly, he tends to use more personal pronouns than he would when writing, except personal essays or letters. Here, of course, degree of formality would determine, both in oral and in written style, the directness of the words chosen.

Because of the temporal aspect of speech, oral style often contains more repetitions than does written style. Avoiding repetitiousness often requires a high degree of originality on the part of the speaker. Although his main idea should be repeated to ensure comprehension, it must not be repeated verbatim or it may become monotonous. Rather, ideas must be *re-stated*, rather than simply repeated.

Since the speaker is saying his words aloud, they should be easily speakable. A formal speech is no place to experiment with tongue twisters or words the speaker is not thoroughly used to saying. Mispronounced words may impede the flow of ideas—they certainly will not help it.

It would be misleading to suggest that good oral and good written style are antithetical to one another. They are not. It may be true that oral style is not "abstract," that it is not "fuzzy," but all this suggests, as one critic points out, is that ". . . good oral style differs from bad written style." [40] It is probably true that linguistic differences between the oral and written discourses of each individual speaker-writer are more pronounced than (1) the general differences between oral and written discourse, and (2) the differences between the oral and written discourses of each individual speaker-writer. Basically, it is not whether language is spoken or written that determines word choice and syntax, but the degree of formality/informality based on the interpersonal relationship between the speaker and his audience.

Summary

Effective oral style possesses three characteristics: It must be clear. It must be appropriate. It must be impressive. To develop all three characteristics the speaker must understand and utilize all the resources of language as he seeks to fulfill his purpose for speaking. Intention (purpose) determines style just as it determines all other means of persuasion which comprise his speech.

Rhetorical Exercises

(1) Prepare a ten to fifteen minute speech in which you attempt to define an abstract concept. Pay particular attention to making your language not only clear and appropriate, but impressive as well.

(2) Select some speeches in class for everyone to read and analyze in terms of style. Compare your analyses. What features did you discuss? Were there disagreements in evaluating the stylistic effectiveness of any given speech? Consider this question: How effective was the style in relation to the audience and occasion on which it was given?

(3) Find a speech you think particularly vivid in style. Analyze the text of the speech carefully. Then, discuss what particular word choices and what particular sentence constructions led you to your overall impression.

(4) Bring to class passages from magazines, books, newspapers, which strike you as unclear. What specific elements in the passage contribute to the lack of clarity? Then, select passages which strike you as very clear. What elements of style contribute to the clarity?

[40] Richard Murphy, "The Speech as Literary Genre," *Quarterly Journal of Speech* (April, 1958), p. 124.

(5) Select a prose passage which you feel lacks vividness and accuracy. Rewrite the passage so that it is both animated and precise. What changes did you make? Discuss each change.

(6) For information concerning the fine points of style keep available a booklet on the elements of style. Which ones are in your library?

(7) Discuss style as "a means of persuasion." Review the section of this chapter entitled "Style and Purpose." Then, explore the following statements of Kenneth Burke:

    a. *It* [rhetoric] *is rooted in an essential function of language itself, a function that is wholly realistic, and is continually born anew; the use of language as a symbolic means of inducing co-operation in beings that by nature respond to symbols.* (From: *The Rhetoric of Motives*)

    b. Style is a mode of "ingratiation." (From: *Permanence and Change*)

Collateral Readings

Cooper, Lane, ed., *Theories of Style* (1907). Republished as *The Art of the Writer*. Ithaca: Cornell University Press, 1952.

Joos, Martin, *The Five Clocks*. Bloomington: Publication 22 of the Indiana University Research Center in Anthropology, Folklore, and Linguistics. Also Part V of the *International Journal of Linguistics* Vol. 28, No. 2 (1962). Especially the first two sections discussing five sorts of style.

Lee, Irving J., ed., *The Language of Wisdom and Folly*. New York: Harper and Row, Publishers, 1949. Especially "Language and the Categorizing of Experience" by Clyde Kluckhohn and Dorothea Leighton and "Language and the Communication of Thought" by Jean Paiget.

Murry, J. Middleton, *The Problem of Style*. Oxford: Oxford University Press, 1925.

Nebergall, Roger, "An Experimental Investigation of Rhetorical Clarity," *Speech Monographs* (November, 1958), pp. 243–54.

Sebeok, Thomas A., ed., *Style in Language*. Cambridge: Harvard University Press, 1952.

Thomas, Gordon L., "Oral Style and Intelligibility," *SM* (March, 1956), pp. 46–54.

Ullmann, Stephen, *Language and Style*. New York: Barnes and Noble, Inc., 1964.

. . . all the study of [rhetoric] is ineffective
unless the other departments of it be
held together by memory as an
animating principle.

QUINTILIAN

VIII   There are two ways of viewing memory as it relates
to the giving of a speech: (1) the committing to
memory of a speech word-by-word; and (2) the storing of
knowledge and evidence for the speech. The "memory" we
are discussing here is not the simple matter of rote memo-
rization. Few, if any, situations would necessitate a memorized speech instead of an extemporaneous speech or a
manuscript speech. Rather, memory is the storing and recall
of the materials and proofs of a speech, both the individual
pieces of evidence and the relationships they bear to each
other. Thus, memory is inextricably associated with the
learning process itself.

Cicero told the story of Simonides [1] who "invented" the
art of memory and it is worth recalling for it has many useful implications. Once, at a banquet, Simonides was called
from the room to receive an urgent message. While he was
gone, the roof of the banquet hall collapsed and crushed all
the guests beyond identification. However when Simonides
returned, he could identify each guest for burial because he

[1] Cicero, *De Oratore*, trans. E. W. Sutton and H. Rackham, 2 vols.,
The Loeb Classical Library (London: W. Heinemann Ltd., 1948),
Book II, lxxxvi.

REMEMBERING
YOUR SPEECH

could remember where each person sat at the table. Cicero comments that this led to the discovery that memory is assisted by the impression of "places" or "localities" on a person's mind. Thus, the ancients taught memory through the concept of place.

There are at least five major reasons why people have trouble with memory during the giving of a speech. Let us explore each of these reasons briefly:

1. The invention process has not been handled adequately.
2. The speaker has failed to prepare a clear, well-organized outline of his materials.
3. Speakers are often general, rather than specific.
4. Speakers sometimes fail to select concrete, descriptive language which vividly expresses their ideas.
5. Delivery assumes too much importance to the speaker and in his "stage fright" he cannot concentrate properly on the materials of his speech.

Relation to Invention

The interdependence of an idea and its recall cannot be overemphasized. If the speaker's ideas are strong, if they are vital, they can be remembered more easily. If the art of invention has been performed effectively, the ideas will be "strong, deep, and vital." It is easy to remember the ideas which interest us, which we know about, which we can relate directly to ourselves and the other things we know. That is why we stressed in the beginning, the selection of the proper topic. If the speaker chooses a topic he is familiar with and has considered at length, he is relaxed and can recall it more easily.

A second aspect of invention is especially closely related to memory. The speaker should take extra care to omit nonpertinent materials. All proofs selected should have a definite relationship to one another. On the other hand, the speaker must include all pertinent material necessary to the full and clear explanation of each of his points.

When ideas are sharply defined, when they have been carefully developed and well explained, they are easier to remember because they are no longer "fuzzy" in the mind, but sharp and clear. The speaker has, in effect, explained his ideas, examined them, explored them until he is familiar with them; that is, until he *knows* them thoroughly.

A speaker should dwell on each idea when preparing a speech to get a very definite impression of it so that it becomes distinct from all other ideas. Principal and subordinate ideas should then be distinguished so that it is obvious how one idea supports another. The speaker must consider each specific support to determine how his evidence operates to prove the principal idea or ideas.

Relation to Arrangement

If the act of arrangement has also been performed efficiently, memory will be still easier. As the famous Roman schoolmaster Quintilian observed, order and arrangement are strong adjuncts to memory: "... if your structure be what it should, the artistic sequence will serve to guide the memory." [2]

In building a brick house, the wall supports the roof, the foundation supports them both; the roof makes the top wall of the enclosure and serves to keep out sun and rain. The windows of the house let in air and light. All components have a definite purpose and that purpose is clearly conceived as the house is built. Each part of the house is in relation to, or, indeed, in many relations to every other part; each has a definite and planned place in the whole and serves the whole.

Every building is erected for a purpose; to serve as a home, a gas station, an office building, and so on. Sometimes a building doubles as both home and grocery but predominantly it fulfills one major purpose. Just so, the speech is concentrated on a definite purpose. All materials in the speech are unified around the purpose and serve to activate it.

To create a speech, one takes a few elements from many and creates a unified, organic whole, centered around a single idea. The whole and all its parts are devoted to the function of developing and presenting that one idea.

Through reading about a speech topic, a conscious awareness should be formed of the associations between ideas and perceived patterns of organization. Read the following statements; then close the text and try writing the points down.

2 Quintilian, *Institutio Oratoria*, trans. H. E. Butler, 4 vols., The Loeb Classical Library (London: W. Heinemann Ltd., 1920–22), Book XI, 2, 39.

(1) Many advantages are to be gained from increasing federal support to higher education.

(2) Loan funds that exist for students often charge a high rate of interest.

(3) The total of above-average students kept from college by a lack of finances is about 150,000 per year.

(4) Corporations, although extending their gifts to higher education, are not increasing them rapidly enough and their gifts are often highly restrictive.

(5) About half of the top 24 per cent of high school graduates do not enter college.

(6) Current scholarships are often too small and many times are restrictive. Moreover, a small percentage of colleges offers the bulk of scholarship funds.

(7) Only the federal government can provide a stable financial base.

(8) The states themselves do not have adequate finances to handle this problem.

(9) Of those who do not enter college, most give financial problems as the reason.

(10) Alumni gifts, although increasing, represent only a small portion of the sum needed.

Could you remember most of them? Probably not. Now, try reading the ideas in this order:

(1) About half of the top 24 per cent of high school graduates do not enter college.

(2) Of those who do not enter college, most give financial problems as the reason.

(3) The total of above-average students kept from college by the lack of finances is about 150,000 per year.

(4) Current scholarships are often too small and many times are restrictive. A small percentage of colleges offers the bulk of scholarship funds.

(5) Loan funds that exist for students often charge a high rate of interest and have other restrictions.

(6) The states themselves do not have adequate finances to handle this problem.

(7) Corporations, although extending their gifts to higher edu-

cation, are not increasing them rapidly enough and their gifts are often highly restrictive.

(8) Alumni gifts, although increasing, represent only a small portion of the sum needed.

(9) Only the federal government can provide a stable financial base.

(10) Many advantages are to be gained from increasing federal support to higher education.

Now, close the text and see how many you can write down. Probably more, not only because you have now read the list twice, but also because there is a more readily grasped sequence to follow. That is, in effect, what memory is—the mastery of material in an orderly sequence.

Relation to Detail

Many times, in preparation, speakers are general rather than specific. Concrete specific details are often easier to remember because they call forth a particular image to mind. Compare the following lists:

a large midwestern city	Cleveland, Ohio
a house	a red brick, two-storied house
a famous statesman	John Adams
about ten years ago	in 1954
Yellowstone National Park is very large.	Yellowstone National Park is as large as the states of Delaware and Rhode Island put together.
writers of western novels	writers of western novels such as Luke Short and Ernest Haycox

Specific names, dates, and places should be used when feasible so that both the speaker and his audience know exactly what he is talking about. Both concreteness and specificity help the speaker to "center" an idea and to clarify it. The use of an example is often helpful for the same reason. The speaker and the audience can remember the specific illustration more easily.

Amplification of an idea, describing a point in more detail to make it vivid, enlarging upon an idea for emphasis—all tend to make the point more memorable, mainly because it forces the speaker to clarify.

Relation to Style

We have already used the words "memorable language" in the chapters on style. The two main qualities of easily remembered language, clarity and vividness, are achieved largely through precision. The speaker must be sure he is saying exactly what he wants to say and that, in fact, he is "saying" all he can say. Every speaker, if he is earnest, is constantly learning and practicing so that his words will more and more become precise, effective tools.

One of the techniques a speaker can develop is *the reiterative pattern*. The repetitive technique makes it easier for him to remember his speech and will tend to make it more "memorable" for his audience. The reiterative pattern can be developed in a number of ways: parallel structure, repetition of key words, alliteration, assonance and rhyme-sound repetition. One of the speeches which almost every one remembers, has in effect "memorized," is the "Gettysburg Address." Why is it so easily remembered? In large part, because Lincoln was a master of the reiterative technique. Note just this short passage from that speech:

> *Four score* and *seven* years ago our *fathers* brought *forth* on this continent, a *new nation, conceived* in Liberty, and dedicated to the *proposition* that all men are *created* equal.
>
> Now we are *engaged* in a great *civil war*, testing whether that (nation), or any (nation) so (conceived) and so (dedicated), can long *endure*. We are met on a (great) battle-*field* of that (war). We have come to (dedicate) a *portion* of that (field), as a *final* resting *place* for those who here gave their *lives* that that (nation) might *live*. It is altogether *fitting* and *proper* that we should do this.[3]

Key words which have been repeated are in parentheses. Examples of alliteration and assonance have been italicized. The reiterative pattern provides clarity and emphasis which aid both the speaker and the hearer.

The reiterative pattern requires willingness to spend time on one's speeches and patience to work carefully and painstakingly with language. It is not easily achieved, but its effectiveness is unmistakable.

[3] *American Speeches*, eds., Wayland Maxfield Parrish and Marie Hochmuth (New York: Longmans, Green and Co., 1954), p. 306. This author's italics and parentheses.

Relation to Delivery

Although we will discuss effective delivery at some length in the following chapter, mention should be made here of stagefright and memory. Although the beginning speaker may have prepared adequately, he sometimes becomes so conscious of the fact that he is giving a speech that he cannot remember all he wants to say.

Recall one of the early concepts of Chapter I—that of the speech as a dialogue. The speaker is speaking *with* his audience, not *at* them. As he is speaking, the members of the audience are responding, sometimes by nodding agreement or smiling, sometimes by frowning when they disagree. This is exactly what happens in a conversation. The speaker and the person or persons he is talking with are actively sharing a common experience; they are thinking about the same information, sharing the same ideas, trying to decide on a course of action. In short, the speaker is not alone with his materials. He is sharing them. As the beginning speaker develops this concept of "dialogue" in his own mind, as he begins to concentrate solely on the *ideas* he is trying to get across, stagefright diminishes. The speaker then has more time to remember what he wants to say because he is concentrating on his ideas—not on overcoming nervousness.

Summary

From the moment the speaker selects his topic and begins his preliminary planning he has started memorizing his speech. As he seeks to clarify his ideas, draw relationships between them, and set them forth in vivid language, he is storing the facts and materials of his speech for use when it is delivered. For memory is, quite literally, the "storehouse" of knowledge. The "storehouse" is only as sturdy as the materials that have gone into it. In the end, the best advice for the beginning speaker to remember is, in Cato's words: "Hold to your matter and the words will come." [4]

Rhetorical Exercises

(1) Prepare a 10-minute speech on any topic of your choice and deliver it with the aid of only one note card.

[4] As cited in Donald Lemen Clark, *Rhetoric in Greco-Roman Education* (New York: Columbia University Press, 1957), p. 67.

(2) Devise outlines similar to the one given in the chapter and test them in class to see which kinds can best be remembered.

(3) Try to recall how you learn new materials. Compile a list of ways in a class discussion. Why are some more effective than others?

(4) Read Cicero's *De Oratore*, Book II. What is to be gained by recalling the traditional incident which supposedly prompted Simonides to "invent" the "art" of memory?

(5) Can you find any useful corollary materials concerning learning theory? Check in your library and report on your results to the class.

(6) Several articles have been written about the ways in which the early classical theorists conceived of memory, such as:

(a) Bromley Smith, "Hippias and a Lost Canon of Rhetoric," *Quarterly Journal of Speech* (June, 1926), pp. 129–45.

(b) Wayne E. Hoogestraat, "Memory: the Lost Canon?", *QJS* (April, 1960), pp. 141–47.

Did the ancients have anything helpful to say to the beginning speaker on this topic?

(7) Recall your last speech. Did you have trouble trying to remember it? If you did, analyze carefully your process of invention, arrangement, and style. Was part of the problem caused by a lack of planning during the early stages of preparing your speech? Or did a problem of delivery interfere with your remembering what you wanted to say? Once the *source* of the problem has been determined, concentrate on trying to correct it in your next speech.

(8) After your next speech, test the audience's recall of your subject. How much of it did they remember? Would they have liked more details? More examples? A clearer outline? More amplification? More sharply focused ideas? More precise choice of words?

(9) As you listen to the speeches in class how carefully do you pay attention to what you hear? A good listener is one who gives his full and undivided attention to what he is hearing. Frequently the best listeners are also the best speakers because they pay attention, they concentrate more fully on what they are doing. Are you a good listener?

Collateral Readings

Bryant, Donald C., and Karl R. Wallace, *Fundamentals of Public Speaking*, 3rd ed. New York: Appleton-Century-Crofts, 1960. Especially pp. 205–8 and pp. 245–48.

Hargis, Donald E., "Memory in Rhetoric," *Southern Speech Journal* (1951), pp. 114–24.

Winans, James A., *Speech-Making*. New York: Appleton-Century-Crofts, 1938. Especially Chapter XX, "Further Study of Delivery," pp. 404–22.

*I wish you to see that public speaking is a perfectly normal act,
which calls for no strange, artificial methods, but only for an
extension and development of that most familiar act,
conversation. If you grasp this idea you will be
saved from much wasted effort.*

JAMES A. WINANS

IX Delivery can be regarded as the whole of the
speaker's overt behavior. Observe what goes on in
conversation. People are animated. They punctuate and emphasize their points with gestures. They look directly at the
people they are talking to. Their whole body is responsive.
They are constantly alert to what they are saying. In short,
they feel a lively sense of communication.[1]

In conversation, attention is focused on the ideas under
discussion not on the way in which they are delivered. The
animation and directness of a speaker are taken for granted;
they are not a feature overlaid on his material. Rather, they
grow out of the vitality of his ideas and his eagerness to
express them to his audience. He is responsive to his ideas,
to his audience, to himself.

Have you ever seen a conversation conducted between
two people "reading aloud" their speeches from manuscript?
Or between two people who have memorized word-for-word
what they want to say to each other? Very probably not,
because in conversation we talk about the things we are

[1] James A. Winans, *Speech-Making* (New York: Appleton-Century-
Crofts, 1938), p. 26.

DELIVERY

interested in, the things we know about, the things we think other people should know about. The speaker's mind is constantly alert to his subject. His "speech" is not something copied down or memorized word for word, then spewed back like a tape recording. He has "vivid realization" of his ideas as he utters them. His mind deals directly and vigorously with his ideas as he discusses them with his audience. Further, he is physically direct. He looks at the people he is talking to. How else can he know whether or not they are dealing with his ideas, whether or not they are responding to what he is saying? This kind of physical directness is termed eye contact.

The speaker's mental alertness is reflected in his eyes and in his face. Through these, the audience receives the cue that he wants to communicate, that he is interested in his topic, that he is concerned with what he is saying. In conversation, we let our audience know what we feel about our topic, what we think about it, what we think they should be feeling—anger, indignation, and the like.

The point of all talk is to convey ideas, and anything which impedes that is a barrier to communication. To say that delivery as such is good or bad is misleading. Delivery should not "stand out"; the ideas of the speech are foremost. If, however, the speaker does not speak loudly enough, his ideas cannot be heard, no matter how important they are. If his pronunciation is not acceptable, his articulation not clear, if he mumbles, the ideas may well be lost or misunderstood. If he is speaking too rapidly, no one in his audience will have time to think about what he is saying.

To suggest that the speaker's attention should not be directed predominantly to his delivery does not mean that the speaker should not pay careful attention to it. The "natural manner," as Whately terms it, is not spontaneously adopted.[2] It is developed by hard work and much practice and, in the final analysis, the natural manner is determined, as are all other rhetorical processes, by the subject, the audience, and the occasion.

If a speaker fully understands the concept of speech as a dialogue, that a speech is part of a circular pattern of stimulus ⟶ response ⟶ stimulus ⟶ response, he will begin to develop the natural manner because he will no longer feel a sense of otherness or differentness from his audience. He will not feel separated from them because he is speaking *with*, not at, his audience. The speaker

[2] Richard Whately, *Elements of Rhetoric*, ed., Douglas Ehninger, Landmarks in Rhetoric and Public Address reprint edition (Carbondale: Southern Illinois University Press, 1963), p. 347. This work was first published in 1828.

is simply engaging in a conversation with his audience. His listeners respond to what he says and he in turn responds to them. They are both constantly concentrating on the same idea, exploring it, moulding it, using it—together. They are experiencing a lively sense of communication.

Lest the problems connected with the process of delivery seem over-simplified, the speaker does need to recognize the importance of the fact that he communicates his ideas through overt behavior, of both an audible and visual nature. One recent experiment to determine the relationship of content and delivery to general effectiveness suggests that: "... delivery is almost twice as important as content in determining the general effectiveness of self-introductions and is almost three times as influential as content in determining the effectiveness of attempts to 'sell' an idea." [3] Still another experiment attempted to check the effect of variations in nonfluency on audience's rating of a speaker's credibility. It reports: "Generally ... as the quantity of nonfluency presented by a speaker increases, audience ratings of perceived source credibility decrease." [4] The report goes on to clarify how it uses the term "source credibility"; it involves three factors: competency, dynamism, and trustworthiness. While lack of fluency generally did not effect judgments of trustworthiness, it did effect the audience's judgment of both competency and dynamism. Much more experimentation is needed concerning the relation of delivery to content and general effectiveness. However, the kinds of experiments mentioned above should indicate this: That through delivery, the speaker gives a series of cues to the audience.

Through delivery, the speaker "tells" an audience: (1) he is interested in his topic; and (2) he is dealing with the topic rigorously and dynamically; that is, that he knows his material, is sure of it, is at ease discussing it with his audience. The end of public speaking is persuasion. To persuade others to believe any point, the speaker must seem firmly convinced of its truth himself. How can he persuade unless he delivers his speech in the manner used by persons who are speaking earnestly? How shall the speaker's words pass for "the truth," when they don't seem like the truth?

[3] Paul Heinberg, "Relationships of Content and Delivery to General Effectiveness," *Speech Monographs* (June, 1963), p. 107.
[4] Gerald R. Miller and Murray Hewgill, "The Effect of Variations in Nonfluency on Audience Ratings of Source Credibility," *Quarterly Journal of Speech* (February, 1964), p. 42.

The Basic Elements of Good Delivery

In his effort to acquire effective delivery, the speaker should: (1) recognize what good delivery is; (2) observe and evaluate himself objectively; and (3) practice, first to eliminate large problems, and then, to refine his skill. Let us briefly discuss each stage.

RECOGNIZE WHAT GOOD
DELIVERY IS

The main way to discover the elements of effective delivery is to observe both poor and good speakers. Try to suggest ways in which they vary. Among the many characteristics of effective delivery to be found in speakers, probably the two major elements were directness and force.

Directness. The quality of directness in conversation and in public speaking stems mainly from two sources: (1) a desire to communicate, to exchange opinions, to talk out ideas; and (2) a concentration on the ideas under discussion which allows the speaker to forget himself. Whately has commented: "The practical rule . . . to be adopted . . . is, not only to pay no studied attention to the Voice, but studiously to *withdraw* the thoughts from it, and to dwell as intently as possible on the Sense; trusting to nature to suggest spontaneously the proper emphases and tones." [5] This natural manner which Whately suggests is the manner which a speaker generally has when he is speaking in earnest, thinking exclusively of what he is going to say.

When the speaker has eliminated all distinct thought of himself, he can concentrate on what he has to say, on his audience, and on the relationship between himself and his audience. He can concentrate on the essential feature of communication, the sharing of an idea, attitude, or opinion. The delivery of most great speakers has been marked by their conversational powers. Consider this comment about the speaking of the great abolitionist orator, Wendell Phillips: "The *character* of his voice—the man in it—had the effect of 'finding' its auditor. It has an *intimate* tone, as if he were speaking to each one as an unknown friend. . . ." [6]

Every day, in conversation, most people manage to convey their

[5] Whately, *Elements of Rhetoric*, p. 352.
[6] *A History and Criticism of American Public Address*, I, ed. William Norwood Brigance (New York: McGraw-Hill Book Company, Inc., 1943), p. 359.

attitudes toward a subject in many ways—tone of voice, word choice, gesture. Why then, when we stand on a platform before an audience to give a speech, should there be a "psychological compulsion" to repress outward manifestations of interest in a subject we have presumably spent time and work preparing specifically for presentation to that audience?

Force. Force is associated with the features often designated as "animation" and "vitality." It stems from a feeling of deep earnestness and communicates to the audience the excitement of a nervous system and a brain working at top form, stimulated by having to think rapidly and aloud, and responding with spontaneity, imagination, and vividness.

Force is motivated by deep interest in the subject. Unless ideas are animated, the delivery of them must necessarily be dull and lifeless. A speaker can experiment with the mechanics of voice and gesture, but they represent no substitute for a strong belief in what one is saying. When beliefs are strong and clearly defined, when the speaker is confident of them, he can rely on them, just as he does in conversation, to convey his feelings and his attitudes about what he is saying. When the speaker has carried over into his public speaking the most desirable qualities of his conversational speaking, he will fully realize the content of his words as he utters them. The force of his ideas will then be naturally manifested in forceful delivery.

OBSERVE AND EVALUATE
YOUR OWN DELIVERY

After the beginning speaker has carefully watched and listened to the delivery of other speakers, he should evaluate himself by listening to himself as he speaks, by tape recordings of his own speech, through teacher criticism, and the criticisms of the other students in the class. He should check especially for directness of communication (both intellectual directness and physical directness):

(1) Is there "vivid-realization-of-idea-at-moment-of-utterance"?
(2) Is there eye contact—direct and sustained?
(3) Is there bodily responsiveness to what is said?
(4) Does pronunuciation meet acceptable standards? Is articulation clear?
(5) Is there vocal variety in rate, inflection, and volume?

When the student knows what particular areas of delivery need work, he can, with the aid of his teacher, plan exercises designed specifically to help him.

Practice to Eliminate Problems and to Refine Skills

The next step is to get as much practice as possible, by speaking often and always objectively evaluating your own performance. The two basic prerequisites to effective delivery must be remembered: (1) preparedness, and (2) a genuine desire to communicate.

Special Problems of
Beginning Speakers

Beginning public speakers face some special problems in delivering a speech. We shall discuss nine. By exploring the causes of the problems, the remedies for them will become clearer.

NERVOUSNESS

Nervousness should be viewed as a natural phenomenon, almost universally felt in the public speaking situation. The speaker's task is not easy, and some degree of tension serves to remind him of this. Insofar as stagefright is controlled, it is basically helpful. As Walter and Scott point out, during stagefright certain physical changes take place that can aid the speaker. They indicate that the body may obtain more than its usual *energy* under tension because of these changes:

1. More blood sugar, which furnishes energy, is made available.
2. Insulin, which increases the permeability of body cells to blood sugar, is secreted so that more food can get inside the cells.
3. Thyroxin, which speeds the burning of sugar inside the cells, is secreted.
4. Blood pressure is increased.
5. The rate of respiration is increased.
6. Nerve conductivity is slightly increased.
7. Poisons are more readily removed from the system, thus reducing toxicity and fatigue.
8. More oxygen is made available to the blood so that more fuel can be oxidized.[7]

[7] Otis M. Walter and Robert L. Scott, *Thinking and Speaking: A Guide to Intelligent Oral Communication* (New York: The Macmillan Co., 1962), p. 84.

Thus, the speaker can potentially think more rapidly about his subject when he is on his feet delivering the speech than he can when sitting quietly in an armchair, thinking about it.

Channeled tension can therefore help the speaker. In great part, uncontrolled stagefright is due to improper emotional conditioning. The beginning speaker often thinks of himself as apart from his audience. He is speaking and they are listening. He views himself as speaking *to* and sometimes even *at*, them—a misconception about the process of communication. We have stressed throughout this book the idea of a public speech as part of a dialogue, carried on between people who are engaged in *sharing* ideas. Both the speaker and his audience are thinking about the same topic at the same time: facing the same problems, trying to find new ways of action, evaluating both old and new ways of action. Thus, the speaker is talking *with* his audience. If the speaker accepts this view of public speaking and if he is well prepared, then the undesirable features of stagefright can be controlled and the helpful and desirable features will remain.

LACK OF EYE CONTACT

The speaker fails to look at his audience mainly for two reasons: (1) He is confined to his notes because of lack of preparedness; or (2) he is suffering from "stagefright." The remedy for the first problem is quite simply to prepare more fully and learn to use notes efficiently. We shall discuss the use of notes in detail later. The remedy for the second problem can be found in learning to accept the implications of the fact that a speech is part of a dialogue. In conversation we normally look at the people we are speaking with because we are sharing an idea, attitude, or opinion with them. We are speaking not at, but *with*, them.

When we look at people, it tells them quite simply that we are interested in them, that we are concentrating on them, that we are communicating directly with them. Eye contact is the speaker's most important means of knowing how an audience is responding to him, or indeed, whether it is responding to him or not. The audience must be a part of the speaking situation. The very idea of communication, of moving another's mind, requires constant sharing of the speaker's ideas with those of the audience. Their minds must be working together on the topic under discussion. One of the surest signs that the speaker wants to work with the members of his audience on a common problem is his direct eye contact with them.

RAPIDITY

The beginning speaker is likely to rush through the materials so he can sit down. You may have heard this question before: "Did the man run because he was frightened or was he frightened because he ran?" The point here is that, by rushing, the speaker accentuates his own nervousness. When he is speaking too rapidly he has less time to think of what he wants to say, less time to consider his ideas himself and to perform the physical act of saying them.

The listener also needs time, time to discriminate between sounds, to listen and to hear, and time to respond, to think about what has been said, to assimilate it, to work with it. If the listener is not given the time he needs to consider the speaker's point, he may well give up trying, and unless his audience is paying attention to what the speaker is saying, he has no reason to be speaking. In short, both the speaker and the audience need time to perform the communication act effectively.

HESITATION PHENOMENA

Most of our speech consists of well-learned sequences of words which make their utterance an automatic activity. As children, most people begin to master the mechanics of speech utterance—the phrases and idioms, the conventionally used and grammatically prescribed sequences of words which soon become habits and "roll off" our tongues automatically, without much premeditation. But at the same time, in near-spontaneous speech, each utterance is a creative act. Any utterance which we say for the first time and which is not an habitual response makes a very great demand on our capacity for improvisation.

Speech, at the most elementary level, demands extensive mental effort. A meaning, before it takes form in speech, is something which is not yet defined. Its communication in speech requires that it be conveyed in some kind of order.

The simple fact is that we rarely achieve a continuous flow of speech. The speaker and the listener cooperate. Listeners concentrate on the message: They integrate elements of the message; they bridge the gaps which divide the groups of words. The speaker, on the other hand, cooperates by trying to minimize the gaps in the stream of words and to make them coincide with semantic groups such as phrases. The point to remember is that pausing is as much a part of speaking as vocal utterance. Pausing is a very basic part of speech production.

Thus, pause has a specific function in the giving of a speech. It permits delay—the time for thinking, for the thought process to take place. There is no need to substitute ah, er, and um, well, now, and the like. The listener will not find a pause unusual. Delay is simply a built-in feature of oral language. Most pauses go unnoticed because they are natural, so there is no reason to have a continuous flow of sound while speaking. Concentrate on the ideas you are dealing with, gain confidence and a sense of rapport with your audience, and your hesitations will be no longer than the minimal delays which we have come to expect, and in fact need, in spontaneous speech.

LAZY ARTICULATION

Many beginning speakers suffer from "lazy" lips, tongue, and jaw; that is, they simply fail to pay enough attention to manipulating the various parts of the articulatory mechanism. Most American-English speech sounds are articulated through activity of the lips and part of the tongue. These moving articulators touch fixed or relatively fixed portions of the roof of the mouth or the upper jaw. Quite often the lazy speaker has never become consciously aware of what happens physically when he speaks. Try first just to feel how these sounds are made: "p" as in pat; "t" as in tin; "c" as in cook; "f" as in fast; "l" as in let. Feel the various parts of the articulatory mechanism move.

However, over-articulation, an overly precise, affected way of speaking should not be developed because it calls attention to delivery and hence detracts from the substance of the speech. The best course of action to follow is this: Simply do not become lazy about articulating the sounds clearly. Make it easy for listeners to listen.

SPEAKING TOO SOFTLY

Common sense tells us that if we speak too softly, our ideas will be lost. Adequate loudness is one of the essential attributes of an effective speaker. Most problems in this respect are a result of the speaker failing to adjust to the size of room he is speaking in and the size of the audience in the room. Practice in speaking under different conditions will give the speaker a good sense of how loudly he must speak in any given situation.

If the speaker makes his audience work just to hear the physical sounds he makes, it may well lose interest in trying to follow the ideas he is expressing. The same thing may happen to the speaker who lets his voice drop at the ends of sentences. Part of his message may be lost and misunderstanding or lack of attention will surely follow.

LACK OF VOCAL VARIETY

Lack of vocal animation is also quite common among beginning speakers. If the speaker speaks in a monotone, he gives no indication that one word, one idea, one point, is more important than others. When a point needs emphasis, a monotone not only fails to help establish degree of importance, but may actually conceal it altogether. The vocally unanimated speaker gives no cues that he is dealing with ideas that are interesting and dynamic.

Most people manage throughout their lives to convey vocal cues to the people they talk with. The question is, then, the one raised earlier, "Why should the speaker, under a kind of 'psychological compulsion' repress animation in the public speaking situation?" There is in fact no reason to believe that this problem cannot be cured with a little effort and concentration on the speaker's part.

Once again, the speaker can refer himself to conversation. Listen to the animation of your own voice—to the change in volume, in pitch, in inflection, in length of pauses. Become consciously aware of what you sound like. A large portion of the problem is unawareness of the problem.

A student suggested a good technique to develop this awareness. Once he and his roommate had been practicing their speeches for class with the aid of a tape recorder. Between speeches the recorder continued to run. When the tape was played back they were surprised to hear the contrast between the animated, dynamic way they spoke in the short conversations between the speeches and the "flat," unanimated way they delivered the speeches. The student was so enthusiastic about his "discovery" that we decided to try an experiment with her whole class, with the aid of the tape recorder. As each person stood ready to deliver his speech he was casually engaged in a short stretch of conversation before giving it. Then he

gave his speech. In the following class session we played the tape
back and asked each person to note the biggest difference he observed between the "conversations" and the speeches. Almost without exception, recognition of the problem proved to be the best way
to alleviate it. Just as a moving object generally attracts more attention than a still one, so an animated voice is a powerful attention-
maintainer and an effective cue-provider.

A speaker must learn to use all his resources—among these is his
voice. No amount of discovery and practice, however, will really aid
a speaker who persistently selects topics for which he has no interest
or enthusiasm. An animated voice and animated ideas usually go
hand in hand.

LACK OF BODILY MOVEMENT

Just as an animated voice proves to be an attention getter, so a
body that is responsive to what is being said shows the audience
what the speaker thinks of his subject and often demonstrates that
he *is* thinking about it. An emphatic gesture underlines, emphasizes,
points to the idea being discussed. Gestures grow naturally from a
desire to use all available means to communicate. They should grow
out of the subject matter rather than being imposed mechanically
on it.

Lack of bodily movement generally stems from a kind of self-
consciousness that a beginning speaker sometimes feels before an
audience. When he becomes at ease in his part of the dialogue, his
body and his voice are freer to return to the totality of communication felt in the most stimulating conversations. That totalness includes an animated voice and unconscious gestures.

Check to become aware of precisely what you do when speaking.
For example, the speaker who at first walks up to the speaker's stand
and places his hands on either side of it quite often never gets
around to gesturing at all. If the hands are free, there is a much
greater chance that the speaker will feel compelled to use them.
The speaker who "clutches" his notes or manuscript, again, has less
chance of feeling the necessity to gesture naturally.

Since gestures grow out of the substance of the speech, the relationship between a responsive body and animated, dynamic ideas
cannot be over-emphasized. Speakers should respond not to a rule
which says it is helpful if speakers gesture, but to the reality that

communicating an important idea is hard work and that the speaker must use all available means of persuasion. The responsiveness of the speaker to what he is saying is surely one of them.

INCORRECT USE OF NOTES

Some notes are generally necessary in extemporaneous speaking to insure accurate and complete statements of fact and opinion, but they should be used unobtrusively. Improperly used notes detract from the import of the speech. If they become a barrier between the speaker and the audience, encouraging him to speak to his notes rather than to communicate directly with his audience, then notes will seriously impede efficient communication.

Notes may also facilitate spotty and/or jerky eye contact and in this way also become a barrier to communication. A common sense rule is to use notes not as a crutch, but as an aid to facilitate the understanding of what you are saying. The speaker who has carefully prepared, who knows what he is talking about, can use them in this advantageous way.

Each speaker should develop his own method of using notes. However, several general suggestions can be made:

1. Make sure the notes are easily readable; otherwise, they are more hindrance than help. Type them if you can; write them legibly in ink if you do not type.
2. Many speakers find it helpful to underline or capitalize or write in a different color ink the key words and ideas so that they stand out clearly.
3. Most speakers find it more helpful to put their notes on small note cards when they are giving an extemporaneous speech. They are less conspicuous and easier to handle than large sheets of paper.
4. Make sure you include only necessary material in your notes. Either a sentence or a topic outline is helpful. Generally, materials quoted verbatim should be included in your notes unless they are very short quotes which are easily remembered.
5. When you practice, practice with your notes. Be very familiar with them before you give your speech.
6. Never direct most of your eye contact at your notes. You are not speaking to them, but to your audience.

Following are examples from student note cards to illustrate several different kinds of notes they have used when delivering speeches in the classroom.

The direct quote:

Carl N. Dengler. Out of Our Past: the Forces that

Shaped Modern America (N.Y.: Harper and Row,

Publishers, 1959), p. 154.

"The very act of being a reformer reveals something

of one's assumption about the world. To work for re-

form implies a belief in the efficacy of making the

world over, even if only in a small corner. To

Americans tomorrow always looked better than today,

not because today was so miserable, but because it

was so good."

The topic outline ("Capitalism in Early Modern Times"):

                                                               Card one

  I. Commerce and a capitalism

    A. Geographical discovery and trade

    B. Mercantilism

    C. Money lending

  II. Industry and capitalism

    A. Fading out of medieval craft guilds

    B. Domestic or putting-out system

    C. Factory system still lacking

III. Agriculture and capitalism

    A. Breaking down of manorial system

    B. Production for profit

    C. Enclosure movement

The complete sentence outline ("Four Aspects of the Puritan Tradition"):

I. The morality and religion of the Puritans was not based wholly on ignorance and superstition.

    A. Their fundamentalism can be viewed as intellectually respectable.

    B. Their fundamentalism did not have to reject biology, physics or historical criticism to maintain its dogma.

II. The Puritan belief in democracy and limited government was rather ambiguous.

    A. They were not really democrats, but they possessed an "irrepressible democratic dynamic."

    B. They supported constitutionalism and limited government, but they were sometimes tempted to claim almost unlimited power.

Card three

Card Three

III. The Puritan "business ethic" was a relatively

stable force in their economy.

A. They believed in the moral dignity of work.

B. They believed that leisure was to be dis-

trusted.

C. They were suspicious that the poor were

ungodly.

Card four

IV. Education, from the beginning, held an important

place in Puritan life.

A. They set up schools and colleges.

B. They produced a variety of different kinds

of literature.

You may want to use more or different kinds of notes. However, keep in mind that they are for the purpose of facilitating, not impeding, communication.

Summary

The delivery of the speech is the culmination of all the work that has gone before: in the act of rhetorical invention, in the arrangement of arguments, in the wording of materials in appropriate language, and in becoming thoroughly aware, through memory, of what the speaker wants to say. If delivery is ineffective, the work which has preceded it has little chance of succeeding.

DELIVERY **176**

If the other steps in the rhetorical act have been handled success-fully, if the speaker fully understands the *nature* of the communi-cative act, then there should be few problems with delivery. If there *are* any, first carefully analyze the causes of the problem and then patiently practice to eliminate them and to refine your skill in delivery.

When analyzing the causes of the problems keep firmly in mind the ways most problems are related to other aspects of the rhetorical process, especially invention. Cicero's conception of delivery, writ-ten in the *De Inventione* when he was a young man, is still one of the most useful to remember. By delivery, he meant "the control of the voice and body in a manner suitable to the dignity of the sub-ject matter and the style." [8]

Rhetorical Exercises

(1) Give a 10-minute extemporaneous speech on a topic which will ne-cessitate the use of notes.

(2) Listen to the speakers in class. Comment on their delivery. Are they direct, animated, conversational? Why or why not?

(3) Listen to a tape of yourself. Check your own communicativeness according to these criteria:
  (a) *Intellectual directness.* Is the speaker vividly aware of what he he is saying? Is he trying to talk his ideas out directly with his audience?
  (b) *Physical directness.* Can he easily be heard? Is he speaking at an understandable, pleasant rate of speed? Does he have vocal variety? Does he have clear articulation? Is his pronunciation of an acceptable standard? Does he maintain eye contact? Is his body responsive?
  Compare your own notes with the other members of the class and with the teacher. Keep your own checksheet or, if the teacher uses a critique sheet, see if you are improving or if the same problems continue to occur.

(4) Make another tape later in the class term. Compare the two tapes according to the criteria set forth above. Have you improved? Where do you still need work?

(5) If you still find it difficult to gesture, to move freely when speaking, try giving a demonstration speech where you have to move; for example, explain badminton strokes, or golf swings, and so on.

(6) If you still have voice and articulation problems, ask your teacher for some additional reading materials. Several of the books listed in the collateral reading list will be especially helpful.

[8] Ray Nadeau, "Delivery in Ancient Times: Homer to Quintilian," *Quarterly Journal of Speech* (February, 1964), p. 58.

(7) Whenever you can, consider the delivery habits of all the speakers you hear, both good and bad, to become aware of their practices and to gain insight into why some are effective and some are not.

Collateral Readings

Bryant, Donald C., and Karl R. Wallace, *Fundamentals of Public Speaking*, 3rd ed. New York: Appleton-Century-Crofts, 1960. Part IV.

Clevenger, Theodore, Jr., "A Synthesis of Experimental Research in Stage Fright," *Quarterly Journal of Speech* (April, 1959), pp. 134–45.

Eisenson, Jon, *The Improvement of Voice and Diction*. New York: The Macmillan Company, 1958.

Heinberg, Paul, "Relationships of Content and Delivery to General Effectiveness," *Speech Monographs* (June, 1963), pp. 103–7.

Hildebrandt, Herbert W., and Walter W. Stevens, "Manuscript and Extemporaneous Delivery in Communicating Information," *SM* (November, 1963), pp. 369–72.

Miller, Gerald R., and Murray Hewgill, "The Effect of Variations in Nonfluency on Audience Ratings of Source Credibility," *QJS* (February, 1964), pp. 36–44.

Mudd, Charles S., and Malcom O. Sillars, *Speech: Content and Communication*. San Francisco, Calif.: Chandler Publishing Co., 1960. Chapters XIII, XIV, XV.

Nadeau, Ray, "Delivery in Ancient Times: Homer to Quintilian," *QJS* (February, 1964), pp. 53–60.

Winans, James A., *Speech-Making*. New York: Appleton-Century-Crofts, 1938. Chapters II and XX.

PART THREE

ANALYSES AND CRITICISMS

*. . . things that are true and things that are just have a
natural tendency to prevail over their opposites, so that
if the decisions of judges are not what they ought to be,
the defeat must be due to the speakers themselves
and they must be blamed accordingly.*

ARISTOTLE

X   We live in a world of speeches. We are literally
        surrounded by them—by short ones when we listen
to the opinions of our friends or to television commercial
announcements, by medium-length ones in meetings, on
radio and television, and sometimes by tediously long ones
by visiting lecturers, professors, and politicians at election
time. In each situation, we are confronted with statements
and we evaluate them. Are they fact or opinion? If opinion,
whose opinion? We listen carefully to those whom we respect and not so carefully to those we do not. Sometimes
we merely reach out and switch off a dial, if not a physical
dial on a television set, then the mental one in our mind.
When we do, we are actually criticizing a speech.

When the beginning speaker learns to evaluate consciously the speeches he hears, he is progressing toward
being an effective speaker. When he understands *why* he
likes or dislikes the speeches he hears, he begins to know
how to give a better speech. Thus, prerequisites to becoming a good speaker are learning to listen carefully and developing a sense of critical awareness. In this chapter, let us
first list guide questions which suggest criteria for evaluating a speech, then read a speech given by a student to two
different audiences and evaluate it in terms of these criteria.

EVALUATING SPEECHES

Guide Questions

First, questions are raised about all five parts of the rhetorical act: invention, arrangement, style, memory, and delivery. Then, questions are asked about total effectiveness. Although, as a critic, you may have more specific points, these questions will serve as guide lines for your further analysis.

RHETORICAL INVENTION

(1) Does the speaker proceed from assumptions and hypotheses which are fair and reasonable?

(2) Is the speaker's analysis of his topic complete and clear?

(3) Does the speaker deal with a reliably established body of material? Is his supporting material accurate? sufficient? recent? well documented?

(4) Does the speaker substitute appeals to the emotions for evidence and argument?

(5) Does the speaker examine through reasoning the implications of his suggestions?

(6) Does the speaker's reasoning meet appropriate tests of validity? Were the materials of the speech internally consistent?

(7) Does the speaker reflect fertility of mind in the suggestions he offers for consideration?

(8) Did the speaker seek to establish identification with his audience?

(9) Did he work effectively to gain and maintain the attention of his audience?

(10) Was the speech appropriate for this particular audience?

ARRANGEMENT

(1) Was the speaker's purpose either made explicit or was it clearly implied?

(2) Was the speaker's thesis clear?

(3) Was there a clear indication of the structural progression which the speaker intended to take?

(4) Was the speech well organized into a clearly definable pattern?

(5) Were there clear transitions to aid in developing the points of relationship between ideas?

STYLE

(1) Was the language clear?

(2) Was the language appropriate to the speaker, audience, and occasion?

(3) Was the language vivid? Did it animate the ideas of the speech?

(4) Was the language persuasive?

MEMORY

(1) Did the speaker appear to be at ease with his materials?

(2) Did he appear to know his subject matter?

DELIVERY

(1) Was the speaker alert to what he was saying? Was there vivid-realization-at-moment-of-utterance?

(2) Was the speaker responsive to his audience? Was there a lively sense of communication?

(3) Was there directness of communication? Did the speaker have good eye contact with his audience?

(4) Was the speaker animated? Was he facially animated? Vocally expressive? Bodily responsive?

(5) Were the mechanical aspects of delivery satisfactory? Did the speaker speak loudly enough? Slowly enough? Were his voice and articulation adequate?

(6) If notes or a manuscript were used, were they effectively used? Or did they present a "barrier" between the speaker and the audience?

TOTAL EFFECTIVENESS

(1) Did the speaker exhibit a real desire to communicate? Did he show real interest in and knowledge of his subject?

(2) Did the speaker use the best available resources to help him convey his point? Or were there better resources available?

(3) Was the audience responsive to the speaker and what he had to say?

(4) Would you like to hear the speaker again?

Although we have listed some guide questions to be used in evaluating a speech, in the end the most important questions are these:

"How well did the speaker carry out what he said or implied that he wanted to do?" "Did he use effective means of persuasion?"

Sample Criticisms

Below are two versions of basically the same speech given by a college student. Her first audience was a group familiar with the topic, whose members had read much information about it and had discussed it at length. They had some training in the use of evidence and argumentation. The second audience was much more general. Its members were not especially familiar with the topic and prob- ably had no previous specific information on it. Some had taken the beginning course in public speaking.

After each paragraph of speech text there is commentary to ex- plain what the student hoped to accomplish and how she hoped to accomplish it. Specific strategies are also criticized for strengths and weaknesses. It is best, in both cases, to read entirely through the speech and then reread the speech with specific criticisms. The criti- cisms are indented to set them apart from the speeches themselves:

FIRST VERSION

The Report of the U.S. Office of Education, which was meant to express the policy of the United States at the Twenty-second Inter- national Conference on Public Education said: "Education in the United States is based on two fundamental principles: (1) every person has an equal right to educational opportunities; and (2) an educated citizenry is essential to freedom and human welfare." How- ever, as the House Committee on Education and Labor commented on this statement: "Opportunities for public education vary widely in the United States." Because there are these wide variations in educational opportunity, I believe that the Federal Government should guarantee an opportunity for higher education to all qualified high school graduates.

[Here, the speaker sets the stage for her topic. She pictures the differences between aims and actualities and orients the audience to her particular position on the topic. Next, she makes a clear statement of purpose and of her position on the topic. Because of the nature of her audience (they had come with the specific intention of working with the topic of her speech immediately after it was given), the speaker included no "attention getter" as such. The opening for basically the same speech given to an- other audience (much more general and less attentive to the sub- ject) is very different. This illustrates the fact that, from the opening remarks, the materials of the speech must be adapted for the particular audience which is hearing it. Note that the speaker does not immediately begin with her thesis sentence, "I believe that the Federal Government should guarantee an opportunity for higher education to all qualified high school students." The reason for this is very simple. The audience needs a chance to adjust to dealing with the topic. Thus, it is seldom a good idea to have your thesis sentence the *first* sentence of your speech. It is too important to be missed.]

I accept as rationale the statement of the Rockefeller Panel on Education that: "Federal programs in education now exist on a large scale and take a great many forms." Thus, it is not a question of whether or not the Federal Government should give aid to higher education, but what direction that aid should take.

[Here, she begins to limit her topic. She says she is not going to discuss the issue of whether or not the Federal Government *should* aid higher education, which is a topic in itself, but rather, will discuss what *direction* the aid should take. The inclusion of an authority is probably a very wise move. The statement that "it is not a question of whether or not the Federal Government should give aid . . . but what direction that aid should take," is not one with which all her audience could agree. Given the added support of an important educational program, they might consider it more carefully.]

Before telling you why I think the Federal Government should *guarantee* an opportunity for higher education, I'd like to explain the way in which I'm using several terms. By "guarantee an opportunity," I mean a rather specific program to give formal assurance by means of federally underwritten loans. By "higher education," I don't mean just college, but post high school education at all institutions designated as institutions of higher education in the *Education Directory* published by the Department of Health, Education, and Welfare. This would, for example, include further work at trade and vocational institutions. By "qualified students," I mean simply those students who are competent to meet the entrance requirements of accredited institutions of higher education.

[Here, she explains how she is using the key terms in her thesis sentence to clarify what she means for her audience. Consider the definition of "opportunity." It could have been rather ambiguously defined as "chance." That, in effect, is not definition because it does not move the audience any further toward understanding the meaning of the term. Rather, the speaker is quite explicit about the meaning: "a formal assurance by means of federally underwritten loans." Again, she limits her topic to more manageable proportions. She also points out that she is not just talking about college education when she says "higher education."

On many topics and in many kinds of speeches, the speaker need not define so many terms. Whenever terms are being used in a specific way or when they may be unclear to the audience, they should be defined.]

I believe that there are three main reasons why you should agree with my position on this matter: (1) Many qualified high school graduates do not receive a higher education because they lack the necessary finances. (2) Existing sources cannot provide this needed financial assistance. (3) Only the Federal Government can provide a stable financial base for needy high school graduates.

[Here, the speaker points out how she will support her thesis and indicates the structural progression of her ideas. The order of materials was dictated by the particular kind of speech she was giving and the particular motivational situation. In this case the speaker limited herself to three main points in order to remember each easily and devote sufficient time to each. Each speaker should include as few main points as possible in his material for those two reasons.]

Under the first reason, that many qualified high school graduates do not receive higher education because they lack the necessary finances, I'll show three things: First, a large proportion of high school graduates do not attend institutions of higher education. Second, this loss is serious enough to warrant immediate action. And, third, the primary cause of this nonattendance is lack of finances.

[The speaker continues to explain how she will handle her materials and points to her line of reasoning. In this particular instance, it was especially necessary because her audience was taking notes and would later discuss her method of handling the materials. The individual situation determines how much explanation of the use of materials must be included in the speech. In all events, the aim should be for clarity. The other "graces" can be developed later. The audience should always be fully aware of the speaker's intention. The point here is that the organization should be clear without being too obviously mechanical.]

Hurst R. Anderson of the American Council of Education, in testimony before the Senate Committee on Labor and Public Welfare in 1960 said, "About half of the top 24 per cent of high school graduates do not enter college."

[The speaker supports her first point with testimony which gives information. She documents her information with name, affiliation, year. In this case no further documentation is necessary. She uses only one support because the statement is not particularly debatable. The speaker, on any subject, should determine how *much* supporting material by this criterion: "How much do I have to use to establish my point?"]

This loss is serious—serious both to the nation as a whole and to the individual. Each year the nation suffers a serious economic loss because of its failure to invest in its human capital. As Theodore Schultz of the University of Chicago states: "It is a simple economic fact that increases in goods and man hours combined appear to account for only a small fraction of the yearly increase in national income. Rather, it is the increase in capital formation by education which accounts for otherwise large, unexplained increases in output."

[Again, she uses one support. Here, she could have usefully indicated Mr. Schultz's special competence to speak on this subject.]

But in addition to talking about national output, let's see how the seriousness of this loss is reflected in each student's potential earning capacity. The *National Education Association Journal* of January 1963 showed what the monetary loss to a student is—that the expected average lifetime earnings of college graduates was $177,000 more, 42 per cent more, than the average of high school graduates. Thus, individual students also suffer serious economic loss.

[Note the transition phrase, ". . . in addition to talking about national output, let's see how the seriousness of this loss is reflected in each student's potential earning capacity." The use of flashback with preview is a particularly good transition type. Here, she also gives one support and uses factual material, whereas she used testimony to support her "loss to the nation" point. There are two very good reasons for the difference: (1) variety, and (2) the nature of the material. There was no specific estimate of the relationship between increases in output and increases in capital formation by education. Thus, the *relationship* between the two was stressed. Since there *was* a specific dollar estimate it was useful to use the estimate itself. When the factual material consists of monetary averages it is relevant that she include the date in her documentation. This particular speaker avoided one of the pitfalls which can be distracting in the presentation of documentation. Note that she cited, not the *NEA Journal* but the *National Education Association Journal*. The avoidance of letter names is important with an audience which may not know the journals in the particular field being discussed. Citing "the *NEA Journal*" to a general audience may be the same as or worse than using no citation at all. Some of the audience may pause to wonder what the letters stand for and miss the substance of the quotation. An audience should never be allowed to "stray" from the point being made in a speech. A lack of understanding or misunderstanding of the point may result.]

While we can talk in averages about economic loss, there is no way to measure the loss of new ideas, of human fulfillment which occurs when this tremendous potential is not realized.

[Again, the speaker uses the flashback ("while we can talk in averages about economic loss") plus the moving forward ("there is no way to measure . . ."). This illustrates the fact that although the same type of transition device is used, the same pattern of wording need not be used. Here, the speaker deals with a generalization. While, in this case, the statement may well be self-evident, some good testimony would have strengthened it considerably. It is a telling point, not easily refuted and should have been amplified and used to better advantage.]

The primary cause for these qualified students not attending college is lack of finances. According to the 1962 Office of Education financed Project Talent, each year between 100 and 200,000 able high school graduates who have high aptitude and interest in college—that is they *are* motivated—fail to continue their education primarily because of the lack of money. Dr. Algo Henderson of the American Council of Education substantiated this fact in his report. Dr. Henderson stated that other studies he had seen, including those by the American Youth Committee, the President's Committee on Higher Education and the Commission on Financing Higher Education, concurred with this statement. The problem is not clearing itself up, for a survey financed by the National Science Foundation in 1958 reported almost the same total of above average students kept from college by lack of finances—about 150,000 annually. Thus, although the figures *do* vary somewhat, the consensus seems to be that approximately 125,000 to 150,000 students do not continue their education because of lack of finances.

[Notice how the speaker keeps the language close to the language she used when explaining what she was going to do, both for clarity and for emphasis. Here, she uses more than one piece of supporting material because of the controversial nature of the point; that is, some may deny the validity of a specific survey. The quoted material from Henderson very neatly adds a number of studies to the picture, without requiring additional citations. It it also a short way to get enough material to support her point. In the Henderson citation note that the speaker gave his credentials rather than the specific source of the quotation. In this case the credentials did more to establish his authority (which is her point) than the name of the magazine containing the quotation would have done. The speaker should avoid cluttering his speech with unnecessary documentation by determining what part of the citation best establishes the worth of the particular support you are using. Observe how the speaker points out an obvious fact that the figures vary. The reason for this is two-fold: (1) for accuracy; and (2) because some of the audience may be so concerned with the variance that they fail to move ahead with the speaker to her next point. The speaker should always tell the audience exactly *how* he arrived at his statement.]

Now, I realize there may be other reasons why students do not attend institutions of higher education and I am not denying that. However, existing evidence seems to indicate that the *primary* reason is financial.

[Here, the speaker acknowledges a qualification to her material. If she hadn't, the thought would probably have occurred to her audience. The carefulness in limiting the claim which she says her materials establish aids in establishing *ethos*, trustworthiness.]

Existing sources cannot provide this needed financial assistance. Here, I'd like to show you first, that they *are* not, and secondly, that they *can* not.

[She establishes her next major point, explaining again, how she intends to handle her materials. She is careful to "bring" the audience along with her on every point. She makes certain that it is she who determines the method of handling the materials.]

In the five years from 1955 to 1960, according to the *World Almanac* for 1963, total scholarships issued increased only 10 per cent. Meanwhile, according to the Department of Health, Education and Welfare, total enrollment increased 25 per cent over this same five-year period. Because of this situation, it is not surprising that hearings before the House of Representatives in 1963 revealed that the percentage of undergraduates benefiting from college-administered assistance programs, the major source of student support, has declined in recent years.

[Here, the speaker feels it is necessary to use three pieces of evidence. This passage is a bit over-documented but this was hard to avoid since each bit of material did come from a different source. Try not to let the documentation, however brief, interfere with the flow of ideas. In this particular case, where the materials were to be examined in detail by the audience, it was hard to avoid. Use good judgment in other situations.]

Not only are scholarships too few and often too small, but also they are concentrated among a relatively small number of schools. The availability of scholarships, in other words, simply does not match the available room in colleges. Elmer D. West pointed this out in his book *Financial Aid to the Undergraduate* which was published in 1963. He states that besides the concentration of scholarship money in schools which may not be able to use it, only six states gave over 80 per cent of the financial assistance to higher education today, thus showing a concentration of scholarship funds geographically.

[Again, the speaker uses the device of a summary of what has been said juxtaposed with a preview or moving forward. The date in the documentation is important here. The audience might like to know who Elmer D. West is. However, in this case, the speaker was presenting strictly factual material which could easily be checked in a variety of sources; that is, she was not using West as an authority (although she could have) but as the source of factual material. Giving the size of the average scholarship would have helped support her statement that "not only are scholarships too few [which she did deal with] and often too small. . . ." The material is easily available and could have been inserted without seeming obtrusive; for example, "and the average scholarship of $——, often too small. . . ." The second sentence of this passage is also not clear.]

Moreover, although some loan funds are available, they cannot hope to solve the problem because of restrictions, high interest rates, and the necessity, in some cases, to start repayment immediately. The *Congressional Digest* of October 1963 pointed out that although the American Medical Association, for instance, has loans for college students, these students must have completed their undergraduate education. Most other loans have some kind of "strings attached." The *Digest* also pointed out that most bank loans require either collateral or a co-signer who does have the collateral—both may be unavailable to a poor student. Even the United Student Aid Fund, the largest private organization designed to underwrite bank loans made to students, requires that colleges must match these funds; thus, if the college is not willing to match them, or cannot, then the student cannot use the loan.

[There could have been a smoother transition between her point concerning scholarships and her point concerning loans, although as the speaker gave the speech, she did *vocally* emphasize "loan funds" to emphasize the fact that she was no longer talking about scholarships. Her decision to use a series of examples to illustrate various limitations in three different kinds of loans was wise. Her use of specific names is good. A better example could have been found than the one using the American Medical Association, which would have been more representative of her undergraduate "strings attached" argument. There was no need to bring in graduate education at all. Also, there was no particular need to quote the *Digest* when saying that most bank loans require either collateral or a co-signer; it's a widely accepted fact. It was particularly good to use a variety of kinds of loan programs: (1) professionally based loan funds; (2) general bank loans; and (3) private loan funds designed specifically for loans to students. The use of the United Student Aid Fund was particularly good because it is "the largest" private organization of its sort.]

Thus, existing sources *are not* solving the problem. And, in fact, they *can not* solve it.

[A summary with a preview used again as a transition device. The words *"are not"* and *"can not"* were underlined in the text because the speaker was particularly careful to emphasize them vocally, both by saying them very forcefully and by pausing a little after them.]

The American Assembly at Columbia University pointed out the obvious variations in wealth among the fifty states, which are great, and that the poorer states are already making a tax effort out of proportion to their ability to pay. The House Committee on Education and Labor reported in 1960 that many states and localities have reached their fiscal limit. Thus, there is a great probability that many states have reached their fiscal limit, not only for higher education funds, but for funds of any kind. The American Assembly concluded that the states in recent years have had only from 13 to 15 per cent of the tax dollar.

[The statement that wealth varies among the states could have gone undocumented as a generally accepted fact. "The American Assembly at Columbia University pointed out the obvious variations in wealth among the fifty states, which are great ..." is an awkward sentence in any event. It was, however, necessary to document the part of the statement: "the poorer states are already making a tax effort out of proportion to their ability to pay." It was also necessary to document the fact that "many states and localities have reached their fiscal limit." Examples might have helped, but the statement is adequate as it stands. The factual material could have been briefly interpreted for maximum effectiveness: "Thus, no matter how well intentioned the states may be, they simply have less to work with than the Federal Government." This amplification would have served two purposes: (1) to indicate very clearly that she is not blaming the states for laxity or ill will but that they do not have sufficient tax revenues to alleviate the problem; and (2) to emphasize her point that since existing sources of income cannot take care of the program, the Federal Government should adopt the program she is advocating.]

State constitutions preclude some states from fully tapping certain tax sources, notably the property tax and personal income tax. An example is Illinois. And, since state tax systems are generally of the regressive variety, attempts to increase them are strongly resisted.

[Since these statements are based on easily checked facts, documentation was not necessary. A *brief* example was all that was necessary at this point, although possibly she could have described the practices of several other states for additional support.]

This excerpt constitutes about half the speech. The speaker went on to point out that, in addition to state revenues and the private sources of educational income she mentioned, corporations have provided funds. They represent, however, only a very small portion of the amount needed and cannot in the future be the stable bases needed to guarantee educational opportunity.

She concluded that since existing sources cannot meet the need, the Federal Government represents the most stable base on which to plan a long-range program. The federal underwriting of student loans would cost the government very little since student borrowers have an excellent record of repaying loans. The program could operate through already existing agencies and would have the obvious advantages of increasing personal income and the gross national product, while at the same time affording personal fulfillment and producing a greater reservoir of new ideas.

> [Here are the rest of the speaker's main arguments to support her basic contention. By this time, her method of analysis, way of handling supporting material, type of outline, and simple functional style can be seen. Each speaker, of course, would handle the topic, the materials, and the presentation in a somewhat different way. The particular value of this speaker's method is that it is extremely clear. What lines of argument did this speaker use? What types of supporting material? As you answer these questions also consider: How would *you* have analyzed this speaker's topic? Would you have supported it in the same manner or can you think of other ways? Would you have used other lines of argument? A different method of presentation? A different sequence of materials within each main point?]

The final remarks were:

> Since many qualified high school graduates do not receive a higher education because they lack the necessary finances, since existing sources cannot provide this needed financial assistance, and since only the Federal Government can provide a stable financial base for needy high school graduates, I urge you to agree with me: that the Federal Government should guarantee an opportunity for education to all qualified high school graduates.
>
> [In this version of the speech, since the speaker knows very precisely *how* her audience will be using the materials, she closes by simply repeating her main lines of argument and by making a straight-forward appeal for the acceptance of the proposal. Note the difference between the summary of this speech and the summary of the other version which you will read. What type and how direct an appeal the speaker uses in closing is, of course, determined by the nature of the topic and the nature of the audience. In this instance, the speaker knew that her audience would be using the materials and arguments of her speech very directly

and at length. Therefore, her appeal could be very direct and very short.]

We shall include and discuss only a small portion of what is basically the same speech as it was delivered to a *general* audience. The purpose of this is to demonstrate the concept of audience analysis and how it determines the speaker's way of handling his materials. As we go along, the basic differences between the two speeches will be noted. Pay particular attention to the amount of amplification several of her ideas receive in the second speech and the care taken to bring her audience more directly into the speech. Also note the slightly more colloquial style and the attempts at "attention getting" which were unnecessary with the first audience.

SECOND VERSION

Every year there are from 100,000 to 200,000 able, qualified students who are denied the opportunity to attend college because they lack the money to do so: from 100,000 to 200,000 students— enough students to fill ten universities with from 10,000 to 20,000 students for one year. Remember, I said, able, qualified students— students who want to go to college, who are capable of going to college but who can not. Why? Because they aren't as lucky as we are. Because their parents can't afford to send them. Because, for a variety of reasons, they can't get a scholarship or a loan. Because a part-time job often just doesn't pay for the expenses of college. Later I will show you how, if by some miraculous chance, they could get all three: the "average" loan, the "average" scholarship, and the "average" part-time job—most of them still would not be financially able to go to college.

[Here, the speaker must work harder to get the audience interested in her topic and to get them involved in the topic. She selects one of the most startling facts of the speech and begins to build around it. The figures 100,000–200,000 are impressive in themselves, but they are made still more impressive by the speaker's amplification that the students would fill ten universities of fairly large size. As soon as possible the speaker brings the members of her audience still more directly into the speech by saying that she is talking about students "who aren't as lucky" as they are. The orientation is longer because this audience needs more time to become adjusted to the topic. In addition, the materials the speaker has selected for the orientation begin to orient the audience toward her particular position. Note also, that the question, "Why?" calls again for the audience to participate rather directly in the speech. They must silently answer a question. In addition, by beginning three sentences with "because," she has the device of parallel structure. Repetition produces the piling up effect of the materials which support her position. Next, these three sentences are separated from the following point, which is that *even if* the students could have the advantages of all sources, they still wouldn't be able to attend college. The parallel structure is now effectively broken by interrupting the sequence of sentences beginning with "because."]

The irony of the situation is that these are students living in a country whose government stated these two fundamental principles as the basis for education in the United States at the 22nd International Conference on Public Education: "(1) Every person has an equal right to educational opportunities; and (2) An educated citizenry is essential to freedom and human welfare." Every person has an equal right to educational opportunities. Yet most of us would agree that in reality, as the House Committee on Education and Labor has commented, ". . . opportunities for public education vary widely in the United States."

[The word "irony" helps to prepare the audience, to put it into the right frame of mind for her next words. She prepares the way for the presentation of her position by contrasting the stated principles with the realities. The word "irony" also reinforces the point. Observe how the speaker works to suggest whenever she can the things most people in the audience would agree with: ". . . most of us would agree that . . . opportunities for public education vary widely." The speaker has anticipated that most of her audience would be *against* federal aid to higher education for a variety of reasons; thus, it became important for her to proceed more slowly than before, maximizing whatever points of agreement were possible at the outset.]

It is precisely because there *are* these wide variations in opportunities, and because existing programs have done all too little to lessen them, that I believe the Federal Government should guarantee an opportunity for higher education to all qualified high school graduates.

[Here, the speaker makes a clear statement of purpose and of her position on the topic. She explains briefly what led her to her position.]

Before telling you in some detail why I think the Federal Government should guarantee an opportunity for higher education, I will explain several of the terms I will be using.

[Next, the speaker begins to define terms. This is especially necessary when the audience is uninformed about the possible differences in meanings of the terms; for instance, that the Federal Government could "guarantee an opportunity" in a variety of ways. They may never have considered a federally underwritten loan

program as one possibility. Here, the definition not only functions
to clarify the term but also, given this early, eliminates a number
of proposals toward which the audience is unfavorably disposed.
Because she says precisely what program she is advocating, her
listeners may not consider other proposals at all.]

The substance of the arguments used in the second version of the
speech were basically the same as those used in the first version. So
let us proceed to the conclusion of version two.

Recently we have heard a lot about television's "vast wasteland."
But, we have heard practically nothing about the 100,000 to 200,000
people each year who inhabit higher education's vast wastelands of
lost human potential, lost chance for economic improvement, lost
new ideas which would benefit the national welfare.

[This conclusion is much different from the brief, simply stated
summary of the other version. The topic of "television's vast wasteland" was, at the time the speech was given, much discussed and
argued. She uses that fact to advantage, both because she has
an effective metaphor (even though the analogy is somewhat
strained) and also to prove her point; that is, that if people are
hearing a lot about "television's vast wasteland" how much more
they should be hearing about what she terms "higher education's
vast wasteland."]

This failure to invest in the most basic resource the nation has,
human potential, would in any time be serious. At a time when we
are competing on every front with another economic-political system, it may prove to be disastrous.

[She adds the point that if the audience is unconcerned with the
problem in general, then it should be concerned with it at this
particular time. Note how she continues to suggest that the
audience is directly concerned with the problem, thus preparing
the way for her next question.]

What can we do about this problem? Several rather specific things.
We can become very much aware of the problem. We can talk
about it with the people we see and we can write about it to our
representative in Congress who can do something about it directly.
They have expressed their good faith in dealing with the problem
by increasing the amount of money in the National Defense Education Loan Fund. But the lack of sufficient funds and the restrictions
on how the loans are used make the NDEA Fund at best only a
partial and temporary measure.

[The speaker is no longer *suggesting* direct involvement; rather,
she questions the audience very directly by using the word "we."
She offers two possible ways in which the audience can use the
speech and also suggests that the majority in Congress is willing to

adopt a somewhat similar plan, thereby giving added authority to the reasonableness of her proposal. This mention of the National Defense Education Act was put into the speech after another student asked, when she heard the speech being practiced: "How do you know the members of Congress would really consider such a program?"]

The realities of our system of education must coincide with the aims of our system of education. Since they do not, since large numbers of qualified high school graduates do not receive a higher education because they can't afford it, since existing sources are not and cannot provide this needed financial assistance, since the Federal Government can provide a stable financial base for needy high school graduates, and since a federally underwritten loan program for students would cost the government almost nothing, but would reap great returns both for the nation and for the individual, I hope you will agree with me that the Federal Government should guarantee an opportunity for higher education to all qualified high school graduates.

Note that first the speaker repeats a fact with which most of her audience would agree. Then, she repeats the line of thinking which led her to her original position that "the Federal Government should guarantee an opportunity for higher education to all qualified high school graduates." She again uses parallel construction with the word "since" to effect a building-up of arguments for added strength before asking for acceptance of her position. The conclusion to this version of the speech is three times longer than that to the other version. Follow her strategy:

1. She calls attention to a problem which most of her audience has been discussing.
2. She says the problem is more serious and calls for more attention than that of "television's vast wasteland."
3. She relates her problem to the general problem of the Cold War and tries to establish just how central it is to the general scheme of things.
4. Presuming that the members of her audience are now impressed by the magnitude and the immediacy of the problem, she offers ways in which they can help. The ways call for no great effort, but are *specific* "ways" that the audience can use the speech after they have left the room.
5. She closes first with a relatively noncontroversial statement, then moves instantly into her main line of argument including: (1) the noncontroversial statement that large numbers of students are not going on to higher education; (2) the statement for which she has offered most of her support; that is, that existing sources cannot provide the money; (3) her conclusion that only the Federal Government can handle the problem;

(4) a "reply" to the most often heard objection to her kind of proposal; and (5) an indication of the possible rewards her proposal could bring. Only then does she restate her position.

Before evaluating the two speeches, one more word must be said concerning version two. Here, we have tried to show how it is possible to attempt identification with an audience that: (1) is general in nature and (2) is somewhat opposed to the speaker's position. The speaker works to seek some agreement before moving into more controversial areas. She works to appeal to the audience without becoming so subservient to it that she weakens her original thesis. Her strategy has been outlined for you to follow. The term "strategy," unfortunately often taken to imply something underhanded and devious, is in fact an honorable and extremely useful term for the speaker. It denotes movement based on the careful analysis of the situation at hand. Thus, after surveying all of the available means of persuasion, the speaker selects those which best aid his purpose. The quality of the speaker's choices determines the value of the speaker's rhetoric.

There are two additional points which should be made before starting an evaluation of these speeches: (1) the speaker's use of notes; and (2) her use of visual aids. This particular speaker chose to use a general outline and small cards with all the materials she wanted to quote verbatim written out for easy handling. Although the speaker could easily remember most of the quoted material without referring to the cards, she decides to read from them, particularly her "testimony," for two reasons: (1) to give added authority to the speech; and (2) to provide a change in bodily movement. When the materials were read from the cards, she was particularly careful to maintain eye contact with her audience, especially at important words or key phrases.

This particular speaker generally feels no special stage fright, and, in fact, is used to speaking to audiences, large and small. However, a few notes do provide added assurance for any speaker and allay the fears of a beginning speaker.

During the speech the speaker used one visual aid, the blackboard. To the left, figures were added up to indicate the amount of money a student could get from all sources: average scholarship + average loan + average amount earned on a part-time job. To the right were the costs of an average year of college at both a private and a public institution. Although these figures could have been handled verbally, the use of visual aids at this point operated in two ways: (1) to call attention, to underline one of her more important points; and (2) to provide a change in bodily movement. Visual aids are effective only as they serve to underline points. They should not become objects of display in and of themselves.

In general, this speaker has done an effective job. In both speeches, she explains what she is going to do and then proceeds to do it. Her organization is clear and she usually has careful transitions between each major idea to show the relationship between her chief points.

One of the speech's outstanding features is the speaker's good judgment about how much supporting material each point requires. When only one piece of support is necessary, she uses only one; when more are necessary, she uses two or three. She avoids using too much supporting material, and thereby filling up her speech-time with unnecessary evidence at less strategic points, and of using too little evidence to support her major points. The speaker also uses a variety of types of supporting material: information, example, testimony, comparison, definition, and visual aids. Thus, she does not rely on any one type of support and at the same time provides a *variety* of supporting materials which maintain attention.

In both versions of the speech this speaker considers her audience. Her first audience came to hear the speech because it was especially interested in the topic and was, in general, fairly well-informed about it. Thus, the speaker did not have to spend so much time getting its attention as she did with the second group. The first group was particularly interested in sources so the speaker gave more detailed documentation in her first version than in the second. In the summary, the first group did not have to be told directly *what* to do with the speech; they came to the speech with the intention of using it in very specific ways. On the other hand, the second group probably needed some prodding to do something about the speech after they left the room. The speeches could have been more impressive stylistically. A speaker should first work, however, to achieve clarity; he can then work for refinements of speaking. The style of these speeches is that of simple functional prose.

Two outstanding points about this particular speaker's delivery should be mentioned. First, the speaker enjoys giving speeches. She conveys this to her audience. Secondly, this particular speaker never speaks without a real feeling of confidence in her knowledge of the topic. She is never unprepared and this confidence allows her audience to sit back relaxed, feeling that it is listening to somebody who knows what she is talking about. One reason for this confidence, in addition to the fact that she is always well-prepared, is that she speaks often: in classes, in meetings, in formal public speaking situations. Nothing can, in the end, replace practice in aiding a beginning speaker become a polished, adept public speaker. But practice without thorough knowledge of principles generally proceeds on a hit-or-miss basis. The more a speaker knows about what *should* be done and *why* it should be done, the more efficiently he can practice to achieve the skill which makes him a vigorous and effective speaker who actively participates in making his environment the kind he would like it to be.

Summary

Throughout this chapter, and the text, we have tried to stress the interrelationships among the five canons of rhetoric and the dependence of the last step, the actual giving of the speech, on all the preceding ones. As the speaker understands this, he begins to acquire a rhetorical perspective.

Only so well as the speaker exhibits that he has chosen the *best* available means of persuasion has he made an effective speech. The available means of persuasion include all the speaker's resources: his proof, his organization of those proofs, the use of clear and vigorous language to animate his ideas, and the fluent, communicative delivery of them. In the final analysis, the key question in evaluating speeches is this: "Has the speaker chosen from *all* the available means of persuasion, the *best* ones for his purpose?" If the answer is yes, he has effectively seen the world through a rhetorical perspective.

Rhetorical Exercises

(1) Design a critique sheet which would be useful in the criticism of speeches given in class. What items would you include? If you already use a critique sheet in class, discuss each item thoroughly. Now that you have had supervised experience in giving speeches, does the critique sheet become more useful? How effectively does the critique reveal the total impact of the speech?

(2) Listen to a contemporary speech which you attend outside of class and try rhetorical criticism. Then, try to evaluate a speech you have

seen on television. What differences were there between your criticism of the first speech and your criticism of the latter? Some of the questions you might want to ask are:

(a) Who spoke? Did the audience know him? Well? Was he given an introduction? Do you think the audience listened in a certain way because of who was speaking? What did the speaker reveal about himself as he spoke?

(b) Who was in the audience? Were they likely to have preconceived ideas about the topic and the speaker? About his position on the topic?

(c) Where did the speech take place? In what kind of immediate environment? In what kind of ideological environment? Did the speaker refer to the place? How did place affect the speech?

(d) At what time was the speech given? Was the time of day relevant? Time in the "life" of the problem being discussed?

(e) What was the purpose of the speech? Was it implied or expressed? Did the speaker fulfill his purpose?

(f) What did the speaker say? Were his main ideas clearly stated? Were they well supported? How would you evaluate the quality of the premises on which the speech was based? Was the content appropriate for the audience?

(g) Was the speech clearly organized? Was it arranged for maximum effectiveness? Were there clear transitions between ideas and internal summaries when necessary? Did he spend enough time on each point to make it meaningful?

(h) Was the style clear? Appropriate to the occasion, the audience and the speaker? Was it vivid and animated? Was it impressive?

(i) Was the speaker direct and communicative? Was he fluent?

(j) What was your overall impression of the speech? Would you like to hear this speaker again?

(3) What can the speaker gain by reading the speeches of the past?

(4) What insights can the critic gain from speaking experience? Discuss your answer in class.

(5) Read several speeches given by the same speaker. Were the audience, the occasion, the time, and the place reflected in the speeches? In what ways?

(6) Read some criticism of famous speeches of the past. See, for example, Marie Hochmuth's "Lincoln's First Inaugural" in *American Speeches*, pp. 21–71. You might also want to look at the criticisms of famous speakers in the three volumnes of *History and Criticism of American Public Address*, and in the *Quarterly Journal of Speech*.

Following is a list of works on criticism and on the nature of criticism.

Collateral Readings

Auer, J. Jeffrey, ed., *Antislavery and Disunion, 1858–1861: Studies in the Rhetoric of Compromise and Conflict.* New York: Harper and Row, Publishers, 1963. Prepared under the auspices of The Speech Association of America.

Baird, A. Craig, and Lester Thonssen, "Methodology in the Criticism of Public Address," *Quarterly Journal of Speech* (April, 1947), pp. 134–38.

Black, Edwin, *Rhetorical Criticism: A Study in Method.* New York: The Macmillan Company, 1965.

Croft, Albert J., "The Functions of Rhetorical Criticism," *QJS* (October, 1956), pp. 283–91.

Goodrich, Chauncey A., *Select British Eloquence.* Photo offset edition. Indianapolis: The Bobbs-Merrill Company, Inc., 1963. Preceding selections of speeches by each speaker, there is a sketch of their lives and critical and explanatory notes. Originally published in 1852.

Mouat, L. H., "An Approach to Rhetorical Criticism," in *The Rhetorical Idiom, Essays Presented to Herbert A. Wichelns,* ed., Donald C. Bryant. Ithaca: Cornell University Press, 1958, pp. 161–77.

Nichols, Marie Hochmuth, *Rhetoric and Criticism.* Baton Rouge: Louisiana State University Press, 1963.

Oliver, Robert, *History of Public Speaking in America.* Boston: Allyn and Bacon, 1965.

Parrish, Wayland Maxfield, "The Study of Speeches," in *American Speeches,* ed., Wayland Maxfield Parrish and Marie Hochmuth. New York: Longmans, Green and Co., 1954, pp. 1–20.

Reid, Loren D., "The Perils of Rhetorical Criticism," *QJS* (December, 1944), pp. 416–22.

Thonssen, Lester, and A. Craig Baird, *Speech Criticism: The Development of Standards for Rhetorical Appraisal.* New York: Ronald Press, 1948.

Wichelns, Herbert A., "The Literary Criticism of Oratory," in the *Rhetorical Idiom,* pp. 5–42.

Wrage, Ernest J., "Public Address: A Study in Social and Intellectual History," *QJS* (December, 1947), pp. 451–57.

APPENDIX

OUR BROKEN MAINSPRING *

A Speech by Adlai E. Stevenson

It is hard indeed to pay adequate homage in words to a man whose own words were so fresh, so apt and fitting to the important issues of the day.

But I am encouraged by one fact. Dr. A. Powell Davies did not feel that his office as a minister of religion debarred him from comment upon contemporary problems. On the contrary, he saw that he could make his message relevant to his people only by showing it at work in the concrete issues of their daily lives.

I think of a story my grandfather Stevenson, a devout Scotch-Presbyterian, told about the preacher who was driving along a back road in the South when he espied a parishioner wearily clearing up a poor, stony field. "That's a fine job you and the Lord have done cleaning up that rocky field," he shouted. "Thank you, parson," the man replied. "But I wish you could have seen it when the Lord had it all to himself."

Dr. Davies believed that God is dependent on man, as man is on God. He believed that the clergy above all were responsible for making a reality of the bond between God and man, and he was fearless in letting his congregation and the world know the truth as he saw it. He had a sensitive awareness of peril to the individual in our day of bigness, of statism and conformity. Therefore he was impelled to fight for the oppressed and the persecuted; to fight for equal justice for all and the rights inherent in our citizenship. Ardently he defended freedom of the mind, free speech, the right of the dissenter to speak, the duty of the conformist to listen. And his compassion was boundless.

It was the tardiness of the American social conscience in understanding the severity of its ordeal, its contest with authoritarianism that made Dr.

---

* A lecture inaugurating the A. Powell Davies Memorial Lectures, established in memory of Dr. Davies, for many years the much respected Minister of the All Souls Unitarian Church in Washington, D.C. It was presented in Constitution Hall, under the title of "The Political Relevance of Moral Principle," in Washington on Sunday, January 18, 1959, and has been somewhat abbreviated for this publication.

Davies impatient, that made him work so hard to awaken us to the perils. He literally wore himself out trying to mobilize public opinion, trying to induce every American to hold himself personally responsible for the preservation of freedom.

From the mountain of his vision, Dr. Davies constantly proclaimed the political relevance of moral principle and of religion as a "judgment of righteousness." From the dusty plain of politics I would like in my turn to reaffirm this relevance. I like to believe that there may be some value in echoing testimony from a layman who has spent his middle life in the press and confusion of great events—in government service, in diplomacy and in politics.

There is a phrase of Dr. Davies that stays in my mind. I do not know when I have heard a more terse and pregnant summing up of our predicament. "The world," he said, "is now too dangerous for anything but the truth, too small for anything but brotherhood." This I believe to be in broad measure a correct estimate of the condition of human society, which is now capable, with a few hydrogen bombs, of extinguishing itself. Today we can all be killed by the same bombs or atomic fallout. In that sense we have attained a desperate physical solidarity. But moral and social solidarity in the family of man is still to be found.

Not so long ago I visited Dr. Albert Schweitzer in his primitive jungle hospital in French Equatorial Africa, and he told me that he considered this the most dangerous period in history. I said, "In contemporary history?" "No," he said, "in all human history." "Why?" "Because," he said, "heretofore nature has controlled man in the last analysis, but now man has learned to control elemental forces of nature—before he has learned to control himself."

Many of us seem, here in our country, to rely on some mythical God-given superiority of the white Western world to save us. And my concern is that there is more evidence that the Communists accept the reality of the human condition than we do.

It is impossible to spend weeks traveling around the Soviet Union, as I did this summer, without taking away an overwhelming impression of thrust and purpose in most aspects of Soviet life. The revolutionary ardor of the early days to be sure has cooled with time but even the very pragmatic political leaders seem to believe profoundly in the truth of their way of life and are quietly confident that it will sweep the whole world in time. I think they sincerely believe that their methods, their aspirations, their dreams, make up the final truth about the nature of man and society; that collective man in the collective state is the ultimate unfolding of human destiny, the end of history, the "far-off divine event" for which mankind has been in long travail, the vision of "all things made new" that has haunted men's minds ever since Christianity thrust into human thought the intoxicating ideal of a perfected humanity.

From this conviction, if I have not overstated it, flow two consequences. The first is that no effort, no dedication, no sacrifice is too great that may help to realize the Communist party's goals in Soviet society. The second is that no corner of humanity can be a matter of indifference to the Communists, because the whole human race is destined to become in time one communist brotherhood.

The energy, the drive, the dedication in the u.s.s.r. spill over into international affairs in ways that we are only now beginning to realize. In part, of course, this is the restless concern which all imperial powers must exercise, especially when the peoples they control are as restive and unreliable as the captive peoples in Russia's European empire. But Communist activity, planning and efforts in trade and aid are not confined to areas of Communist control. They are world-wide, and there is no corner of the earth's surface which the Russians think too insignificant for their attention, none.

All this we know—or begin to know. But I wonder how often we try to grasp the scale of dedication that lies behind it. Why should they be so busy? Why so much work and thought? Why such diversion of precious resources? Why such patience through every setback, such forward thrusts through every point of Western weakness? Heaven knows, we only want to stay home. Why don't they? Why do we never meet an isolationist Communist? These are some of the questions that haunted me when I confronted at first hand this iron, forceful, formidable way of life.

And I do not think that there is any doubt about the answer. Part of it is simply needed foreign trade. Part is fear, the search for security through friends. And part is the historical centrifugal forces in Russia which have been pressing outward for two hundred years—to the Pacific, the Balkans, the Middle East, the Straits, and so on. But the important thing is that the Soviet Russians believe in their truth, as the men of the Western world once believed in theirs. They, not we, are firing the shots that are heard round the world—and also the satellites that orbit above it. The fact that their faith is in many ways an evil perversion of the great propositions that once made the blood course in Western veins does not alter the fact that their tempo is dynamic and rapid, ours sluggish—even, I think, to ourselves.

Surely, the reason cannot be that we Americans have lost our vision of truth and brotherhood. No country on earth owes the sense of community more explicitly to the fact that it is united not by race or nationality but by fidelity to an idea. We were born "dedicated to a proposition" and our greatest leaders—the Jeffersons, the Lincolns, the Wilsons—were not great because they achieved purely American purposes, but because they were able to speak for humanity at large and extend their vision to the whole family of man.

Nor, I believe, can we find fault with the substance of what we have endearingly called the American dream. Its truths are still "self-evident." The possession of liberty and the pursuit of happiness—rightly understood —these have not been overthrown as the highest goods of human society. Indeed, the ferment of our freedom works inexorably and dangerously in the Communist world. No one can have visited Poland without seeing how little the Polish people really accept their servitude and how they look beyond their neighbors to the free world as the reservoir of power and hope.

But, alas, on the basis of the record, one would hardly suspect that the Western world possessed so powerful a weapon. Our talk—in diplomacy, in strategy, in aid and trade, in all of the intricacies of our world-wide relations—has been to a depressing degree purely defensive. We have offered aid not to help others but to shield ourselves. We have reacted to countless Soviet initiatives; acted on our own initiative barely at all. We watch the skies for other people's Sputniks and listen to the telegraph wires for other people's moves. Yet we are the free men of this universe; we are the children of liberty, the beneficiaries of unequaled abundance, and heirs of the highest, proudest political tradition ever known to man!

Why this lack of initiative? Why this paralysis of will? What have we done to our truth, our brotherhood—the supreme truth of freedom, the Christian truth of brotherly love? Have they failed? Or have we?

There is no more urgent duty than to discover why we have failed, if we have, and I think we have, and to get back into the arena, aspiring, striving, fighting, if you please, once more for what we believe. An examination of what you might call our collective conscience is to my mind far more important than particular projects or programs. You can have a perfect assembly of pieces in your watch, but they are worthless if the mainspring is broken. I am not worried about our various pieces—our technology, our science, our machines, our resources. But I am concerned, desperately concerned, about our mainspring. That it has run down, we know. But is it broken; is it broken beyond repair? In the last analysis, no question is worth more consideration in America today.

And I would like to suggest some of the ways in which it seems to me we have enfeebled the great central pulse of our freedom, the great truth of liberty, which, more than any other nation, we first set working in the modern world.

Goethe, who also lived through a crisis of freedom, said to his generation: "What you have inherited from your fathers, earn over again for yourselves or it will not be yours." We inherited this freedom we talk about so glibly. We seem unaware that it has to be remade and re-earned in each generation of man. One reason for this failure is, I believe, passing at last. In recent years we were stifled with complacent self-confidence. We believed ourselves dominant in every field. We talked of "the American Century." We forgot the ardors and the efforts that had given us a measure of pre-eminence. Complacency made us impervious to ideas, even the obvious idea that we are in danger. So we assumed that all we needed was to sit still and enjoy the "peace and prosperity" that was our right.

I believe that phase is now passing. Our foolish languor has been shaken, if not shattered. We are more ready to examine ourselves and our record.

And it is a privilege of our society that every citizen should make his own inquiry. If I stress one or the other aspect of the problem, this is simply my angle of vision. You will have yours. The urgent thing is to feel the need for re-thinking and to set to work the ultimate energies of a free society—which cannot be done by the fiat of government but only by the troubled conscience of responsible men and women.

I believe—as I have said before—that we have confused the free with the free and easy. If freedom had been the happy, simple, relaxed state of ordinary humanity, man would have everywhere been free—whereas through most of time and space he has been in chains. Do not let us make any mistake about this. The natural government of man is servitude. Tyranny is the normal pattern of government. It is only by intense thought, by great effort, by burning idealism and unlimited sacrifice that freedom has prevailed as a system of government. And the efforts which were first necessary to create it are fully as necessary to sustain it in our own day.

He who offers this thing that we call freedom as the soft option is a deceiver or himself deceived. He who sells it cheap or offers it as the by-product of this or that economic system is knave or fool. For freedom demands infinitely more care and devotion than any other political system. It puts consent and personal initiative in the place of command and obedience. By relying upon the devotion and initiative of ordinary citizens, it gives up the harsh but effective disciplines that underpin all the tyrannies which over the millennia have stunted the full stature of man.

But of what use is escape from external restraint if given the opportunity man simply stunts himself? If freedom means ease alone, if it means shirking the hard disciplines of learning, if it means evading the rigors and rewards of creative activity, if it means more expenditure on advertising than on education, if it means "bachelor cooking" and "life adjustment" courses in the schools, and the steady cult of the trivial and the mediocre, if it means—worst of all—indifference, even contempt for all but athletic excellence in our educational system, we may keep for a time the forms of free society, but its spirit will be dead.

I believe we have had enough of adjustment, of conformity, of easy options and the least common denominator in our system. We need instead to see the "pursuit of happiness" in terms which are historically proven and psychologically correct. The dreary failure in history of all classes committed to pleasure and profit alone, the vacuity and misery accompanying the sole pursuit of ease—the collapse of the French aristocracy, the corruption of imperial Rome, the decline and fall of the resplendent Manchus—all these facts of history do not lose their point because the pleasures of today are mass pleasures and no longer the enjoyments of an elite. If we become a nation of Bourbons, numbers will not save us. We shall go their way, too. Vacuity and indifference are not redeemed by the fact that everyone can share in them. They merely restrict the circle from which regeneration can come.

I say this—I hope you will believe me—in no Puritan or pleasure-hating spirit. On the contrary, there is no boredom, no misery to equal the pursuit of distraction alone. We do not slip into happiness. It is strenuously sought and earned. A nation glued to recreation, to the television screen, is not simply at a loss before the iron pioneers of the new collective society. It is not even having a good time. No society has ever spent as much as we do on drink and tranquilizers. Can one argue that this is evidence of universal fun? I ran across a quotation from La Bruyère on the court of Louis XIV which struck me as relevant: *"Les joies sont visibles, mais fausses, et les chagrins cachés, mais réels"*—its joys are visible, but artificial, and its sorrows hidden, but real.

But perhaps this misunderstanding of the true nature of happiness and of the conditions of its pursuit is simply an aspect of something else—our misunderstanding of the real nature of freedom. I recall the words of the wise Judge Learned Hand, who warned us that freedom would not survive in our Constitution if it had already died in the hearts of the people. We shall not have a free society unless we have free men.

And how often do we reflect upon what this inner freedom entails? "Give me the man," cries Hamlet, "who is not passion's slave." But this is what we are in danger of becoming, slaves to a tyranny more intimate and inescapable than any that Stalin or Mao Tse-tung could impose. We can be made slaves simply by the clutter and complexity of modern living—which notoriously leaves no time for serious thought and offers every means of distraction so that we can avoid such thought. Between aircraft that take us everywhere more rapidly, newspapers that grow in weight and coverage, news that flashes round the globe, ceaseless and competitive entertainment, fashions—God help us!—that change from sack to trapeze and back again, we can fill up every "unforgiving minute" with enough trash and preoccupation to still forever the deeper voices of the soul. Like Matthew Arnold, we can

> ... see all sights from pole to pole,
> And glance and nod and hustle by,
> And never once possess our soul
> Before we die.

How are we to defend freedom if, for the tyranny of external control we substitute the clattering, cluttering tyranny of internal aimlessness and fuss? This freedom of our souls, freedom at the profoundest level of our being, is not a gift to us by our contemporary way of life. On the contrary, much of this life is a direct conspiracy against it. And if we cannot—by a certain discipline, by readiness for reflection and quiet, by determination to do the difficult and aim at a lasting good—rediscover the real purpose and direction of our existence, we shall not be free. Our society will not be free. And between a chaotic, selfish, indifferent, commercial society and the iron discipline of the Communist world, I would not like to predict the outcome. Outer tyranny with purpose may well triumph over the inner, purposeless tyranny of a confused and aimless way of life.

I doubt if any society in history has faced so great a moral challenge as ours, or needed more desperately to draw on the deepest sources of courage and responsibility. Ours is the first human community in which resources are so abundant that almost no policies lie beyond our capacity for purely physical reasons. What we decide to do, we can do. The inhibitions of poverty—lack of resources, lack of capital, lack of power—do not hold us back. We can accomplish what we aim at. Thus, perhaps for the first time in the world, choice, not means, ends, not instruments, are decisive.

Then again we have proved—drably and dangerously—over the last decade that defensiveness is not a sufficient reason for action. All the policies we have pursued in self-defense have left us still on the defensive. But if we do not act from fear, we must find some other motivation. In free society there is no other alternative but to tap the vigor, the faith, the imagination of the people themselves. We must find out once more who we are, as the psychologists say.

But perhaps the most urgent reason why the quality of our moral response has become the decisive issue in politics is quite simply that most of the major problems of our day present themselves in moral terms, and are probably insoluble without some stirring of generosity, some measure of vision. Let me give you three instances. In the wealthiest nation in the world, at least five million families still live in squalid but remediable poverty. They are a minority. They do not have the votes to force the issue of their misfortune into the front rank of public issues. They depend, for remedies, upon the alert conscience of the majority. But how do we keep the conscience sensitive and alert? By concentrating on our own concerns? By adding the dishwasher to the television set to the air conditioner? By griping over taxes and attacking that great bogey we call "the welfare state"? By closing our minds every time our shiny car takes us through a slum? No—we shall have the dedication, the drive to wipe poverty out of this rich land only if the well-to-do majority of today do not repeat the selfish indifference which, in many communities, has been the epitaph of the well-to-do of yesterday.

Or take the issue of the rights and status of our colored citizens. This is our small share of a world-wide problem. The four hundred years of dominance of men of white skin is ending. The vast colored majority of mankind are seeking the opportunity and the respect which white people have been lucky enough to enjoy for so long—sometimes at the colored people's expense. But, within this world-wide crisis, we in America, with our colored minority, have a major role to play—for good or evil. "The unfinished work" which Lincoln left us, of creating a society in which all men can hold up their heads as equals and self-respecting citizens, can never be accomplished unless there are enough white men and women who resist to the core of their being the moral evil of treating any of God's children as essentially inferior.

Nor is this simply a question of our own national community. I come back to the painful fact that the Communists show a world-wide concern which is largely lacking among the men of the West. The whole human race is their horizon. Their "brotherhood" is materialist, collectivist, atheist, and we dislike it, but it embraces everybody, and it is the framework of policies which take the missionaries of their new order to the ends of the earth. I say with all the emphasis that I can command that we have no corresponding commitment to our fellow man. For hundreds of years, we have preached the Christian promise of brotherhood, but today, when vanishing space and scientific revolution have turned our planet into a single neighborhood, the ideal means little in terms of concern or conviction, in terms of policy or of action.

Here we are in the Atlantic world, 16 per cent of the world's peoples consuming 70 per cent of the world's wealth. We cannot be indifferent to the moral implications of this gigantic gap. I do not know how we can gain a new perspective about the narrow world of plenty and of poverty in which we live unless moral insights of justice and compassion stir us to understand the privileged position in which we live.

We are not going to be stirred to action by our own needs. We are the cushioned, the protected, the fortunate minority. It is not the measure of our morals or the lesson of our history to be spurred on only by fear of Russian encroachment. What we have done has largely been from this motivation, and it has left us on the defensive. Our hope is to accept the implications of our own faith, to make concrete the image of brotherhood which we profess, to set to work to express our dedication in whatever effort or sacrifice the world's needs may dictate. And, if we must always think in terms of contest with the Soviets, let us bear in mind that the ability to create the good life for the greatest numbers will be decisive. This age has been defined in many ways—as a time of conflict in ideology, as a time of ferment in technology, as a period of revolution in science, as an era when at last the means lie at hand to free mankind from the ancient shackles of pain and of hunger. It is all these things—but I believe the true crisis of our time lies at a deeper level. We have indeed conquered means and resources unknown at earlier ages. We have had thrown open to us frontiers of choice which would have left earlier ages stupefied by their scale and their scope.

But all this freedom and elbow room only thrusts onto us with more force the fundamental issue of the truth that is within us. We can use our wealth, our capacity for some vision of truth, some ideal of brotherhood, or we can imprison ourselves within the selfishness of our own concerns and the limitations of a narrow nationhood. This is the dimension of our crisis.

You may argue that these qualities of dedication, of selflessness, are pretty remote from the realities of politics. They are all very well for private life, but what part can they play in the rough and tumble of partisanship, of primaries, conventions and election campaigns? Ambition, drive, material interests, political skills, the arts of maneuver—all these, you say, have their part, but do not let us pretend that the democratic process is primarily a school of virtue or an arena of moral combat.

And yet, I wonder. It has been the view of great philosophers and great statesmen that our system of free government depends in the first instance upon the virtue of its citizens. Montesquieu made virtue the condition of republican government; Washington declared that it could not survive without it. We have had a hundred and seventy-five years of it and no one can deny that the system has survived a remarkable amount of skulduggery. In fact, it is probably a tougher system than its founders imagined. Yet I believe they are right. For no democratic system can survive without at least a large and an active leaven of citizens in whom dedication and selflessness are not confined to private life but are the fundamental principles of their activity in the public sphere.

Naked interest and ambition will carry a lot of people naturally and inevitably into politics. We do not need societies for the promotion of lobbies. Interests, good and bad, will promote themselves. Nor, in any generation do we lack politicians whose only principle of action is the advancement of their own career—the starry-eyed opportunists and all the other eager men in a hurry to the top. But into what state must politics degenerate if that is all we find active in the political arena? That and sectional interests played upon by personal ambitions? There have been such periods, but our democratic system survived them because such epochs were followed and cleansed by periods of disinterested reform.

But there has never been any disinterested reform without disinterested reformers. And here we come to the essential contribution made by dedication and selflessness to the public good. No one ever did any good in politics without readiness for endless hard work—for the grinding, boring, tedious work, as well as the glamorous, high-sounding, headline-hitting work. The painstaking hours collecting the facts, the hours in committee and conference, the hours in persuasion and argument, the hours of defeat and disappointment, the hours of disgust and revulsion at the darker sides of human behavior—these cannot be supported without energy and devotion. No reform comes easy; even the most obvious will have its entrenched enemies. Each one is carried to us on the bent and the weary backs of patient, dedicated men and women.

They are not only dedicated in their readiness to give energy and work to the cause; they must also have sufficiently clear sight and open minds and hearts to see the need for reform in the first place. But clear sight or an open heart for the needs of others is again something that hardly "comes naturally." We have so many needs of our own—our families, our jobs, our homes, our fortunes, our prospects. We are hemmed in with needs and interests, weighty, urgent, honorable, human needs and interests, even if they are exclusively our own. It takes an extra dimension of vision to see beyond our inner circle of personal interest. Most people, most of the time, do not possess it, that extra dimension of vision, which is one reason why self-regarding interests make up so much of the stuff of politics. And this, I suppose, is why the men and women of genuine, imperturbable public spirit seem so few and far between.

I sometimes think there is a danger of this element of vision vanishing almost wholly from our political life. In the main we are so comfortable; so many evils of the past have shrunk in size and almost out of sight. At the same time, people marry much younger; they have larger families and are profoundly involved in earning a living, making careers and safeguarding the future of their children. It is more difficult, they say, to give time to public affairs when private life is so urgent and so absorbing. Yet is it, I wonder, more urgent and absorbing than it was a hundred years ago, when men not only married young, had large families, built up careers, but also opened up the new frontiers, created new cities out of the wilderness and gave to new states and communities the framework of active political life?

If one reads the story of young Abraham Lincoln, it is hard to believe that his struggles as a young lawyer, his difficulties as a young parent were less than those of young men today. Yet there was no time when the deepest issues of the day did not occupy his mind or the call of statecraft make itself heard above the claims and clamor of everyday life. Nor was he alone or exceptional. Stephen Douglas' life was no different. The prairie towns were filled with earnest, active citizens deeply, profoundly concerned with the great issues of a nation "half slave, half free." When the multitudes gathered, a hundred years ago, to listen in rapt attention for hours to the Lincoln-Douglas debates, had they fewer responsibilities and duties than the citizens of today to many of whom the great issues of politics seem to be most usefully conveyed in a fifteen-second television flash of subliminal advertising?

Is it not possible that the pressures of personal responsibilities are not greater but that the dedication and selflessness needed to discern and to influence public issues have shrunk? In a century in which so many of the mentors of the public mind—from the psychiatrists to the ad-men—speak to us in terms of "what we owe ourselves," may there not indeed have been a slackening of devotion compared with those days, not so long distant, when what man owes to God and his neighbor was a common theme of public discourse?

If so, this is a dangerous hour for our politics and for government by consent of the governed. For at no time have so many of the great issues of the day demanded clear, real moral vision to bring them into focus—the vision, if you please, of A. Powell Davies, who loved the truth and believed in man's capacity and right to govern himself.

INDEX

A

Accuracy and clarity, 123–24
Acoustic level, in communication, 6
Adams, Samuel, 30, 69, 71
Aeschines, 94
Alliteration, 116
Ambiguity and clarity, 122–23
Ambiguity, syntactical, 125–29
Amplification, 67–68
Analogy, use of, 59–61
Anti-climax order, in sequencing ideas, 91–92
Antithesis, technique of, 137–38
Antony, Marc, 147–48
Appropriateness, and style, 129–32
Arguments, "both-sides presentation," 46–48
Aristotle, 3, 24, 25, 27, 32, 62, 121
Arrangement (*see* Organization)
Articulation, lazy, 169
Assonance, 117
Attention-getters, 76–77
Attitude change, in audiences, 37–39, 92–93
Audiences:
    analyzing attitudes of, 37–39, 92–93
    and the communicative event, 9–10
    eye contact with, 167–68
    identification with, 80–81
    size of, 169
Authoritative definition, 64
Authorities, and testimony, 64–65

B

Bacon, Francis, 3
Barrier situations, 44, 83
Beardsley, Monroe C., 79
Beginners, problems of, 166–75
Beveridge, Albert, 53
Blaine, James G., 69–70
Bodily movement, in delivery, 171–72
"Both-sides presentation" of arguments, 46–48
Bowen, Catherine, 64–65
Bright, John, 138
Brockriede, Wayne, 62
Brooks, Preston, 16
Burke, Kenneth, 152
Burns, James M., 42

C

Calhoun, John C., 30
Cause-effect relationship, 85
Cerf, Bennett, 140
Chicago Tribune, 20, 98
Choate, Rufus, 6
Churchill, Winston, 18, 30, 33, 63–64, 112, 114, 118, 121, 138
Cicero, 3, 20, 30, 33, 71, 153, 154, 176
Clarity, and oral style, 122–29
Classification, in definition, 62
Clay, Henry, 25, 30, 148–49
Climax order, in sequencing ideas, 91–92

INDEX

Comfortable Words, 129–30
Communication:
  communicative event, 8–21
    audience, 9–10
    content, 17–18
    delivery, 19–21
    identity of speaker, 8–9
    place, 16–17
    purpose, 11–12
    speaker, 8–9
    style of speaker, 18–19
    time, 13–16
  failures in, 7–8
  interstimulation, 4
  levels, 6
  nature of, 3–21
  process of, 3–8
Comparison and contrast, in definition,
  62
Conclusions, 90–91
Concrete language, and impressive-
  ness, 133
Concreteness, and clarity, 124
Connotation of words, 106–8
Conrad, Joseph, 141
Content, 17–18, 163
Context of words, 108
Contrast and antithesis, technique of,
  137–38
Conversation and delivery, 161–63
Coolidge, Calvin, 122
Corax, 3
Correlatives and syntactical ambiguity,
  126
Credentials of speaker (*see* Proofs)
Criticisms, samples of, 184–99

                    D

Darrow, Clarence, 26
Data (*see* Statistics)
Davis, John W., 42
Definitions (*see* Proofs, definitions)
De Inventione, 176
Delivery:
  beginners, problems of, 166–76
  bodily movement, 171–72
  and communication, 19–21
  and conversation, 161–63
  directness, 164–65
  evaluation of, 165–66, 183
  eye contact, 167–68

Delivery (*Cont.*)
  examples of notes, 173–75
  force, 165
  hesitation phenomena, 168–69
  lazy articulation, 169
  loudness, 169–70
  nervousness, 166–67
  nonfluency, 163
  notes, 172–75
  observation of own delivery, 165–66
  pausing, 169
  practice, 166
  rapidity of, 168
  recognition of good delivery, 164–65
  relation to memory, 159
  relationship of content to, 163
  speaking too softly, 169–70
  speech as dialogue, 162–63
  tape recorders, 170–71
  vocal variety, 170–71
*Demographic Yearbook of the United
  Nations,* 57
Demosthenes, 25, 30, 94
Denotation, of words, 105–6
DeQuincey, Thomas, 123
Detail, relation to memory, 157
Deuteronomy, 98
DeVoto, Bernard, 64–65
Dialogue concept:
  and communication, 6
  and delivery, 162–63
  and memory, 159
Dickinson, G. Lowes, 136, 137–38
*Dictionary of Contemporary American
  Usage,* 98
Difficulty situation, 44
Direct suggestion, 92–93
Directness in delivery, 164–65
Disagreements, as motivation, 45–46
Discussions, 82–90 (*see also* Organi-
  zation)
Duration, and sound, 112–13

                    E

Edwards, Jonathan, 61, 136
Effectiveness, evaluation of, 183
Ehninger, Douglas, 62
Eisenhower, Dwight D., 113
Emerson, Ralph Waldo, 33, 132
Emotional appeal, 91
Emotional proof, 68–73, 147–48

Emphasis, technique of, 136–37
Ethics:
    and proof, 52–56
    and rhetoric, 28–29, 32
Etymology, in definition, 63
Evaluation of speeches:
    arrangement of material, 182
    delivery, 183
    effectiveness, 183
    guide questions, 182–84
    memory, 183
    of own delivery, 165–66
    rhetorical invention, 182
    sample criticisms, 184–99
    style, 183
Evans, Bergen, 98, 129
Evans, Cornelia, 98
Events, historical and present, 56–57
Example, in definition, 64
Examples, use of, 58–59
Eye contact, in delivery, 167–68

F

Facts (see Proofs)
Failure points, in communication, 7–8
Familiarity, and clarity, 124–25
Faneuil Hall, Boston, 17
"Farewell Address," Lincoln, 116
Faulkner, William, 18, 33
Feedback, in communication, 4
First Commandment, 98
"First Inaugural Address," Jefferson, 54
"First Inaugural Address," Lincoln, 19, 20, 63, 69, 145
Flanders, Ralph, 136
Fluency, in delivery, 163
Force, in delivery, 165

G

Gettysburg, Pa., 17
Gettysburg Address, 101–4, 117, 123, 128, 158
Gladstone, William E., 72
Goal-oriented situation, 44
Godkin, E. L., 31
Goodyear Tire and Rubber Co., 10
Grady, Henry, 69, 70–71, 116, 148
Greece, 32

H

"Happy Warrior Speech," Roosevelt, 42
Hayne, Robert Young, 139
Henry, Patrick, 11, 30, 61, 112, 136
Hesitation phenomena, in delivery, 168–69
Historical events, 56–57
History, and rhetoric, 29–33
Hitler, 114
Huxley, Thomas, 39–40

I

Identification, with audience, 80–81
Identification situation, 45, 84
Imagery, and impressiveness, 133–34
Impressiveness, and style, 132–39
"Inaugural Address," Kennedy, 130–31
Inference, 67
Information-giving situation, 43, 82
Information Please Almanac, 57
Ingersoll, Robert, 69–70, 71
Interstimulation in communication, 4
Introductions, 76–81 (see also Organization)
Invention, relation to memory, 154–55
Isocrates, 3, 23–24, 37, 52

J

Jefferson, Thomas, 28, 54
Johnson, Lyndon, 128
Julius Caesar, 33, 147–48

K

Kazantzakis, Nikos, 128
Kennedy, John F., 19, 121, 130–31
Khrushchev, Nikita S., 8

L

La Bruyère, Jean de, 137
Landor, Walter Savage, 30
Language (see also Oral style; Style, theoretical aspects)
    definition, 104
    signals, 109–10
    sound, characteristics of, 111–14

Language (*Cont.*)
  sound devices, 114–16
  usage, and interpersonal relation-
    ships, 99
  usage, professional styles, 99–101
Lasswell, Harold D., 31
Leighton, Dorothea, 146
Leiserson, Avery, 31
Length, and clarity, 128–29
Lincoln, Abraham, 17, 19, 20, 30, 47,
    63, 69, 102–3, 104, 116, 123,
    128, 145–46, 158
Lines of argument, development of,
    43–46
Linguistic level in communication, 6
Lippmann, Walter, 60
Logic:
  and oral style, 147
  and proof, 56
  and rhetoric, 32
Loudness, in delivery, 169–70
Loudness, and stress, 111–12
Lovejoy, Elijah, 17

M

McAdoo, W. G., 42
Mann, Thomas, 3
Marshall, John, 26
Material:
  arrangement (*see* Organization)
  modes of presenting, 46–48
  supporting, 56–68 (*see also* Proofs)
Meaning of meaning, 104–5
Memory:
  arrangement, 155–57
  delivery, 159
  detail, 157
  evaluation of, 183
  invention, 154–55
  reiterative pattern technique, 158
  stagefright, 159
  style, 158
Metaphors, and impressiveness, 134–
    36
Metaphors, use of, 61
Miller, H. P., 64
Modifiers and syntactical ambiguity,
    125–26
Motivational situations, 43–45, 82–84
Murphy, Richard, 80
Mussolini, 114

N

Necessary conditions, definition by, 63
Negation, in definition, 63
Nervousness and delivery, 166–67
Nevins, Allan, 51
Nichols, Marie H., 148–49
*The 1964 Manpower Report of the
    President,* 57
Nixon-Kennedy debates, 31, 150
"Nobel Prize Acceptance Speech,"
    Faulkner, 33
Nobel Prize for Literature, Churchill,
    33
Notes, in delivery, 172–75
Notes, examples of, 173–75

O

The Odyssey—A Modern Sequel, 128
"On Conciliation with America," 137
"On Knocking at the Gate of *Mac-
    beth,*" 123
Onomatopoeia, 114
Operational description, in definition,
    63–64
Oral style (*see also* Style, theoretical
    aspects)
  accuracy, 123–24
  appropriateness, 129–32
  clarity, 122–29
  concrete language, 133
  concreteness, 124
  differences from written style, 149–
    51
  emotional proof, 147–48
  familiarity, 124–25
  formality, degrees of, 130–32
  imagery, 133–34
  impressiveness, 132–39
  logical proof, 147
  metaphors and similes, 134–36
  proofs, 146–49
  purpose, 139–46
  reiterative pattern technique, 158
  structural impressiveness, 136–39
  syntactical ambiguity, 125–29
  valuative words, 148–49
"Ordeal of the Mid-Century," 138–39
Organization:
  conclusions, 90–91
  direct suggestion, 92–93

Organization (*Cont.*)
 discussions, 82–90
  barrier situations, 83
  causal pattern, 85
  identification situations, 84
  information situations, 82
  motivational situations, outlining
   for, 82–84
  problem situations, 82–83
  problem-solution pattern, 85
  relationships, outlining for, 84–86
  sample outlines, 86–90
  solution situations, 83
  space pattern, 85
  threat situations, 84
  time pattern, 85
  topic pattern, 85
 evaluation of arrangement, 182
 introductions, 76–81
  attention-getters, 76–77
  identification, 80
  orientation, 77–78
  partition, 79–80
  statement of purpose, 78
  thesis sentence, 78–79
 memory, 155–57
 proportion, 92
 sequencing materials, 91–92
 summaries, 90–91
 transitions, 90
Orientation, 77–78
Osgood, Charles E., 107, 108
Otis, James, 30
"Our Broken Mainspring," 205–14

P

Parallels and syntactical ambiguity,
 126
Partition, 80
Pauses, in delivery, 169
Pericles, 30, 33
Perkins, Frances, 19
Phaedrus (Socrates), 38
Phillips, Wendell, 17, 20, 61, 132, 135,
 164
Philosophy and rhetoric, 32
Physiological level, in communication,
 6
Pitch and sound, 112
Pitt, William (Lord Chatham), 14–16,
 20, 30, 40, 121
Place, importance of, 16–17

Planning (*see also* Organization)
 analyzing attitudes of audience, 37–
  39
 first steps, 37–43
 focusing on purpose, 41–43
 lines of argument, 43–46
 modes of presentation, 46–48
 subject selection, 39–41
Plato, 3, 32, 75
Political science, and rhetoric, 30–31
Practice, in delivery, 166
Presentation, 46–48
Prestige of speaker, 55–56
Problem situations, 82–83
Problem-solution relationship, 85
Pronoun references and syntactical
 ambiguity, 127
Proofs:
 amplification, 67–68
 analogies, 59–61
 authorities and testimony, 64–65
 comparison and contrast, 59–61
 definitions, 61–64
  authoritative, 64
  classification, 62
  comparison and contrast, 62
  etymology, 63
  example, 64
  necessary conditions, 63
  negation, 63
  operational description, 63–64
 emotional, 68–73
 emotional, and oral style, 147–48
 ethical, 52–56
 events, 56–57
 examples, use of, 58–59
 fairness of sampling, 60
 inference, 67
 kinds of, 51–52
 logical, 56–58
 logical, and oral style, 147
 metaphors, 61
 selection of, 51–73
 similes, 61
 statistics, 57–58
 stereotyping, 60–61
 test of supporting material, 66
 testimony, 64–65
 and valuative words, 148–49
 and values, 71
 visual aids, 65–66
Proportion, 92
Psychology, and rhetoric, 31–32

Purpose:
  in communication, 11–12
  focusing on, 41–43
  and oral style, 139–46
  statement of, 78
Pyramidal order, in sequencing ideas, 91–92

Q

Quality and sound, 113–14
Quintilian, 3, 153, 155

R

Rapidity, in delivery, 168
Refutative technique, 47–48
Reiterative pattern technique, 158
Relationships, outlining for, 84–86
Rhetoric:
  definitions of, 24–25
  and ethics, 32
  and fine arts, 32–33
  and history, 29–33
  and logic, 32
  nature and scope of, 25–28
  as participation, 28–29
  and philosophy, 32
  and political science, 30–31
  and psychology, 31–32
  relationship to other subjects, 29–33
  and social psychology, 32
  and sociology, 32
  writers on, 3
Rhetoric (Aristotle), 27
Rhetorical invention, evaluation of, 182
Rhythm, 117–18
Richard II, 129
Roosevelt, Eleanor, 25
Roosevelt, Franklin D., 19, 42, 113–14, 137, 142–44, 150
Roosevelt, Theodore, 9, 20, 80
Roosevelt: The Lion and the Fox, 42
Russell, Bertrand, 62, 140–42

S

St. Augustine, 3, 32
Sainte-Beuve, C. A., 63
Sampling, fairness of, 60
"The Scholar in a Republic," 132
Schramm, Wilbur, 92

Schweitzer, Albert, 33
Scott, Robert L., 166
"Second Inaugural Address," Eisenhower, 113
"Selling Appeals," 10
Semantic Differential word scale, 107–8
Semantic meaning, 105–8
Seneca, 98
Sequencing materials, 91–92
Seward, W. H., 145–46
Shakespeare, 98, 129
Shift in point of view, and syntactical ambiguity, 126–27
Sicily, 3
Signals, and language, 109–10
Silence, in speech, 112–13
Similes, and impressiveness, 136
Simonides, 153–54
Situations, motivational, 43–45
Smith, Alfred E., 42
Social psychology, and rhetoric, 32
Sociology, and rhetoric, 32
Socrates, 37
Solution situations, 83
Sound:
  characteristics of, 111–14
  meaning, 111–18
  repetition, 116–18
  suggestion, 114–16
Spatial relationship, 85
"Speech on Conciliation," 117
Stagefright and memory, 159
Stasis, in disagreements, 45–46
The Statistical Abstract of the United States, 57
Statistical Yearbook of the United Nations, 57
Statistics, 57–58
Stereotyping, 60–61
Stevenson, Adlai, 13–14, 33, 81, 121, 138, 205–14
Stress emphasis, and sound, 111–12
Structural meaning, 109–10
Style:
  definitions, 18–19
  evaluation of, 183
  practical applications (*see* Oral style)
  theoretical aspects, 99–119
    dimensions, 103
    individual, 101–4
    language usage, 99–101

Style (*Cont.*)
  theoretical aspects (*Cont.*)
    meaning of meaning, 104–5
    semantic meaning, 105–8
    sound meaning, 111–18
    structural meaning, 109–10
Subject, selection of, 39–41
Suggestion, 92–93
Summaries, 90–91
Sumner, Charles, 16
Supporting materials, 56–68 (*see also* Proofs)
Suspense, technique of, 138
Syntactical ambiguity, 125–29

T

Tape recorders, use of, 170–71
Testimony, 64–65
Thant, U, 12
Thesis sentence, 78–79
Threat appeal, 91
Threat situations, 44–45, 84
Thucydides, 33
Time:
  in communication, 13–16
  order of words, 110
  relationship, 85
Topical relationship, 85
Transitions, 90
Transitions, and syntactical ambiguity, 127–28
Truman, Harry, 131
Truth (*see* Proofs)
Tyler, John, 28

U

United Nations Statistical Office, 57
United States Bureau of the Census, 57
United States Bureau of Labor Statistics, 57

V

"Valedictory," Truman, 131
Valuative words, and oral style, 148–49
Values and emotional proof, 71
Variety, technique of, 138–39
Verres, 59
Virginia Convention, 26
Visual aids, 65–66
Vocal variety, 170–71
Voice quality, 113–14

W

Wallace, Karl R., 23
Walter, Otis M., 166
"War Message," Roosevelt, 142–44
Washington, George, 16, 66
Weaver, Richard, 48, 119
Webster, Daniel, 8, 11–12, 26, 30, 53–54, 139
"What Is a Classic?" 63
Whately, Richard, 162, 164
Whitehead, Alfred North, 121
Winans, James A., 6
Wolfe, Thomas, 128
Words:
  connotative meaning, 106–8
  context, 108
  denotative meaning, 105–6
  Semantic Differential scale, 107–8
  space order, 110
  time order, 110
  word-word relationships, 110
World Almanac, 57
Written style, differences from oral style, 149–51

Y

Young, Kimball, 38